Signers of the Declaration

For Jo & Hutch, about the only people we know nowadays who are worthy of the efforts of the signers.

John Bakeless
Katherine Bakeless

30 December 1969

Signers of the Declaration

JOHN and KATHERINE BAKELESS

1969

Houghton Mifflin Company Boston

Also by John Bakeless

The Adventures of Lewis and Clark

To Fyle Edberg

CONTENTS

TABLE OF DATES   xi

INTRODUCTION: The Glorious Fourth and the Men Who
     Made It Glorious   1

PART I	MASSACHUSETTS	15
	Samuel Adams	17
	John Hancock	33
	John Adams	45
	Elbridge Gerry	59
	Robert Treat Paine	64

PART II	VIRGINIA	69
	Thomas Jefferson	71
	Richard Henry Lee	79
	Benjamin Harrison	87
	Francis Lightfoot Lee	91
	Thomas Nelson	92
	George Wythe	96
	Carter Braxton	101

PART III	PENNSYLVANIA	105
	Benjamin Franklin	107
	Robert Morris	127
	Benjamin Rush	136
	John Morton	141
	George Clymer	143
	James Smith	146
	George Taylor	148
	James Wilson	150
	George Ross	155

PART IV	NEW JERSEY	159
	John Witherspoon	161
	Richard Stockton	166
	Francis Hopkinson	169
	John Hart	173
	Abraham Clark	175
PART V	NEW YORK	179
	Philip Livingston	181
	Lewis Morris	184
	William Floyd	187
	Francis Lewis	188
PART VI	CONNECTICUT	193
	Roger Sherman	195
	Samuel Huntington	202
	William Williams	204
	Oliver Wolcott	206
PART VII	RHODE ISLAND	211
	Stephen Hopkins	213
	William Ellery	216
PART VIII	NEW HAMPSHIRE	221
	Josiah Bartlett	223
	William Whipple	225
	Matthew Thornton	227
PART IX	MARYLAND	231
	Charles Carroll	233
	Thomas Stone	240
	William Paca	242
	Samuel Chase	244

PART X   DELAWARE   249

              Caesar Rodney   251
              Thomas McKean   255
              George Read   259

PART XI   NORTH CAROLINA   263

              William Hooper   265
              Joseph Hewes   267
              John Penn   270

PART XII   SOUTH CAROLINA   273

              Thomas Heyward, Jr.   275
              Arthur Middleton   277
              Edward Rutledge   280
              Thomas Lynch, Jr.   282

PART XIII   GEORGIA   285

              Lyman Hall   287
              Button Guinnett   290
              George Walton   296

BIBLIOGRAPHY   299

DATES

1760	OCTOBER 26	George III ascends the British throne.
1764	APRIL 5	The Sugar Act is passed by Parliament; the colonies protest.
	APRIL 19	The Currency Act forbids the colonists to issue paper money as legal tender.
	DECEMBER 22	Stephen Hopkins, Governor of Rhode Island, publishes "The Rights of Colonies Examined."
1765	MARCH 22	The Stamp Act becomes law. The Sons of Liberty organize throughout the colonies a resistance to its enforcement.
	MAY 15	The Quartering Act orders the colonists to provide barracks and supplies for British troops.
	JUNE 8	The Massachusetts General Court adopts a circular letter calling representatives from all colonies to a Congress in New York in October.
	OCTOBER 7	The Stamp Act Congress meets in New York.
	NOVEMBER 1	The Stamp Act goes into effect to the sound of the tolling of muffled bells and flags at half staff.
1766	FEBRUARY 13	Benjamin Franklin, examined before the House of Commons in London, declares the Stamp Act cannot be enforced.
	MARCH 18	England repeals the Stamp Act.
1767	JUNE 29	Charles Townshend, British Chancelor of the Exchequer, imposes in his Revenue Act duties to be paid on glass, lead, tea, paper, and painters' colors imported into the colonies.
	SEPTEMBER 4	Charles Townshend dies. Lord North succeeds him.
	OCTOBER 28	The Boston Town-Meeting renews its *non-importation* agreement; an action followed in other colonies to compel a repeal of the Townshend Acts.

1768 FEBRUARY 11   The Massachusetts House of Representatives adopts Samuel Adams's circular letter and orders it sent to the assemblies of other colonies, suggesting united opposition to Great Britain by discussion and petition.

      JULY 18   A "Song for American Freedom" by John Dickinson is published by the *Boston Gazette*.

      OCTOBER 1   Two regiments of British soldiers land in Boston to enforce the customs laws.

1769 MAY 18   Virginia agrees to non-importation of British goods.

1770 JANUARY 31   Lord North becomes Prime Minister of Great Britain.

      MARCH 5   The Boston Massacre takes place; five killed, six injured.

      APRIL 12   The Townshend Revenue Act is repealed, except for the tax on tea.

1772 NOVEMBER 2   Committees of Correspondence are first organized by Samuel Adams and Joseph Warren in Massachusetts and later followed by similar committees in the other colonies.

1773 DECEMBER 16   The Boston Tea Party takes place.

1774   Benjamin Franklin's articles, "On the Rise and Progress of the Differences between Great Britain and Her American Colonies," are published in London.

      MARCH 31   The Boston Port Act, first of Britain's coercive acts, receives the King's assent.

      MAY 12   The Boston Committee of Correspondence recommends suspension of trade with Great Britain by all colonies.

      MAY 13   General Gage arrives in Boston to command British troops quartered there.

      MAY 27   The Virginia House of Burgesses, meeting unofficially in Williamsburg, adopts a resolution calling for an annual intercolonial congress.

JUNE 1   Boston harbor is closed to exports and imports by the Boston Port Act of March 31.

JUNE 2   The Quartering Act is passed by Parliament. The colonists must house and feed the British soldiers.

JUNE 17   Massachusetts elects delegates to an intercolonial congress to meet September 1 in Philadelphia.

SEPTEMBER 1   General Gage seizes Massachusetts's stock of powder at Charlestown.

SEPTEMBER 5   The First Continental Congress assembles in Philadelphia with all colonies except Georgia represented.

OCTOBER 14   The Declaration of Rights and Grievances is adopted by Congress.

OCTOBER 26   The First Continental Congress adjourns to meet again May 10, 1775, if found to be necessary at that date.

1775

      The words of "Yankee Doodle" are written by Edward Barnes and set to an old English tune.

APRIL 18/19   Paul Revere takes his midnight ride.

APRIL 19   The battles of Lexington and Concord take place.

MAY 10   The Second Continental Congress meets in Philadelphia. All thirteen colonies send representatives.

MAY 24   John Hancock of Massachusetts is chosen president of this Congress.

JUNE 15   George Washington of Virginia is appointed by Congress to be Commander in Chief of the Continental Army.

JUNE 17   The battle of Bunker Hill ends in a British victory.

JULY 3   After traveling twelve days from Philadelphia, Washington takes command of the Continental Army on the Cambridge (Massachusetts) Common.

JULY 6   Congress adopts a "Declaration of the Causes and Necessity of Taking up Arms."

	JULY 8	Congress adopts a petition to the king, offering reconciliation. (Samuel Adams and Benjamin Franklin think this a futile gesture, but consent to yield to the "moderates" of the middle colonies.)
	SEPTEMBER 1	This petition of July 8 to the king from Congress is refused.
1776	JANUARY 1	A Continental flag with thirteen stripes is raised by Washington before his headquarters in Cambridge.
	APRIL 6	Congress opens the ports of all colonies to all countries "not subject to the King of Great Britain" and prohibits the importation of slaves.
	APRIL 12	North Carolina is the first colony to instruct her delegates to support independence.
	MAY 15	Virginia instructs her delegates to propose independence.
	JUNE 7	Richard Henry Lee, chairman of the Virginia delegation, offers a resolution in Congress: "That these United Colonies are and of right ought to be free and independent states."
	JUNE 11	A committee is appointed in Congress to draft a Declaration of Independence. Thomas Jefferson is chairman.
	JULY 2	Lee's resolution of June 7 is adopted by Congress.
	JULY 4	The Declaration of Independence, as drafted by Thomas Jefferson, and amended, is adopted by Congress and signed by its president, John Hancock.
	AUGUST 2	The Declaration of Independence, having been engrossed on parchment, is signed by the members of Congress then present.

The Glorious Fourth

and the

Men Who Made it Glorious

THE FOURTH OF JULY is the day on which Americans commemorate
the independence of their country. Though there are several
other days we *might* celebrate as Independence Day, the Second
Continental Congress, in 1776, formally adopted the final revision
of the Declaration of Independence on the Fourth of July. The
United Colonies were already independent, for Congress had
passed a resolution declaring independence two days before, on
July 2, 1776. All the formal Declaration of Independence did was
to state formally to the world, and especially to the British Empire, what Congress had decided and why.

We could celebrate July 2, the day independence was actually
voted. We could celebrate June 7, the day Richard Henry Lee of
Virginia submitted to Congress his resolution "that these United
Colonies are, and of right ought to be, free and independent
states, that they are absolved from all allegiance to the British
Crown, and that all political connection between them and the
State of Great Britain is, and ought to be, totally dissolved."

When Thomas Jefferson was writing the Declaration of Independence, some weeks after Lee's resolution, he took these words,
almost without change, as the final, ringing paragraph of his immortal document. But Lee's resolution was only *submitted* to Congress on June 7. There was no vote. Congress took nearly a month
to think it over, before formally and officially adopting it. John
Adams expected July 2 to be the day formally celebrated. But
there was only a vote of Congress that day. American independence was not officially announced to the world until July Fourth.

It wasn't really necessary to have a Declaration of Independence
at all. If the Second Continental Congress was the legitimate
government of the Thirteen Colonies, then the colonies became
independent the moment Congress — when it finally passed Lee's

resolution — said it was independent. But the delegates in Congress thought they ought to give reasons for so serious a step. That is what the Declaration means when it says that "a decent respect to the opinions of mankind requires that they should declare the causes which impel them to the separation" from Great Britain.

There was a great deal to do before Independence could be declared. Not every one, even among the delegates to the Second Continental Congress, favored it. They were good Americans. They were sound patriots. But they were mostly of British blood and they had been bred in a tradition of loyalty to King and Country. They knew the king and his government were treating them outrageously, but they still hoped the dispute could be settled peaceably.

Though Samuel Adams and a few others wanted to set up a new and independent country almost as soon as disputes with the royal government began, many leading American patriots — some of them among the greatest heroes of the Revolution — did not want to be independent at all, even after fighting had started. All they wanted was what every Briton back home in the British Isles had always wanted: self-government, the right to tax himself, protection against injustice in the courts of law.

In the beginning, both Washington and Jefferson had declared openly they did not favor independence. But they, like Franklin and many other moderates, began to change their minds not long after the fighting started. Within a year or two, the British were offering to concede nearly everything the patriots had ever demanded, except independence. But it was too late then. America had won independence by that time and meant to stay independent.

It was true, however, that a few Americans had been talking about independence long before the Revolution, though no one either in England or America took them very seriously. As early as 1764, Christopher Gadsden of South Carolina, later a delegate to the First Continental Congress in 1774, was discussing the possible independence of the colonies, though only among his friends. In 1766, Gadsden began to discuss the subject again. Samuel Adams apparently had made up his mind by 1768. When Patrick Henry, in 1773, also suggested American independence, the people

where browsers are always welcome

MAXAE'S
BOOKS

John Dunn House–Bent St.
Box 1872 (505) 758-4018
Taos, NM 87571

Made in U.S.A.

who heard him "appeared to be startled; for they had never heard anything of the kind even suggested."

Jonathan Trumbull, the war governor of Connecticut whom Washington liked to address as "Brother Jonathan," wrote the Earl of Dartmouth, "We consider the interest of the two countries as inseperable, [sic] and are shocked at the idea of any disunion between them." Dr. Joseph Warren, not long before he was killed at Bunker Hill, declared that independence was "not our aim." The people of Portsmouth thought their delegates in the Provincial New Hampshire Congress should "totally disavow" any desire to separate from Britain. The New York Provincial Congress formally denied that it wished "to cast off the connexion and dependence of the Colonies on Great Britain."

Naturally, after fighting began, this loyalty to the old country swiftly cooled. The redcoats were now killing Americans. One of General Gage's spies in the American lines outside Boston reported on July 23, 1775: "A view to independence seems more and more general." This was less than a year before the Declaration of Independence. Yet even then all the spy could report was that the desire for independence was "more general." He didn't report any overwhelming demand for it. In late October, 1775, General Nathanael Greene wrote Washington that people were *beginning* "heartily to wish a declaration of Independence." But it was December before General Greene was willing to tell the commander in chief frankly: "We are now driven to the necessity of making a declaration of independence."

Because his wife was very seriously ill, Thomas Jefferson, soon to be the author of the Declaration, did not take his seat in the Second Continental Congress till May 14, 1776. Next day, he heard Congress adopt a resolution denouncing King George (in almost the same terms Jefferson himself would use in the Declaration of Independence a few weeks later) and recommending that Congress assume all the powers of government. This resolution did not go so far as to demand outright American independence but it did very nearly the same thing. If the American Congress assumed all the powers of government and made war on the King's army, the country would be practically independent.

On that same day, far away in Virginia, something else happened. In Williamsburg, the Virginia Convention (that is, the state legislature) passed an official resolution, urging Congress to "declare the United Colonies free and independent states."

It took some time for the news to reach the Virginia delegates in Congress. In those days, people traveled on horseback or in carriages, over roads that were sometimes stretches of log "corduroy," at other times mere patches of mud and stone, crossing streams by fords or clumsy ferries, for there were usually no bridges. Hence it took time for news, even official news as important as this, to spread; and these instructions did not reach the Virginia delegates in Philadelphia until May 27, 1776.

All through those first months of 1776, a good deal had been happening to incline the thoughts of the patriots toward independence. Important among these events was the publication of a little pamphlet called *Common Sense* by an English immigrant who had come to America in 1774. His name was Thomas Paine. He had hardly reached this country when he became an intense patriot, ardent in the cause of independence. *Common Sense,* published January 9, 1776, is said to have sold 300,000 copies in its first three months and another 200,000 copies immediately afterward. Even today, with our enormous population, any publisher would be delighted with such a sale. In those days, amid the thin populace of the eastern seaboard, it was almost a miracle.

It meant that, in the first few months of '76, as the idea of independence took greater and greater hold of the people and of Congress, practically every one was reading Paine's fiery arguments.

The scene was now set for independence. No matter how much they might protest they were only loyal Britons demanding only the rights of Englishmen, the colonists had refused to pay British taxes, they had driven out British governors, they had been shooting British soldiers, and they had taken over the government. No wonder Samuel Adams asked: "Is not America already independent? Why then not declare it?"

The Virginia delegates in Congress took their time about complying with the instructions that state had sent them. The resolution for independence that they were to present had to be carefully thought out and carefully worded. It was June 7, 1776, before Richard Henry Lee, senior member of the Virginia delegation, rose to propose it.

The New England advocates of independence were glad enough
to see a Virginian make the first move. As John Adams said,
long afterward, "the eastern members" had been viewed askance,
"because they had been suspected from the beginning of having
independence in contemplation." As a matter of fact, that was
exactly what most of the "eastern" — that is, New England —
delegates actually had favored for some time.

John Adams promptly seconded Lee's resolution. The two had
probably fixed that little matter up beforehand. They knew well
enough that this public co-operation of a Massachusetts Yankee
democrat and a Virginian aristocrat would serve as a strong hint to
the central Atlantic colonies that the most important New England colony and the most important Southern colony were working
together to support independence. The delegates would also
know that if the largest New England colony and the largest
Southern colony felt that way, the rest of New England and the
South would probably join them.

After it had heard the resolution, Congress did not rush matters.
In fact, it did nothing at all until the next day. Then it decided
to resolve itself into a "committee of the whole," to discuss what
Richard Henry Lee had proposed. Legislative bodies often do
that to make discussion easier and freer than it is under strict
parliamentary procedure.

On June 7, 1776, the committee of the whole reported to Congress and there was a more formal discussion of the resolution.
Among those who argued against independence were John Dickinson, James Wilson, and Robert R. Livingston. They felt sure that
the middle colonies were not yet ready for so bold a move.

But there was one strong argument for not delaying the declaration of independence. The colonists would soon reach the end
of their resources. They badly needed foreign arms, foreign soldiers, and foreign money. The only countries that might possibly
give such help were England's enemies, France and Spain. Both
had fought the British not many years before. Though no longer
at war, both were still hostile to Great Britain. Both would be
glad to do anything they could to cause the British trouble. Either
one might be willing to supply arms, money, or soldiers. If America declared herself an independent nation, France and Spain
might be willing to recognize her independence and aid her

against Great Britain. But they certainly would not go openly to the aid of American rebels who admitted they were still subjects of King George. (In the end, France provided all three necessities and Spain went to war with Great Britain, which assisted the Colonies, even if there was no formal American alliance with Spain as there was with France.)

After debating till seven o'clock in the evening of Saturday, June 8, Congress decided to go back into committee of the whole on June 10. Following this second day of discussion, the committee of the whole at last decided in favor of Richard Henry Lee's proposal.

Congress decided, after hearing this report, to postpone any decision for three weeks, which meant until July 1. It seemed likely that the central colonies, which were still hesitating at the thought of complete independence, would soon change their minds. Hence, as Thomas Jefferson said later, "it was thought most prudent to wait a while for them." Edward Rutledge, of South Carolina, even thought that at this time "the sensible part of the House opposed the motion."

Though Congress postponed the vote and though there was certainly some hesitation, the delegates appointed a committee of five to decide on the wording of a future Declaration of Independence — in case Congress should ever pass it. Four members of this committee, Thomas Jefferson, Benjamin Franklin, John Adams, and Roger Sherman, favored independence. The fifth member, Robert R. Livingston, still had his doubts. In fact, he did not vote for the Declaration when it was finally submitted to Congress, and never signed it — though it was he who later, in 1789, administered the oath of office for President of the United States to George Washington. In 1776, however, Livingston was so doubtful about the whole thing that he left Philadelphia before the committee had finished revising the Declaration.

The rest of the committee had no doubt about independence at all. As soon as they met, they assigned Thomas Jefferson to write the first draft. Jefferson had been very silent during the debates, since he did not care for public speaking. John Adams later said: "During the whole time I sat with him in Congress, I never heard him utter three sentences together." But Jefferson was already known as one of the best writers in North America, or, as John

Adams put it, he had "a happy talent of composition."

Jefferson wrote the Declaration of Independence in the simple lodgings he had rented for himself — a parlor and a bedroom in the house of Jacob Graff, Jr., a Philadelphia bricklayer. Richard Henry Lee, though he had offered the original resolution for independence, had nothing to do with writing the Declaration that made his resolution effective. While Jefferson and his fellow-committeemen were busy with that task, Lee had gone back to Williamsburg to attend the Virginia Convention. This was not so odd as it seems today. To most of these men the affairs of their own colonies were quite as important as the affairs of America as a whole, especially since no one was then quite sure what was meant by America.

Many years afterward, when John Adams and Thomas Jefferson were both old men and both ex-Presidents, John Adams thought he remembered that the committee had made Jefferson and himself a committee of two to write the first draft. Adams was perfectly sincere when he said this, and a warm friend of Jefferson's, whom he greatly admired, but he was very, very old and was apparently confused. There is no doubt that Thomas Jefferson did write the Declaration of Independence, though the committee, especially Adams and Franklin, suggested certain verbal changes, and Congress eventually made some very important changes of its own.

Jefferson, in later years, had his own notes, made at the time, to prove his authorship; and the earliest draft of the Declaration now known (Jefferson may have torn up a good many sheets of paper while he was at work) is in his handwriting. Adams had no such record, only a very old man's memory of things long, long ago. No record, official or otherwise, suggests that there ever was a subcommittee to make the first draft of the Declaration.

As a literary composition, the Declaration of Independence is not particularly original. There is nothing surprising about that. Jefferson was not trying to say anything startlingly new. He was trying to state clearly some old but fundamental principles that justified the American fight for freedom. These had been stated many times before — by the English philosopher, John Locke; by the Swiss jurist, Jean Jacques Burlamqui; and by the Swiss diplomat, Emmerich de Vattel, years earlier. Tom Paine had repeated them vigorously in America in his best-selling pamphlet. *Common*

Sense stated the American case so vigorously that Washington had the whole pamphlet read aloud to his troops.

Practically every idea in the Declaration of Independence had also been discussed for a long time by speakers in Congress. John Adams, though himself on the committee to draft it, admitted long afterward that the Declaration contained nothing whatever that had not been "hackneyed over in Congress a hundred times."

Not only did Thomas Jefferson borrow the ideas in the Declaration of Independence, he also borrowed a good deal of the language. The list of wrongs the colonists had suffered from King George III was based on an earlier list of similar charges Jefferson had himself written for the new Virginia Constitution. From the Virginia Constitution Jefferson also borrowed part of the Bill of Rights, which George Mason had largely written in its original Virginian form, adding some new charges against the king. Everybody was discussing citizens' rights by that time and all these ideas were more or less familiar.

In writing the Declaration of Independence, Jefferson sometimes followed his models very closely. For instance, the first paragraph of Mason's Virginia Bill of Rights asserted "that all men are born equally free and independant." Mason also declared that every man had a right to "the Enjoyment of Life and Liberty, with the Means of Acquiring and possessing property, and pursuing and obtaining Happiness and Safety." Everyone knows the familiar sentences in which Jefferson repeated these ideas in the Declaration of Independence.

There is no reason for thinking that Roger Sherman did any of the drafting. If he did, it was very little. And Robert R. Livingston probably had as little to do with the Declaration as possible. Benjamin Franklin, who admired the Declaration of Independence as a literary production so much that he said he wished he had written it himself, wrote in a few changes in his own handwriting. A few others appear to be changes by John Adams; and Thomas Jefferson made some last-minute changes himself. All these alterations can easily be noted in the original manuscript, which still survives.

Since the other two members of the committee seem to have had no changes to suggest, the committee were able to lay their approved form of Jefferson's draft before Congress on June 28, 1776.

Congress merely received it formally and ordered it "laid on the table." For the moment, nothing could be done about a *declaration* of independence, since Congress had not yet voted in favor of independence. Richard Henry Lee's resolution had also been "lying on the table" ever since he had introduced it.

On July 2, however, Congress voted in favor of Lee's resolution and thus put itself on record as favoring independence. Congress went right on, that same day, to begin discussion of the exact wording of the Declaration. Thomas Jefferson's draft was now minutely scrutinized, line by line.

It was not very pleasant for Thomas Jefferson. His friend, John Adams, spoke vigorously in favor of the text of the Declaration, as the committee had submitted it. But, as usually happens, everybody else thought he knew exactly how to improve the manuscript; and, as also always happens, everybody had a different way of doing it. Jefferson, having done his best, had nothing whatever to say. He listened in unhappy silence.

Franklin, sitting beside him and seeing his annoyance, tried to comfort him with a funny story. (Franklin was a little like Lincoln in one respect: He always had a joke or a story to tell, especially when a touch of humor might relieve a delicate or difficult situation.)

While the other delegates were slashing various words, sentences, and whole sections of Jefferson's draft, Franklin told him about a hatter who asked a friend to write a sign advertising the hatter's business. The sign, as written, read: "John Thomson, Hatter, Makes and Sells Hats for Ready Money." On it was also a picture of a hat. Then the man's friends began to make suggestions. One wanted the word "Hatter" removed, because the words "Sells Hats" implied he was a hatter, anyway. Another thought the word "Makes" ought to be cut out. You can't sell a hat until it is made, he pointed out. Another struck out the words "for Ready Money." Another said: "Sells hats? Why no one would expect you to give them away!" Another thought the word "Hat" was needless. The picture was enough. In the end, all that was left of the original sign was the man's name and the picture!

The change that probably disturbed Jefferson most was Congress's insistence on striking out a passage denouncing King George III for continuing the African slave trade. Like all Southern land-owners, Thomas Jefferson owned slaves. But he treated them well and at least he wanted to end the dreadful practice of kidnaping free Negroes in Africa and shipping them — under the dreadful conditions existing on the slaving ships — to be sold in supposedly free America. Though most of the colonies had long since prohibited the slave trade, permitting only the sale of the Negroes already here (which was bad enough), South Carolina and Georgia still allowed importation of Negroes from Africa. Besides, many of the ships that were still bringing in kidnaped slaves belonged to ship-owners in "free" New England, who thus made a great deal of money. If Jefferson's denunciation was allowed to remain in the Declaration of Independence, South Carolina and Georgia might vote against it. It was also possible that the resentful Yankee owners of slaving ships might persuade New England delegates to oppose it. In the end, the passage denouncing the slave trade was cut out.

Congress also struck out Jefferson's last paragraph and substituted almost the exact wording of the resolution for independence that Richard Henry Lee had proposed in June. Other changes were largely verbal. Jefferson, who like many other patriots regretted leaving the British Empire, had said in his original draft, "We must forget our former love for them," and had added sadly, "We might have been a free and a great people together." Both these passages were struck out. The words, "a people who mean to be free" were changed to "a free people." The words "Scotch and other mercenaries" were dropped so as not to offend patriots of Scottish descent, especially Dr. Witherspoon, of New Jersey.

Jefferson's criticisms of the British Parliament were also eliminated. Congress did not want to annoy the members of Parliament any more than it had to. The delegates knew they might have to negotiate with them later on. Thomas Jefferson thought this great nonsense: "The pusillanimous idea that we had friends in England worth keeping still haunted the minds of many. For this reason, those passages which conveyed censure on the people of England were struck out, lest they should give them offense." Congress continued its discussion all day on July 3 and on into July 4, 1776, which was to become the most famous date in American history.

The vote was taken by states — or rather, by colonies, for the colonies did not become states until they had formally proclaimed their independence. Each had only one vote, no matter how many delegates it had sent. The delegates from each had to agree among themselves how they would cast the vote for their colony.

Secretary Thomson called the roll, from North to South, beginning with New Hampshire and ending with Georgia. Twelve colonies had voted in favor of independence and only twelve now voted for the text of the Declaration. In each case, the New York delegates abstained from voting because their Provincial Congress had instructed them to take no action, either for or against independence. Pennsylvania would not have voted for independence except that John Dickinson and Robert Morris purposely disappeared on the day the vote was taken, allowing the other members of the Pennsylvania delegation to cast an aye vote. Yet Dickinson later fought bravely for America and Morris became the financial mainstay of the War.

The Declaration of Independence was at first signed only by John Hancock, as President of Congress, and Charles Thomson, as Secretary. When all the revision was finished, the actual paper of Thomas Jefferson's draft was pretty well scratched up, and Congress ordered that the whole Declaration be written in a clear copy and engrossed on parchment for signing. This is the copy now shown at the National Archives, with the actual signatures. Not all the signatures were affixed at once, however. The engrossed parchment copy of the Declaration was not ready till August 2. Most of the fifty-six signatures were affixed then, but others were added later. Matthew Thornton, of New Hampshire, who had not been a member of Congress when the Declaration was passed, did not sign it until November, 1776.

There was no formal proclamation of America's independence on July 4, and it is very doubtful that the Liberty Bell rang at all that day. Congress had some other business to handle and it went right ahead. It ordered the Declaration printed and also ordered the printed copies sent to Washington's army, to all state assemblies, and to various churches.

A corrected copy of the Declaration of Independence was rushed off to John Dunlap, a Philadelphia printer. Dunlap worked all night to get the type set (by hand, of course) and, in the morning, was able to send a proof to Jefferson's lodgings. An hour later, the author of the Declaration of Independence returned it, after correcting a few typographical errors. Dunlap ran his press all day on July 5, but he did not wait to finish the press run before beginning to send forty or fifty copies at a time — as they came off the old, slow handpress — to Secretary Charles Thomson.

Late that afternoon, a delegation of chiefs of the Six Nations of the Iroquois appeared in Congress, were given seats and welcomed, listened to an explanation of the Declaration of Independence and what it meant, and were given the presents indispensable at all Indian councils. Chiefs and delegates then made speeches and John Hancock, the dapper Boston merchant, was formally adopted as a member of the tribe of the Onondagas.

Though the Declaration of Independence was published in the Philadelphia *Evening Post* on July 6, it was not officially proclaimed until July 8. Behind Independence Hall stood a large platform built for the Philadelphia astronomer, David Rittenhouse, to use in his observations. Here, on the eighth, the people gathered, while Colonel John Nixon, of the Committee of Safety, read the Declaration of Independence publicly and officially for the first time, though every one must have known for several days what Congress had done. July 8 was an appropriate date, for that was also election day in Pennsylvania — the first election as a free and independent state, no longer a British colony.

Post riders saddled their horses and rode off through the states in all directions, carrying printed copies of the Declaration, spreading the news as they went, and sometimes pausing to let the Declaration be publicly read before riding on.

People are likely to imagine that, as soon as the Declaration was adopted on July 4, 1776, the delegates went up, one by one, and affixed their signatures. That was quite impossible. All that Congress had, at the moment, was Jefferson's draft, much corrected and scribbled upon with all the changes Congress had made. The signed Declaration of Independence, now displayed in the National Archives in Washington, is a copy of Jefferson's manuscript as changed by Congress, beautifully engrossed on parchment, by a skilled professional penman.

It was not formally signed by the delegates until August 2, 1776. That is probably when John Hancock, affixing his usual big, bold signature, remarked that King George would have no trouble reading it — though he could have said the same thing when he signed Jefferson's draft, as amended. There is also a story that when Charles Carroll signed, someone remarked that there were so many Charles Carrolls in Maryland, no one would know which one it was. Then, the story goes, Carroll seized his pen and added "of Carrollton," so that there could be no possible doubt who the signer was. But a good many of Charles Carroll's signatures have survived, and they show that he often added "of Carrollton" for this very reason.

There was a certain solemnity as the signatures were affixed. All the signers knew that if the American army won and America became free they would be national heroes. They also knew that if America lost most of them would be executed as traitors. There would be no doubt about their treason. There were their signatures on the Declaration — enough to hang them, without other evidence. Indeed, if America had lost the Revolutionary War, the Signers of the Declaration of Independence would have been lucky to get off with hanging. The legal penalty for treason was still hanging, drawing, and quartering. That is, hanging the victim till he was half dead from strangling, then disembowelling him and cutting his body into four quarters while he was still alive.

Thinking of this, some one remarked that, after the signing there must be complete co-operation for victory:

"We must all hang together."

"Yes," replied Benjamin Franklin, who loved his little joke, even if it was a rather grim one. "We must all hang together or we shall all hang separately."

To make sure they were in earnest as patriots, new delegates elected to Congress continued to sign the Declaration of Independence when they took their seats, even if they had not been members when it was passed. This continued at least as late as November, 1776.

That is the story of the Declaration of Independence, to which our country owes its freedom and almost two hundred years of successful democratic living.

But what of the men who made the Declaration?

I

MASSACHUSETTS

Saml Adams

John Hancock

John Adams

Elbridge Gerry

Robt Treat Paine

Samuel Adams

Sam͂ Adams

September 27, 1722 — October 2, 1803

THE GREATEST WORLD EVENT of the eighteenth century was the birth of a new nation. It was a hard struggle, and the new nation was long a-borning. But in the end the whole world benefited by ideals of human liberty that had been long developing and were now given practical application.

The first Signer's voice to give utterance to the profoundly stirring and revolutionary demand for American freedom was that of Samuel Adams, an unsuccessful businessman but an ardent talker and very persuasive reasoner in the town meetings of Boston. One of the Tories was quite correct when he remarked: "Independence, it is true, was declared in Congress in 1776, but it was settled in Boston in 1768 by Adams and his Junto."

For that reason we turn our attention to him first among the fifty-six representatives of the Thirteen Colonies in the Second Continental Congress of 1776, the Signers of the Declaration of Independence.

Like most of the 250,000 inhabitants of Massachusetts (which in those days included Maine), Samuel Adams's forebears were English.

Henry Adams of Devonshire was the first of the Adams family — which was to become both numerous and distinguished — to reach American shores. Arriving about 1636, with a family of eight children, he settled at Mt. Wollaston, in a part of Braintree, Massachusetts, which later became the modern town of Quincy.

This first Henry Adams had two grandsons. One, Joseph, became the grandfather of John Adams, a Signer and the second President of the United States. The second, John, became a sea-captain and the grandfather of Samuel, the other Signer bearing the Adams name. Samuel's father was another Samuel, a successful Yankee businessman who, with his wife Mary Fifield Adams, lived in a fine house on Purchase Street, Boston, overlooking the harbor.

The father Samuel was a prosperous brewer and merchant, a prominent man in Boston town — justice of the peace, deacon of the Old South Church, member of the Massachusetts Bay Assembly, landowner, a leader in public affairs.

His son, Samuel, born in the Purchase Street house on September 27, 1722, was given the usual education thought best for Boston's sons: the Boston Grammar School and then Harvard. He entered Harvard College when he was fourteen, studied Latin and Greek, and learned to admire the ancient classical heroes. Graduating in 1740, he took an M.A. degree three years later, then started to study law in spite of his father's wish that he become a theologian. Since in that harbor city business offered a more substantial career than law, young Sam Adams entered the counting-house of Thomas Cushing. This lasted only until his father gave him £1000 to start a business of his own. But that business did not last long either. After loaning one half of his £1000 to a friend who never repaid it, Adams lost the other half in his own operations. He then went into his father's brewery but even there he failed. Money simply got away from him. Generous to a fault, he was always loaning any money he had to others who never paid it back.

Actually, Samuel Adams did not have money on his mind. He did not care for clothes or style or fine living. He was no status-seeker, but a man of ideas, a dreamer.

Where could such a man succeed?

In the local taverns and clubs and town meetings, Adams was at his best. Night after night found him among groups of men discussing questions of the day, Boston's needs, and possible civic improvements. Though no one realized it, this was Samuel Adams's real training for his life work. In about twenty years serious questions were going to arise — not only for the town of Boston, but for the colony of Massachusetts and for all the colonies of America. Here already a great politician was in the making.

When his father and mother died, Samuel, at twenty-six, inherited a third of the family property, including the malt-house and the handsome estate on Purchase Street. The next year, 1749, he married Elizabeth Checkley, daughter of the "New South"

Church minister. Eight years later she died, leaving two children. Seven years passed before Adams married again. Elizabeth Wells became the second Mrs. Adams, a loyal, hard-working wife, and — what was especially good for Adams — a strict economist. It was she who managed to keep the household going, though there were times when neighbors' gifts of food and clothing were gratefully accepted.

Through all these years, Adams was an indifferent manager of the malt-house. Always in debt, a thinker and student, he was more interested in public matters than in private business, as was shown by the articles he wrote and sent to the papers. He was devoted to the discussions in the debating clubs, devoted to the welfare of his town. He was, his cousin John Adams once said, "a universal good character"; but John Adams qualified that by adding, "unless it should be admitted that he is too attentive to the public, and not enough to himself and his family." He served in various offices: on committees to see to the proper inspection of chimneys, and to take precautions against small-pox. His first official public duty was the modest one of keeping the town clean.

Though he seemed shiftless in managing the business in which his father had been successful, friends and townsmen apparently had faith in him, since they elected him a tax collector year after year.

Significant happenings in Sam Adams's life came in the year 1764. He was now forty-two, already turning grey. He had a peculiar tremor of hands and head that made him seem older still. But in spite of all that, he was vigorous enough to live on for almost forty years more, and his greatest work was still to come. He was of medium height, muscular and hardy, with grey, clear eyes and a prominent nose. His gaze was at times intense and stern, again genial and benign. He had been through hard times. His malt-house had failed, and everything else his father had left him had been gradually vanishing. He still lived in the Purchase Street house with its lovely harbor view, but it badly needed repairs. He owed so much that the Sheriff put it up for sale four times — though Adams managed to save it. Now, however, when Britain's arbitrary treatment of her American colonies was becoming increasingly annoying, Samuel Adams's great hour had come.

In April of 1764, the British Parliament passed a "Sugar Act," which laid a tax on sugar and molasses imported into the colonies. There had always been a tax on molasses, large quantities of which were brought into Massachusetts for distilling rum. The new law cut the tax on molasses in half. It may seem odd that the colonists should object to a law that reduced taxes. But under the older law, the tax on molasses had been so high nobody could collect it. Hence ship-owners made huge profits on smuggled molasses that paid no duty at all. The British hoped that if they reduced taxes, they might be able to collect them. They hoped smuggling would become less profitable and more cargoes would be brought in legally, if taxed at a lower rate.

The Sugar Act was, nevertheless, an objectionable law. A Yankee sea-captain had to give bond at a British customs house every time he loaded his ship for sea — whether his cargo included sugar and molasses or not! This was troublesome, especially as customs officials found the new law a profitable source of graft, frequently extorting tax payments that were not really due.

But the real grievance of the colonists was that they were being taxed in America by an English Parliament in which they were not represented. There was an immediate and violent protest against taxation without representation.

The Sugar Act marked the beginning of Samuel Adams's rise to fame. He and all the other Massachusetts Yankees reacted instantly and indignantly. In May, a Boston town meeting appointed a committee to instruct its representatives in the General Court (that is, the colonial legislature) to oppose the Sugar Act.

Town meetings, the freest and most democratic of all forms of government, were universal in colonial New England.* In a town meeting, all citizens appear in person to decide public questions — not through Senators or representatives, but by direct, free, public, open discussion among themselves. Each citizen has the right to speak and vote. He cannot be "silenced or brow-beaten by a richer or greater townsman than himself." In the perilous years before the Revolution, this gave citizens a splendid chance to speak out boldly against their tyrannical king.

*Town meetings still survive in some New England towns. The authors of this book live in a Connecticut town that still governs itself directly, by this completely democratic system.

Such a system of government is, understandably, possible only in rather small communities, but in the 1760's and 1770's Boston was still a small community. It was entirely possible for Bostonians to meet together in Faneuil Hall.

The free speech of these free citizens in these little New England town meetings probably did more than anything else in America to promote resistance to oppressive British rule. The British knew it only too well. As one of the Tories wrote: "The town-meeting at Boston is the hot-bed of sedition. It is there that all their dangerous insurrections are engendered; it is there that the flame of discord and rebellion was first lighted up and disseminated over the provinces." And the town-meeting voice in Boston was the voice of Sam Adams.

The committee which the Boston town meeting had selected to draft instructions to Boston's representatives in the General Court in turn chose Samuel Adams to do the actual writing. On old yellow paper, one may still read in his fine handwriting:

> "What still heightens our apprehensions is, that these unexpected Proceedings may be preparatory to more extensive Taxations upon us: For if our Trade may be taxed, why not our Lands? Why not the Produce of our Lands & everything we possess or make use of? This, we apprehend, annihilates our Charter Right to govern & tax ourselves. . . . If Taxes are laid upon us in any shape without our having a legal Representation where they are laid, are we not reduced from the Character of free Subjects to the miserable State of tributary Slaves?"

Here was a flat public denial of the British Parliament's right to tax colonists who were not represented in Parliament.

> "As His Majesty's other Northern American Colonys are embarked with us . . . we further desire you to use your Endeavors, that their weight may be added to that of this Province: that by the united Applications of all who are Aggrieved, All may happily attain Redress."

And here was a very early suggestion for a union of the colonies.

When England sent Commissioners of the Customs to Boston to collect the duties, Samuel Adams kept up a running fire of opposition in controversial articles in the *Boston Gazette* and other journals. He also wrote letters to official persons both in England and America.

But in spite of all these protests, the hated Stamp Act became law in March of 1765. Two months later, the Quartering Act ordered the colonists to provide supplies and barracks for British troops that were to be sent over. Indignation became so hot that delegates from nine colonies met in a Stamp Act Congress in New York in early October to prepare a "declaration of rights and grievances." Still, in spite of all protests, the Stamp Act went into effect on November 1. Flags were lowered to half staff, bells tolled mournfully.

In the Stamp Act year, 1765, Samuel Adams was elected to fill a vacancy as representative in the House. His influence spread until the royal governor, Thomas Hutchinson, became alarmed and described him as a dangerous "incendiary." Disapproval was mutual. Adams regarded the governor as an "enemy of liberty." Indeed, Adams's influence, which had started among the dock workers and "mechanics" of Boston where he had been a rabble-rouser, had during the years spread over the colony and into others.

After Benjamin Franklin patiently explained to the House of Commons in London in 1766 why the Stamp Act could never be enforced, it was repealed in March.*

But this was only one concession. The next year England imposed more duties on imported goods and the Boston town meeting decided to do without the imports. No one was to bring in any English goods. Other colonies followed suit.

Here was something to worry England, for trade with the colonies was important to British merchants, who made great profit out of it.

There was more trouble when, in the autumn of 1768, two regiments of British soldiers landed in Boston to help the Governor enforce the law in unruly Massachusetts, especially in Boston. The colonists had not yet completed arrangements to cut off British imports. Some British goods were still coming in, and there was much difficulty in collecting duty on them. The government in London hoped, by suppressing resistance in Boston, to end it throughout the colonies.

* See the chapter on Benjamin Franklin for the colonists' grievances over the Stamp Act.

Now the leader of a patriotic group called the Sons of Liberty, Sam Adams began to use his influence to stir up feeling against the redcoats. Eventually friction between the people and the soldiers grew so bitter that in 1770 soldiers fired on an American group who defied a British sentry. Probably without orders, the soldiers fired, killing four men and wounding seven. Two of the wounded Bostonians died later. This was the Boston Massacre. Some of the soldiers were arrested, though later tried and almost all acquitted, and the governor agreed to remove one regiment from the town.

After this, for about two years, disputes with the mother country cooled off. The most objectionable laws were repealed, though not the duty on tea. Sam Adams's cousin, John Adams, withdrew from politics for a time, disgusted because he was criticized for having done his duty as a lawyer by serving as attorney for the soldiers implicated in the Massacre.

But Samuel Adams, like an Old Testament prophet, kept steadfastly sounding the warnings of the wrath to come. In some forty articles in Boston newspapers, he warned the people of the "concealed conspiracy intended to deprive them of their liberty." He told them that the greatest danger was in thinking that there was no danger; that, though unaware of it, they were being made slaves.

At a Boston meeting on November 2, 1772, on Adams's motion, a committee of correspondence was appointed to state the rights of the colonists, "and of this Province in particular, as men, as Christians, and as Subjects; and to communicate the same to the several towns and to the world."

In London, Parliament passed the tax on tea the next day. Though it would take some weeks for this news to reach the American side of the Atlantic, the foresight of Samuel Adams caused him to begin at once to work for an assembly of the colonies, in other words, a Continental Congress. With his clear logic, he explained, persuaded, and wrote hundreds of articles, keeping his ideas before the public. Four months later, an article entitled "Observation," which was attributed to Samuel Adams, appeared in the *Boston Gazette*. It proposed that "a congress of American states be assembled as soon as possible; draw up a Bill of Rights — choose an ambassador to reside at the British

Court to act for the united colonies; appoint where the congress shall annually meet."

Adams knew the coming of the tea ships that very autumn would bring trouble, might even create a crisis. In early November, the Boston Committee of Correspondence voted that it would not allow the tea shipped by the East India Company (for whose benefit Parliament had imposed the tea tax) even to be unloaded. The next day, Sam Adams and others of the Sons of Liberty committee requested the resignation of the "consignees" — that is, the merchants who were to accept the consignments of tea when they reached Boston. The consignees refused to resign. Two days later, November 5, Adams drafted a resolution declaring all who helped in landing or selling the tea to be enemies of America.

The first of the tea ships, *Dartmouth,* arrived November 28. Next day there was a mass meeting in Faneuil Hall. Guesses were that from one thousand to five thousand people were present, either in the hall or in the square outside. Adams moved that the tea should be sent back to England, and the motion was carried. A meeting next day chose a directing committee, Sam Adams being included. During the next two weeks many meetings took place. All this time the tea remained on the ships. Finally the time was up. Under customs law, the cargo had to be either landed or confiscated by December 16.

Excitement was now at fever heat. A mass meeting of about seven thousand people filled the Old South Church, the adjoining streets, and Boston Common. It was like a swarming of bees. Nothing like it had ever been seen. Adams presided. The meeting lasted from ten in the morning until six in the evening. When a messenger came, saying that Governor Hutchinson still refused to have the ships return to England, Samuel Adams declared, "This meeting can do nothing more to save the country."

As if this had been a pre-arranged signal, a number of men rose and left the meeting. Presently a group, probably the same men, many now dressed as Indians, appeared on the wharf and dumped all the tea overboard. This was the famous Boston Tea Party.

In our coffee-drinking century, we may doubt that the rejection of the tea was very hard on the colonists. But tea had long been the favorite hot beverage of the English, and most New Englanders had come from the British Isles, or had English forebears. Some now tried to brew a tea from catnip and pennyroyal but it was not at all the same. They really missed their tea.

The Boston Tea Party had far-reaching effects. Philadelphia, New York, and Charleston also resisted the landing of tea. In England, the Parliament, King George, and his adviser, Lord North, were incensed. Retaliation was bound to come. The Boston Port Act, which would close the port entirely, was approved by the King at the end of March. Six weeks later, the Boston Committee retaliated by recommending that all colonies suspend trade with Great Britain entirely.

In the Massachusetts General Court, Adams moved to appoint delegates to a Continental Congress "to deliberate and determine upon all measures." Five delegates were chosen, Adams himself being one.

It was well that Samuel Adams, who never much cared how he looked, had some friends who did care. He could hardly go to Philadelphia and meet representatives from all the other colonies, looking the way he usually looked at home. Bostonians were used to his unkempt, slovenly personal appearance. After all, what did it matter? Sam Adams had brains, a wonderful single-ness of purpose, spirit, and a capacity for indefatigable work — all for the cause of "the people," whose deep respect he commanded. He had education. They knew him; many loved him. Already in 1774, one friend had built him a new barn; another had repaired his house. Now, when he was about to take the first long trip of his life to attend the Congress for which he had labored so hard and so long, friends outfitted him with a new suit, new shoes, and several pairs of silk hose. People appreciated him, and when he needed help they helped him. Samuel Adams was now fifty-two, and he had never been outside Massachusetts, and never even far from home.

When the Massachusetts delegates reached Philadelphia, they were warned to keep themselves a bit in the background for a while. Some delegates from more "moderate" colonies felt that the Massachusetts patriots had been too rash. Pennsylvania, with her large Quaker population, was one of the moderate middle colonies.

In fact, the moderates and Tories believed that Samuel Adams "managed things both in and out of Congress." The Pennsylvania

lawyer, Joseph Galloway, who had been Speaker of the Pennsylvania Assembly and was now a leader in Congress of the party
who still wanted reconciliation with Britain, wrote later in his
book on the rise and progress of the American Revolution that
it was Samuel Adams who managed the expresses (mails) which
were continually moving between Philadelphia and Boston during
the seven weeks this first Congress convened. "These were," he
wrote, "under the management of Samuel Adams . . . He eats
little, drinks little, sleeps little, thinks much, and is most decisive
and indefatigable in the pursuit of his objects. It was this man,
who, by his superior application, managed at once the faction in
Congress at Philadelphia and the factions in New England."

During the seven weeks session of the First Congress, the
deliberators prepared a Declaration of Rights and Grievances,
addresses to the king, to the people of England, of Canada, and
of other British American colonies, as well as a letter to the agent
of the colonies in England. Comparatively few men felt, as yet,
that it would be impossible to deal with king and Parliament.
Hence the colonies still begged Britain to understand their position, give them their rights, and allow them to be represented
where their laws were made, that is, in Parliament. But Samuel
Adams knew this would never be done, that Britain would never
be conciliatory. Benjamin Franklin, in England at the time, also
felt this way. Congress was adjourned October 26 to meet again
May 10, 1775.

Returning to Boston in early November, these first Massachusetts congressmen were greeted with public demonstrations. Surviving letters of the time show the regard, even reverence, that
Boston patriots felt toward Samuel Adams. Indeed, it was said
that the uneducated people came to think he had a prophetic
power and that even war and peace might rest with him.

Once back in Boston, Sam Adams had a busy winter in the
Provincial Congress, which had now come into being. The redcoats under British General Gage were now all over Boston.
Against this state of affairs, the colonists had been storing up
guns and ammunition in secret. Adams led the local congress in
making people aware of the ever approaching outburst of conflict. He pointed out the danger of allowing British soldiers to
march into the country and recommended opposition if they went

even ten miles from Boston. General Gage could not help realizing that Adams and John Hancock were two patriotic firebrands. He also was aware that the patriots were storing ammunition. He moved his regulars out to Lexington and Concord on the never-to-be-forgotten night of April 18/19, in order to seize those stores. That caused those first "shots heard round the world." He was hoping, too, to capture Hancock and Adams.

For some time tension in Boston had been tightening, what with the presence of British soldiers all through the streets, and more always coming. A silversmith named Paul Revere had already set up the first American intelligence net of about thirty "mechanics" * whose purpose, Revere reported, was to watch "the movements of the British soldiers" and keep a close eye on the Tories. That fateful Spring, these volunteers "frequently took turns, two and two, to watch the soldiers, by patrolling the streets all night."

On the evening of April 18, 1775, news spread around town that the British regulars were going out into the country. Samuel Adams and John Hancock were staying that night in the old parsonage at Lexington, at that time the home of the Reverend Jonas Clark.

Every American knows the story of Paul Revere's ride. When he galloped up to the Lexington Green, he found the parsonage dark, and every one asleep. A sergeant stationed at the house told Revere that the family did not want to be disturbed by any noise.

"Noise!" cried Paul Revere. "You'll have enough noise before long. The regulars are coming out."

The British infantry arrived about dawn and firing started. While the smoke was clearing away, Hancock and Adams escaped across the fields to Woburn. As the white sun of that Spring morning rose over the horizon, Adams exclaimed: "What a glorious morning is this!" Within the next few days, the Massachusetts representatives were again on their way to Philadelphia.

The Second Continental Congress convened May 10, 1775. Samuel Adams was now fifty-four, and he had travelled a long, hard road. Through all those years of persuading, discussing, debating,

* John and Katherine Bakeless, *Spies of the Revolution*, J. B. Lippincott Co., Phila., and New York, 1962, p. 44. "Mechanics" was the term for men who "made" things.

writing articles, getting poorer all the time, while trying to open people's minds to the danger of an increasing British tyranny, and showing them the desirability of American independence he had been a true servant of the people. Long after the war, Dr. Benjamin Rush, a Pennsylvania Signer, wrote in a letter to John Adams that "Samuel Adams once told me that the independence of British America had been the first wish of his heart seven years before the commencement of the American Revolutionary War in 1774." At the time of the Second Congress, Dr. Rush supposed Adams to be "near sixty," but he wrote that Adams "possessed all the vigor of mind of a young man of five and twenty." He said Adams "loved simplicity and oeconomy [sic] in the administration of government, and despised the appeals which are made to the eyes and ears of the common people in order to govern them . . . Ambition and avarice, the usual vices of politicians, seem to have no place in his breast."

One of the most important acts of the Second Continental Congress was the appointment of George Washington as commander in chief. And for this perfect appointment Americans must always feel grateful to the "brace of Adamses," for it was John who nominated the tall Virginian and Samuel who seconded the motion. This was a long and busy period for Congress. Two days after this appointment was made in Philadelphia, the Battle of Bunker Hill took place outside Boston. This was a British victory in which Samuel Adams's beloved friend, General (and Doctor) Joseph Warren was killed. Two weeks later, Washington, having traveled twelve days from Philadelphia, took command of all American armed forces in Cambridge.

Even after these clashes of arms, there were still insistent demands from the moderate middle colonies that Congress should send still more petitions to the king. Samuel Adams was out of patience with the Pennsylvania Quakers for such delays when war had already begun. Benjamin Franklin, now sitting in Congress after many years in London, also knew that further petition was useless; that Lord North, the king's prime minister, would concede nothing. But in July, Congress decided to send still another petition to George III. When it arrived in London, it was refused at once. Adams had been right. Franklin had been right. It had been of no use.

This Congress adjourned August 1 until September 5, and Adams returned home for a few busy weeks. But the Massachusetts delegates took back with them $500,000 for Washington's army.

Soon, however, Sam Adams was in the saddle on a horse loaned him by his cousin John for the three-hundred-mile ride back to Philadelphia. Some historians call this September, 1775, session of Congress the Third Continental Congress, while others refer to it as the Second. The confusion no doubt arises because there were no elections for representatives such as we have today. Instead, they were chosen by the state assemblies.

Adams was in favor of immediate independence. But a declaration of independence was a declaration of rebellion, and the middle colonies still could not bring themselves to accept this appalling idea. Persuasions, discussions, debates increased. The various committees in Congress were busy day and night. At the end of November Congress founded an American Navy. On January 1, 1776, Lord Dunmore, royal governor of Virginia, bombarded and burned Norfolk. And on that same day, in Cambridge, Massachusetts, Washington raised the Continental flag with thirteen stripes before his headquarters. Ten days later, Thomas Paine published his famous pamphlet, *Common Sense*. In April, North Carolina definitely instructed her delegates to stand for independence. She was the first to venture upon this bold course. Congress buzzed with excitement. A month later, a second colony, Virginia, took the same stand, and went further. Virginia instructed her delegates to make a formal proposal of separation from the mother country.

By the end of the first week of June the Virginia delegates were ready. On June 7, Richard Henry Lee of Virginia took the floor and offered to Congress the resolution for independence. This must have been the sweetest of music to the ears of Samuel Adams. After all those years . . .

The next day the debate on the resolution began.

Long after, Elbridge Gerry told Samuel Adams's daughter that the success of Lee's measure was largely due to the "timely remarks" of her father arguing in favor of independence. Gerry added that in one unusually long speech, Adams won over two or three wavering members.

Edward Rutledge of South Carolina moved for a postponement of this all-important question for three weeks to enable the hesitating delegates to consult their constituents and gauge the feelings of the people in their respective colonies.

During those three weeks, Samuel Adams's peculiar powers were brought to the fore in personal conferences. He labored long hours stating his views clearly, logically, over and over again. Patiently, he "button-holed" the moderates and those less stout of heart. Hot July arrived and the steadily ripening sentiment of the country made itself felt in Congress. They were ready to vote.

Then some late arrivals, who had not heard the previous discussions, asked to have certain points clarified. All eyes turned to Samuel Adams's cousin John who had just finished a formal address to Congress on these very matters. Since he had every point clearly in mind, he was asked to enlighten the newcomers and he obliged.

In the end, Delaware's representatives needed the absent Caesar Rodney to complete that colony's vote in favor of independence. Congress would be voting the next day and a messenger was sent off to get him. All through the night of July 1, through thunderstorms and driving rain, Rodney rode back to Philadelphia. He arrived in time on July 2 when Lee's resolution declaring independence was adopted by Congress. On the Fourth, the Declaration of Independence, as drafted by Thomas Jefferson and subsequently amended, was adopted and signed by John Hancock, President of Congress.

At once, the atmosphere in the hall changed. A wave of relief washed away the tenseness of worry, apprehension, fear of not doing the right thing. Now it was done. The anguish of decision was past. The men laughed and joked.

This then was the career of Samuel Adams, America's first great genius in politics. This was the part of his life that has given his name an exalted place in American history. It began with the resistance to mounting British tyranny and ended, really, when the war began. Adams had been the foremost revolutionary agitator, but his talent did not lie in the direction of constructive statesmanship, although he remained in Congress until 1781, serving ably on many committees, the most important of which dealt with the Articles of Confederation.

In April of 1781, he returned home to his beloved Boston. He was a delegate to the Convention which drafted the Massachusetts Constitution. Under the new government he became a senator, and from 1789 to 1793 he was lieutenant-governor of his state. When Governor John Hancock died in 1793, Adams became governor and was elected again for three terms.

In 1796, during his last term as Governor of Massachusetts, Virginia cast fifteen votes for Samuel Adams for President of the United States. Thomas Jefferson had twenty votes. But Adams, now seventy-four, was soon to announce his retirement from public life. When Thomas Jefferson became President in 1801, he would have liked the old congressman in his cabinet. He wrote Adams: "How much I lament that time has deprived me of your aid! It would have been a day of glory which should have called you to the first office of my administration. But give us your counsel, my friend, and give us your blessing, and be assured that there exists not in the heart of man a more faithful esteem than mine to you, and that I shall ever bear you the most affectionate veneration and respect."

Samuel Adams was a strange combination of qualities rarely seen in one person. In religion he was the narrowest of Puritans; in manner easy and genial. Absolutely rigid in his opinions, he could express them with a flexibility that was often compliant. Most conservative of men, he was at the same time a vigorous revolutionary. At political maneuvering he was wily as a fox. With no foresight or push in business, he was a power of force and shrewdness in politics, where his foresight was keen and accurate. No one could be more skillful than he in the managing of men. So adroit was he that his followers were often not even aware that they were being managed. Though he was not considered eloquent as an orator and could not match his cousin, John Adams, as a debater, he could, when his deeper feelings were aroused, speak with a "purity, correctness and nervous elegance" of style that strongly impressed all who heard and saw him. John Adams said that Samuel had "an exquisite ear for music, and a charming voice when he pleased to exert it." But when Boston wanted a theatre Samuel Adams was Puritan enough to oppose it strongly.

Thomas Jefferson has told us that, as a speaker, Samuel Adams could not be compared with his cousin John, who, in Congress, was "our bulwark in debate. But Mr. Samuel Adams," he continued, "although not of fluent elocution, was so rigorously logical, so clear in his views, abundant in good sense, and master always of his subject, that he commanded the most profound attention whenever he rose in an assembly."

The last years of the old revolutionist were filled with honor and expressions of regard. Even the Federalists — the opposing party — honored him. In 1800, when the new Governor of Massachusetts, Caleb Strong, moved through Winter Street in a large procession which was probably his inaugural parade, old Mr. Adams sat at his window looking out at the pageant. The governor ordered a halt, stopped the music, got out of his carriage, and went to the door to shake the hand of the old hero. With head bared, the new governor expressed his reverence for the man who embodied the Spirit of '76. The soldiers presented arms. The crowd stood silent with uncovered heads.

Years later, in an oration in Lexington, Edward Everett described the beginnings of Samuel Adams's work in the 1760's.

"The throne of his ascendency was in Faneuil Hall," he said. These were the town meetings. "As each new measure of arbitrary power was announced from across the Atlantic, or each new act of menace and violence on the part of the officers of the government or of the army occurred in Boston, its citizens, oftentimes in astonishment and perplexity, rallied to the sound of his voice in Faneuil Hall; and there, as from the crowded gallery or the moderator's chair he animated, enlightened, fortified, and roused the admiring throng, he seemed to gather them together beneath the aegis of his indomitable spirit, as a hen gathereth her chickens under her wings."

During the summer of 1803, the old man grew more and more feeble. Early on Sunday morning, October 2, the bells of Boston tolled for his death. Samuel Adams had reached his eighty-first year.

The funeral procession, headed by the Independent Cadets and followed by many dignitaries and friends, moved through the streets as minute guns were fired from the old fort and muffled drums beat a dirge at Faneuil Hall. At the old State House, the cortège turned up Tremont Street toward the Old Granary Burying Ground.

Samuel Adams's unmarked grave is appropriately near that of the victims of the Boston Massacre, which had taken place thirty-three years before, and almost beneath the feet of passers-by along the busy modern thoroughfare of Uncle Sam's beloved Boston town.

John Hancock

January 23, 1737 — October 8, 1793

"I WRITE SO THAT George the Third may read without his spectacles," John Hancock is supposed to have said when he signed his name, in his big, bold, careful handwriting, to the Declaration of Independence. Infinitely relieved and happy that the Declaration was now an accomplished fact, he obviously felt like flaunting it before the king of England.

The first American Hancock was Nathaniel, the Signer's great-great-grandfather, who came from England. He probably came in 1633 — at any rate, he was granted two acres of land in Newtown (now Cambridge), Massachusetts, on January 5, 1634. He improved his two-acre patch and thrived as a small farmer. When his children came along, he was no doubt glad that a grammar school had started next to the first American college, Harvard, founded in 1636.

The early settlers' activities revolved about their church, in which succeeding generations of Hancocks became leaders. By the time John Hancock, the Signer, was born on January 23, 1737, a hundred years after Nathaniel Hancock's arrival as an immigrant, he had an ancestral background of ministers. He was born in Braintree, Massachusetts, where his father, the Reverend John Hancock, was minister of the Congregational Church. His mother had been Mary Hawke Thaxter when she married the minister. The Signer's grandfather was another John Hancock, pastor of the Congregational Church in Lexington. In that house, which had been his grandfather's parsonage, John Hancock and Samuel

Adams were sleeping on the April night of Paul Revere's ride in 1775.

John Hancock was only seven when his father died, leaving his mother almost penniless with three small children: Mary, John, and Ebenezer. His father's brother, the boy's Uncle Thomas, took his elder nephew, John, to raise in his own home in Boston. This made a great change in the boy's life. His Uncle Thomas Hancock was the wealthiest merchant in Boston and his house was a large mansion on Beacon Hill. Moreover, since he and his wife had no children of their own, Aunt Lydia lavished her affection on their nephew. She fussed over him, buying him the finest of clothes, and kept him home from school a year, probably because he was not a very strong child. From this time on, John Hancock grew up amid elegant and luxurious surroundings. At nine years of age, he was sent to the Public Latin School, now the oldest school in the country.

In the next five years he was required to cover much more than boys of today study in eight years. Recitations lasted from seven in the morning until five in the afternoon. There were one-week vacations at Thanksgiving and Christmas and three weeks in August. At first young John worked on grammar, spelling, penmanship (to good effect as we can see), and other familiar subjects, but then came Latin and Greek and studies we hear little of today, including the New Testament in Greek.

From the Latin School he was sent to Harvard, where he had to get up in time for six o'clock chapel, listen to Scripture reading in Hebrew or Greek, and report for his first recitation at 6:30. Students had six weeks' vacation in summer, five in winter. If they lived within ten miles of Cambridge, as Hancock did, they could go home for four days each month. Nevertheless, work was more intense than the study students complain about today.

Many other things were different: The college gave boys beer for their evening meal. They also drank wines and spirits. Rum punch was popular, and so was "flip," a horrid concoction of ale, beer, cider, "etc." — which apparently meant anything else they had at hand to pour in. It is no wonder Hancock began to suffer from gout in his fifties.

With an M.A. degree at seventeen, John Hancock was ready to take a job, but that was no problem at all, for the job was all ready. He had only to enter his uncle's counting-house and learn the business from the ground up. But it was a complex business, which included shipping, book-keeping, importing, buying and selling; and Uncle Thomas had built it up from scratch, without the advantage of a Harvard degree. From England, Thomas Hancock was importing tea, cloth, paper, cutlery, and sending back American codfish, whale oil, whale bone, and lumber. His merchandizing had spread to include Nova Scotia and the West Indies on this side of the Atlantic, and Holland and Spain besides Great Britain on the other. As there was very little money in New England, most of these deals had to be accomplished by trading. Shiploads of goods were not bought with money, but traded for something else, and this brought about a great deal of smuggling. It seems strange to us today that in the land of the Puritans smuggling was almost respectable, that it was rather taken for granted, and that many of the merchant princes of those days gained their great fortunes in illicit dealing. Four large Hancock ships were always sailing between Old and New England. It was a big business.

After six years of studying and working in the local part of the business, John went to England to meet business connections and to settle accounts for the House of Hancock. He was therefore in London when King George II died. He attended the great state funeral and remained to see the coronation of George III, because, as he wrote home, it would be "the grandest thing I shall ever meet with."

Back home in Boston in October, 1761, young Hancock found his uncle's health had badly deteriorated. Uncle Thomas, now suffering from frequent attacks of gout, took John into partnership; and when he died, three years later, John inherited the vast business. Though he was still only twenty-eight years old, he now possessed a fortune comparable to that of a modern millionaire.

The responsibility, however, was heavy and growing heavier because under George III British relations with the American colonies soon began to deteriorate. Times were getting worse for businessmen and especially so for merchants. The very next year the Stamp Act went into effect.

John Hancock's first political interests probably began when he joined several lodges. Men in those times spent their evenings with friends in various clubs, which met in taverns and coffee-houses. A man usually belonged to several — at all of which current events were discussed, and public questions were debated. In 1762, the year after he returned from England, John Hancock became a member of the Masonic Lodge of St. Andrews. He also joined St. John's Lodge, the Long Room Club, and the Merchants' Club. Influential citizens in business and the professions met monthly or weekly in these and other clubs, and, as time went on, they aired more and more grievances against mounting trade restrictions placed upon them by the mother country. "Out of these talks came some of the earliest rebellious ideas," writes Herbert S. Allan, John Hancock's biographer, "although most of the men who took part in them, including Hancock, had then no conscious thought of disloyalty to the Crown." In the Long Room Club were Paul Revere, Thomas Dawes, Samuel Adams, Dr. Benjamin Church (later found guilty of treason to America), and others who became the leaders of the Revolution.

Here was the beginning of colonial resentment of the heavy British import duties and other taxes that Parliament was forcing upon her American colonies. It was also the beginning of Hancock's political career. Association and discussion with these men led him to run for the office of selectman when the opportunity arose. He won and from then on, for the remainder of his life, paid more attention to his exhausting work as a statesman than to his profitable private business.

Then came the Stamp Act, which aroused such indignation as to bring the first show of violence against England by the Sons of Liberty. Samuel Adams is supposed to have inspired the gathering of a mob under the "Liberty Tree," a large elm at the corner of Washington and Essex streets. As yet, Hancock was opposed to violence, but Sam Adams was a rabble-rouser from the beginning. The mob destroyed the house and property of Thomas Hutchinson, the royal lieutenant-governor, and with it his library and collection of irreplaceable American historical manuscripts.

Hancock protested the Stamp Act not by violence but in letters to his English correspondents. In England, Benjamin Franklin was explaining to Parliament why the Stamp Act could not be enforced. But their efforts were fruitless. Though the Stamp Act was repealed, more oppressive acts of Parliament eventually convinced

Hancock that the colonists would have to resort to arms.

In the meantime, he was elected to the General Court, as Massachusetts still called its legislature.

In 1767 John Hancock gave Harvard £500 worth of books, fulfilling a promise his uncle had made, and adding some books of his own. The next year he was in difficulty over importing a large cargo of Madeira wine in his sloop *Liberty*. Accused of having smuggled some of the cargo ashore, he engaged John Adams to defend him. After some months the case was dropped (smuggling was common among the merchants of those times and not much frowned upon), but the *Liberty* was condemned, converted into a coast guard vessel, and later burned by a mob in Newport. The publicity made Hancock all the more popular with the common people. After a frightful fire in Boston in February, 1767, which destroyed more than twenty buildings, including some of Hancock's, he contributed a large sum of money to the relief of homeless families. He also gave many gifts to meeting-houses and churches — others as well as his own. People came to look upon him as a generous benefactor.

After the Boston Massacre, Hancock was chosen to head the town committee. Samuel Adams, ever active in keeping patriotic feelings stirred up, saw the great advantage in having Boston's wealthiest man on the side of the patriots. For if anything were to be lost in being a patriot, Hancock surely had the most to lose. To the British, the word patriot had come to mean those Americans who were disloyal to the Crown. But all most patriots wanted as yet was to have some say in the laws that governed them. Most of them were still loyal British subjects who were not thinking of separation from the mother country.

As Sam Adams's influence spread, he helped his friend Hancock become a local favorite, winning election to various minor offices. After the General Court became the Provincial Congress in 1774, he was chosen president.

Hancock was a militia officer himself. In 1772, he had been made "Captain of the Company of Cadets with the rank of Colonel," the cadets being a small military unit that served as honor guard to the governor. This he loved because he could dress up in a resplendent military uniform. For John Hancock was a vain little man. Slight of build, he had a dapper, neat appearance and,

of course, he could afford the finest of clothing. Perhaps his Aunt
Lydia had stirred this harmless vanity in him when he was a small
child, for she took great pleasure in keeping the boy well dressed.
However that may have been, Hancock was always generous and
supplied uniforms and arms to his Cadets at his own expense.
They loved him for it. He gave generously everywhere. He supplied Boston with its first street lamps, and also gave the town its
first concert hall — stipulating that no British officers, whether of
the army, navy, or revenue service, should ever be admitted!

Then, in the autumn of 1774, John Hancock cut himself off from
the Crown. At this same time, Samuel Adams and other Massachusetts delegates to the First Continental Congress were on their
way to Philadelphia. Hancock saw more excitement at home in
Boston. Threats against his life were now being made. The Boston
Port Bill had gone into effect. The British government had closed
the harbor to all imports and exports. Whigs and Tories were more
hostile than ever. Undaunted by all these signs that his life was
in danger, Hancock accepted appointment as chairman of the
provincial Committee of Safety and proceeded to provoke the redcoats still further. As chairman of the Committee of Safety, he had
the power to call out the militia. When more British troops came to
Boston, he suggested burning the city to get rid of them, though
most of his own property would have been lost. But the patriots
gave up this idea.

Early in the following March, a farmer visiting Boston was
seized by British soldiers on false charges of having tried to influence a soldier to desert. They tarred and feathered him and
paraded him on a wagon through the streets. A British regimental
band led the procession, playing for the first time for the American public, an old English tune to which new words had been set.
The military escort sang:

> *Yankee Doodle came to town*
> *For to buy a firelock;*
> *We will tar and feather him,*
> *And so we will John Hancock.*

Within a month, it was plain that events were mounting to a
climax. Whig leaders were leaving town and sending wives and

families away. Hancock and Samuel Adams went out to Lexington and spent the night of April 18/19 in the old Hancock parsonage. But at Paul Revere's warning they were forced to flee at dawn. These two most wanted rebels escaped through woods and swamps while the first shots were exchanged on the Lexington Common in front of the parsonage. The British went on to Concord hoping to seize the patriots' ammunition but were stopped by the "embattled farmers." Meanwhile, Hancock and Adams were making their way safely to Woburn.

About two weeks later, chosen a delegate to the Second Continental Congress, Hancock was on his way to Philadelphia. The British General Gage had for a short time permitted Boston inhabitants to leave the city, and Hancock's Aunt Lydia and his fiancée, Dorothy Quincy, had gone to the home of an old friend of the family in Fairfield, Connecticut. From New York, Hancock sent letters back to his "Dolly," describing the rousing reception he was given in New York. The reception was meant for all the delegates, naturally, but Hancock was vain enough to make it appear as if it were especially for him. Perhaps he wanted to impress Dolly. And perhaps a good deal of the homage was indeed meant for him, for Hancock was very popular and was now known throughout the colonies for his many defiant gestures toward the British government. While Samuel Adams, equally defiant and a devotee of complete independence long before Hancock, had always worked quietly, Hancock deliberately provoked publicity.

He wrote Dorothy that when he was within a mile of New York, his carriage was stopped by people who wanted to unhitch the horses and pull his carriage into the city. He begged off from that, but "when I got to the entrance of the city," he wrote, "the number of spectators increased to perhaps 7000 or more."

The delegates from New England, now numbering fourteen (those from Connecticut, New York, and probably Rhode Island having joined those from Massachusetts), were all greeted by groups both military and civilian. Silas Deane of Connecticut wrote: "A battalion of about eight hundred men in uniform and bayonets fixed, with a band of music, received us with a military salute — led us down the main street to the corner of Wall Street; up that and down the Broadway by the fort; then up to Fraunces'

Tavern." At ten o'clock that night, John Hancock sat down there to a supper of fried oysters. Fraunces'. Tavern is still one of New York's most interesting landmarks — and still a restaurant.

Approaching Philadelphia on May 10, the delegates were met by about two hundred "principal gentlemen on horseback." Hancock and Adams — already famous not only because of their own achievements but also because they came from the center of revolution — rode, surrounded by this escort, in a phaeton drawn by a pair of horses. As they entered the Pennsylvania city, all the church bells were ringing to greet them.

There was to be no rest for the travelers. Having washed up after riding through "the greatest cloud of dust I ever saw," Hancock wrote there was just time to have dinner before these founding fathers had to be in Independence Hall for the opening of the Second Continental Congress.

Philadelphia was the largest city in the colonies in those days. Its houses and streets reflected the prosperity of the rich countryside surrounding it, where ideal farmlands produced food more abundantly and more easily than did the colder and stonier New England the Massachusetts delegation knew. Though it had a certain refinement due to its Quaker origin, all kinds of people were to be seen in the streets: Indians wrapped in blankets; Pennsylvania Dutch in wooden shoes; Germans, Swedes, and Welsh farmers from the surrounding countryside; hunters from the "back country" wearing leather shirts and carrying their long rifles. Slaves were still bought and sold at Philadelphia auctions. On top of all this was the silk-and-satin aristocracy.

Such a mixture meant also a mixture of opinion; much more so than in Boston, whose inhabitants were mostly of a kind and mostly of English ancestry.

John Hancock, now forty-five years old, was unanimously chosen President of the Congress. Though he was vastly pleased by this great honor, he soon found that he would have to earn it by laborious and discouraging endeavor. The next two and a half years were extremely difficult for him. The role of president was arduous, and the atmosphere uncongenial. A good many Philadelphians were far from enthusiastic about the approaching Revolution. Philadelphia businessmen were ultra-conservative and willing to put up with things as they were. They did not like British trade restrictions any more than the Yankees did; but because they had greater resources for export in their corner of fertile Pennsylvania, they could stand the higher import duties better than New Englanders could. Besides, the Quakers, who were the dominant part of the population and pacifist by religious principle, preferred to accept whatever restrictions were put upon them rather than fight. Pennsylvania was therefore unsympathetic to the bold, new, radical ideas that Samuel Adams most ardently urged. Hancock labored under a tremendous handicap as president of a dissident assemblage that was struggling with some of the most difficult problems ever undertaken by statesmen. Moreover, rich as he was, he was intellectually inferior to some of the other statesmen sitting in the Congress over which he was presiding.

A month later, in mid-June, he suffered a bitter disappointment. It was necessary to appoint a commander in chief for the new American Army.

Strange as it now seems, Hancock wanted this appointment for himself, although his only military experience had been as colonel of the Cadets. In addition to his lack of experience, he was not a strong man physically and could never have endured such a heavy military responsibility nor withstood the rigors of army life. Even his friends the Adamses did not favor this idea.

When this discussion came up, a tall, robust figure in uniform, who had been listening to congressional business, rose and left the room. This was Colonel George Washington of the Virginia Militia, who had fought in the French and Indian War, had saved Braddock's army, and had long defended the Virginia frontier. After the colonel left the room, John Adams moved that Washington be appointed. Samuel Adams seconded the motion. Hancock was so bitterly disappointed he could not keep from showing it, and it affected his friendship with the Adamses, at least for a time. His truly great service to the country was his ability to mediate between the antagonistic factions in the Congress, and keep its business moving smoothly, with an appearance of unity through all the heated arguments and debates that preceded the day of the all-important vote on independence.

It was his duty, too, to see that all the thirteen provincial assemblies back home were kept informed of what was going on in Congress; to persuade them to comply with congressional resolutions;

to appease them when their own pet projects were by-passed. This meant a vast amount of daily letter-writing.

Even after the first shots had been fired at Lexington and Concord, and at Bunker Hill, there were ultra-conservatives in the middle colonies who still insisted on trying one more time to settle peacefully with Britain for American self-government within the Empire, rather than war over complete independence. In July, John Hancock signed their "Olive Branch" petition, as did a majority of delegates. But it was useless — George III would not even read their petition when it was presented to him.

Then the committees in Congress began to work long hours, day and night, making plans for the needs of a new country. Besides an army, there would have to be a navy. There was the problem of friendly relations with foreign countries and with the Indians. If a long war came, the colonies would have to have money and they looked to France for loans. Constant communications had to be maintained between the delegates in Philadelphia and the thirteen provincial congresses.

In April, North Carolina sent instructions to her delegates to stand for independence, the first colony to do so. A month later, Virginia instructed her delegates to *propose* independence. The atmosphere grew more intense as the days became warmer. On June 7, the chairman of the Virginia delegation, Richard Henry Lee, offered the great resolution. Three weeks were given to its consideration. It was a hot July first when Lee's resolution was reopened in Congress.

The leaders of the independence movement asked for a delay in the vote, hoping that a little more time would win a unanimous or near-unanimous vote. They almost had it when Pennsylvania and South Carolina moved over into line, and when Delaware's Caesar Rodney arrived on the morning of July 2 after an all-night ride through heavy rain and thunderstorms. His vote carried Delaware for independence.

After the black night, the vote came *yea*.

It was unanimous — with twelve colonies voting. New York representatives abstained from the vote. They themselves favored independence; but they were bound by their instructions to keep the way open for reconciliation with Great Britain.

Two more days of impassioned oratory followed, until, about

two o'clock on the afternoon of the Fourth, "the great white paper was reported out of committee to the House with a recommendation for approval, and was immediately ratified."

It was done.

John Hancock and Secretary Charles Thomson were ordered to sign the paper. It was then that Hancock made the remark that opens this chapter.

After about two and a half years of arduous work in Congress, John Hancock resigned, feeling that his indifferent health required rest. For all the demanding, worrisome labor he had done, he never received a cent of pay, though he was given $1392 in repayment of his own personal loans to the treasury. Six years later he was reimbursed for his incidental and household expenses.

Simple good manners demanded a polite vote of thanks from that body of public men as a gesture of gratitude to a leader who had been faithful to his trust. But here Samuel Adams, with his fanatically narrow conception of democracy, intervened. Confusing gratitude with homage, he thought no special tribute should be paid to any person in a democracy. To him, that smacked of treatment given to royalty! Samuel Adams had great influence among the members of the Congress and when he raised the issue, a vote of thanks to their presiding member was opposed. Hancock was given no public thanks and no formal credit for his excellent work as mediator in what was perhaps the most agitated, unhappy, uncertain Congress we have ever had. Keenly hurt, he was never able to feel so friendly as before toward his boyhood friend. But his own farewell speech to Congress was a model of restraint and good will.

From this time on, though he was again elected to Congress, Hancock spent more time in Boston and, in the latter war years, became primarily interested in the politics of his own state. In 1778, he had brief military experience when he commanded the Massachusetts contingent of five thousand men who were to move against the British in Rhode Island. But as a major general in charge of troops, he was not a success and, besides, he was already suffering from the gout.

John Hancock was a great favorite with the people, though he had some severe critics among his associates. Part of their feeling was due to his vanity, obvious to those who knew him but unknown to the mass of the people who could not see this side of his character.

In 1780, he was a member of the Massachusetts Constitutional Convention, and in September was elected governor. After serving five years, he resigned during the post-war economic depression, but was later re-elected. He presided at the 1788 convention for ratifying the Federal Constitution. His prestige increased as the years passed until he died at the age of fifty-six, on October 8, 1793, while serving his ninth term as governor.

No one had ever been given such funeral honors in Massachusetts by the state's elect, and with such expressions of sorrow by the people. Governor Hancock, who in life had shown himself a vain lover of pomp, luxury, and flattering appreciation, had asked for a quiet funeral with no public display, no firing of the salute customarily given at the grave of a chief magistrate. But this time he was not granted his wish.

Instead, his body lay in state in the Hancock mansion on Beacon Hill for almost a week while thousands of mourners from all over the commonwealth filed by for their last view of this "founding father." At sunrise on the day of the funeral, the bells of Boston began tolling and continued for an hour. Flags flew at half-staff; all ships in the harbor flew flags at half-mast. At one o'clock all stores closed. Every military unit in Boston was assembled on beautiful Boston Common. Units from nearby towns, under the command of General William Hull, who had served in the Revolution, were also there.

When the procession marched out of the Common, all the state functionaries and various citizens of national standing followed the military units. In the center of these walked seventy-one-year-old Samuel Adams, now the acting governor. An artillery guard of honor followed the coffin, drawing a shining brass fieldpiece draped in black. This fieldpiece was named the *Hancock*. It had been stolen from the local British arsenal at the instigation of young John Hancock almost forty years before when war clouds were gathering.

Then came the family, in twenty-one carriages. Then the Vice-President of the United States, John Adams; the justices of the courts; ministers of foreign governments; Harvard College representatives; the city officers; churchmen; other notables. And after them the people — a column marching four abreast and stretching for half a mile, people who had loved, admired, trusted John Hancock.

At two o'clock they moved off to the dirge of muffled drums. Across the Common to Boylston Street (then called Frog Lane), to Washington Street, and around the State House. Here Samuel Adams had to drop out, too tired to go on and, perhaps, overcome with emotion and memories. On to the Old Granary Burying Ground — the last stop. All this long lugubrious time the boom of cannons sounded from nearby hills, until John Hancock was placed beside his uncle in the ancestral tomb.

As one walks today along Tremont Street and passes this truly hallowed ground, one may see on a stone, among other remembered famous names, the one who among those dreamers of a new nation was the real Yankee Doodle Dandy.

John Adams

John Adams

October 19, 1735 — July 4, 1826

To SIGNER JOHN ADAMS, second President of the United States, America is indebted for much more than his work during the critical years that saw the launching of a new nation. For John Adams was a man of multifarious achievement. We are indebted to him for his ceaseless writing — his diary, the numerous letters he wrote to his wife, his autobiography — all of which give us much information which we, today, would not otherwise have.

Like his second cousin, Samuel, John Adams was descended from the Henry Adams who came from England about a hundred years before John was born. On October 19, 1735, the Signer John was born in the old family farmhouse at Braintree. His father was another John who had married Susanna Boylston. Her more urban and sophisticated family, of Brookline and Boston, had already become prominent in medicine.

The Adamses had been hard-working Puritan farmers, and John,

Senior, was a prominent citizen — selectman for many years, lieutenant in the militia, deacon in the church, and a good father. His
influence on his son was very great. John considered his father
"the honestest man I ever knew," and wrote after his father died
that he had managed almost all the business of the town for twenty
years.

The elder John himself taught his son to read before sending
him to one of the "dame schools" which little boys and girls customarily attended. The school mistress, a certain Dame Belcher,
taught reading, writing, and arithmetic, and guided her pupils
through the traditional *New England Primer*. Then young John
was sent to a Latin School, taught by a sour and uninspiring
schoolmaster called Joseph Cleverly, a teacher so dull that John
Adams came to hate all Latin studies, preferring mathematics.
But his father had set his heart on his son's going to Harvard,
which required Latin for entrance. When the boy admitted to
his father that he could not bear Mr. Cleverly and preferred another teacher, his father consented. Under a teacher he really
liked, John Adams was ready to enter Harvard in less than a year,
at the age of fourteen.

In those days, Harvard College had four tutors, each carrying
one class through its four-year curriculum. The day began with
prayers at six, every student taking his turn reading from the
Bible. Breakfast, usually "bread, biscuit and milk," followed, and
classes started with a lecture at eight. Then came study and
recitations until a light lunch at noon, followed by more study until evening prayers at five and a thin supper at 7:30. Students who
could afford it "lived out" and took their meals in a tavern. After
supper the students were free to entertain themselves for about an
hour, until the college bell rang at nine, when they had to go to
their rooms.

Greek, Latin, logic, rhetoric, and ethics were John Adams's
freshman studies. Later, he had natural philosophy (elementary
physics and chemistry), more philosophy, metaphysics, and geog-
raphy. Every Saturday during the whole four years was given over
to theology.

Upon graduation in 1755, he became a teacher in Worcester, a
larger town than Braintree, with a population of about fifteen hundred. But school teaching did not greatly appeal to this ambitious

young man. His parents wanted him to become a Congregational minister, but he himself hesitated between medicine and the law. In the end the law won out and, while he was still teaching school, the young pedagogue began reading in the office of James Putnam, a Worcester attorney.

John Adams was never an idler. Beginning his second year of teaching, he wrote in his diary: "I am resolved not to neglect my time as I did last year. I am resolved to rise with the sun and to study the Scriptures on Thursday, Friday, Saturday and Sunday mornings, and to study some Latin author the other three mornings." This was before school opened for the day, of course. Then: "Noons and nights I intend to read English authors. . . . I will strive with all my soul to be something more than persons who have had less advantages than myself." Though he frequently fell short of these exceedingly strict hours, the young man was preparing for a distinguished career. One Friday his diary says briefly, "A very rainy day. Dreamed away the time." But some of this kind of day-dreaming was useful, too, for in it came ideas and plans for the future.

Teaching, studying law, reading the classics, engaging in conversations, debates, discussions with the best company in the town (for a school-teacher gets to know everybody), John Adams, by 1758, was ready for his bar examination in Boston. Admitted then to the bar, he decided to practice in his home town and returned to Braintree. But since practice came slowly in so small a place, and since there wasn't much of it, the twenty-three-year-old Adams helped in the fields on his father's farm and enjoyed it. He also took an interest in public affairs and began writing articles for the newspapers.

After six years, he married Miss Abigail Smith, daughter of the Reverend William and Elizabeth Quincy Smith of Weymouth. This marriage widened the young lawyer's connections with other prominent families. Abigail was to prove a true helpmeet and companion for her husband in the difficult periods of his career. Theirs was a marriage of real partnership. They were to have four children, a girl and three boys, one of whom would be John Quincy Adams, the sixth President of the United States.

The year after the pair were married, the colonists were infuriated by the Stamp Act. Adams considered the Stamp Act unlawful, since the colonists had not consented to it, but he disapproved of the riots that followed its enactment. He contributed essays to the *Boston Gazette* on various legal points concerning the act and prepared the resolutions of protest for Braintree which were imitated throughout the Bay Colony. This led to a long contest between him and the royal lieutenant-governor, Thomas Hutchinson.

Two years after the Stamp Act was repealed, the Adamses moved to Boston and lived in the "White House" on Brattle Square. But before long, Adams, considering city life unwholesome, became homesick for Braintree. Then, for about a year he found himself commuting between the two places.

When his boyhood friend John Hancock, now the wealthiest businessman in the city, was charged with smuggling, he engaged Adams to defend him. Other important legal cases drew him into patriotic causes. He was elected to the General Court as representative of Boston, and, though he devoted himself to the law and soon achieved a leading position at the bar, times and events were pulling him into public life.

By the time the Boston Tea Party took place, Adams considered it "the grandest event which has yet happened since the controversy with Britain opened." Tension mounted higher and higher. By mid-May, the Boston Committee of Correspondence recommended to all colonies a suspension of trade with Great Britain.

When the Massachusetts delegates were chosen for the First Continental Congress, John Adams was among the number, and when he took his seat in Carpenter's Hall, Philadelphia, where the first Congress met, he lacked about a month to his fortieth birthday.

He had anticipated the adventure of traveling so far with great pleasure. It was going to be most interesting to see other towns and cities; to meet the representatives of the other colonies; to take part in the greatest discussions and decisions that ever faced a group of men, who were about to lay the foundations for a new nation. But who knew what this near future might bring? War? Very likely. Failure? Who knew?

Pausing in his southward journey to go sight-seeing in various cities and meet local political leaders, Adams reported in his letters home on the welcome the Massachusetts representatives received in

Hartford, New Haven, Milford, and Stratford in Connecticut. He was enraptured by New York, where he and his companions stayed for a few days. They also visited Princeton and finally arrived in Philadelphia, "dirty, dusty, and fatigued." Seeing the rich New Yorkers and their great estates made him feel, as he wrote his wife, that he had not much to show for all his labors. He kept contrasting his simple Braintree life with that of the wealthy merchants in the larger towns and cities he passed through. But he made up his mind he was going to "enjoy good company, good conversation and — a fine ride and see a little more of the world than I have seen before."

If doubts and fears like those of John Adams ever troubled John Hancock and Samuel Adams, they seem never to have mentioned them. But John Adams was a man often assailed by doubts — though he always conquered them. Perhaps he had the kind of imagination that caused him to look inward. Perhaps this was because he had studied more than either of the other two. At any rate, he confessed his feelings to his Abigail in his letters.

After a short while in Philadelphia, Adams wrote her: "We have numberless prejudices to remove here. We have been obliged to act with great delicacy and caution. We have been obliged to keep ourselves out of sight, and to feel pulses and sound the depths, to insinuate our sentiments, designs and desires by means of other persons." He was disturbed because "great things are wanted to be done, and little things only I fear can be done." To Abigail he admitted, "I confess myself to be full of fears that the ministry and their friends . . . will prevail and crush the cause and friends of liberty."

Meeting the representatives of all the colonies, except Georgia, for the first time in Carpenters' Hall, John Adams saw in that body of men "a great spirit." Two committees were formed: One was instructed to "state the rights of the colonies in general, the several instances in which these rights are violated or infringed, and the means most proper to be pursued for obtaining a restoration of them." The two Adamses were the Massachusetts representatives on this important committee. The other committee was to examine and report on the regulations which affected the trade and manufactures of the colonies. And then began the tedious long hours of discussions.

There was little time now to write letters to his wife. He explained that he had "the characters and tempers, the principles and views, of fifty gentlemen, total strangers to me, to study, and the trade, policy and whole interest of a dozen provinces to learn." But some of his time was given to happier hours of relaxation, when the Philadelphia patriots were eager to entertain the Massachusetts delegates whom they lionized. After much wining and dining, Adams reported on the good food, the good company, and the fraternal spirit. When a false rumor spread that Boston had been bombarded by the British fleet, expressions of sympathy and support touched him to tears. He wrote his wife: "The spirit, the firmness, the prudence of our Province are vastly applauded, and we are universally acknowledged the saviors and defenders of American liberty."

When Congress adjourned after many seemingly endless sessions at which, Adams thought, too many men talked too much, John Adams was eager to go home.

No sooner was he back in Braintree than he was re-elected to the Provincial Congress. When articles written by a Tory using the pen-name "Massachusettensis," began to appear in the Boston paper *Post Boy*, attacking the patriot position, Adams wrote essays in rebuttal under the name "Novanglus," which were published in the *Boston Gazette*.

On May 10, 1775, John Adams was again in Philadelphia for the opening of the Second Continental Congress. There was much to do. The business of Congress, he wrote Abigail, was "as great and important as can be trusted to man, and the difficulty and intricacy of it prodigious. When fifty or sixty men have a constitution to form for a great empire, at the same time that they have a country of fifteen hundred miles in extent to fortify, millions to arm and train, a naval power to begin, and extensive commerce to regulate, numerous tribes of Indians to negotiate with, a standing army of twenty-seven thousand men to raise, pay, victual, and officer, I really shall pity those fifty or sixty men." Yet he was one of them.

While the thinkers and planners were hard at work in Philadelphia, fighting was breaking out in the north. John Adams often wished he could be a soldier and see some action instead of sitting in Congress listening to endless talk. However, according to his good friend, Dr. Benjamin Rush of Philadelphia, he was in the place where he was most needed and doing the most good. Said Rush: "He was a most sensible and forcible speaker. Every member of Congress . . . acknowledged him to be the first man in the House. . . . Dr. Brownson used to say when he spoke, he fancied an angel was let down from heaven to illumine the Congress. He saw the whole of a subject at a single glance, and by a happy union of the powers of reasoning and persuasion often succeeded in carrying measures which were at first sight of an unpopular nature . . . he was a real American in principle and conduct."

Often at work from seven in the morning until eleven at night, the forty-year-old Adams frequently complained of ill health, and his eyes bothered him. When Congress adjourned for the month of August, he hurried home for a short visit, to ramble "all alone, through the fields, groves, meadows . . . of peaceful, happy Braintree." Best of all was to be back with Abigail and the children. In those days, when forty miles a day was fast traveling, and Philadelphia and Boston were twelve days apart, Adams could have only a taste of home before he had to start off again on his third trip to Philadelphia.

For three autumn months congressional work occupied all his time until, in the first week of December, he asked for a short leave to return home. So eager was he to be on his way that he broke his rule about not traveling on Sundays. He had Christmas with his family, made a trip to Cambridge to inspect the army, saw George Washington, and talked with people to learn their opinions.

Before the end of the month he was on his way back to Congress. He stopped first in Framingham to inspect the artillery that was captured at Fort Ticonderoga by Ethan Allen, then continued traveling over what had become a familiar route until he at last reached Philadelphia after a cold journey of eighteen days during which he stopped all along the way to talk to patriots.

In Philadelphia he found the delegates in "deep anxiety." He himself was now eager for independence. He knew it had to come, though it meant all-out war. War, after all, had now been going on for more than a year, not only in Massachusetts, but in New Hampshire and Virginia. Norfolk had been burned and cannonaded on the order of Lord Dunmore, and the Virginians were ready to demand independence. Adams was impatient at the backwardness of the middle colonies. After the fighting at Dorchester Heights in early March, 1776, a letter from his wife told him how the house shook with the thunder of distant cannon fire even while she sat at her desk writing. Then Abigail had gone out to climb Penn's Hill near their Braintree home to watch the artillery fire between the American and British batteries. The middle colonies simply *had* to be brought round to Adams's views which were, by this time, the views of the majority.

When committees were appointed to prepare a declaration of independence and to plan treaties with foreign powers, Adams was on both. He was also appointed to the Board of War.

After Richard Henry Lee placed the motion for independence before Congress on June 7, the question was to wait for three weeks to "ripen." Most of the colonies were now in favor of it. South Carolina, Pennsylvania, Delaware, and New York were still definitely reluctant.

The day came. John Adams was up early that morning of July 1. He rehearsed his own remarks in case he should have to speak. He and Samuel Adams and Richard Henry Lee reviewed their plans for working the resolution through the Congress. He wrote a letter to the Governor of Georgia, Archibald Bullock, who had been a delegate, in which he said: "This morning is assigned for the greatest debate of all."

As leader of the opposition to independence, John Dickinson of Pennsylvania spoke first in the fight against the resolution. He spoke with "ardent zeal," with "politeness and candor," at great length "with all his eloquence." After he sat down there was a long pause. It became uncomfortable. Who should answer this "orator of reconciliation?"

John Adams could not let this great moment pass. He stood up and began by saying that he had not the talents of the orators of ancient times, that he was no Pericles, Cicero, nor Demosthenes, but since the issue to be discussed might be safely left to the guidance of "plain understanding and common sense," he launched forth and made the "most notable speech of his life."

He reviewed the legal and constitutional arguments. He pointed out the measures the British Parliament had taken to curtail the liberties of their American colonies. He described the deepening crisis over the recent past years, the tyranny which had led to armed conflict. He mentioned past efforts at reconciliation, which had been in vain. Then he said that independence was inevitable and spoke of the advantages to be gained by declaring it at once.

Just as the moment came for the final question, the New Jersey delegates entered the hall. Though their instructions gave them permission to vote for independence, they wanted to hear a summary of the arguments. During the pause that followed, every one looked at John Adams. Laughingly approaching him, Edward Rutledge of South Carolina told Adams he must "satisfy the gentlemen from New Jersey." For, he continued, "Nobody will speak but you upon this subject, Mr. Adams. You have the topics so ready." Adams hated to repeat what he had just been saying — what he had, indeed, said in Congress twenty times over; but, when Dr. Witherspoon of New Jersey pressed him, he yielded. Afterwards, another New Jersey delegate, Richard Stockton, wrote his son: "The man to whom the country is most indebted for the great measure of independency is Mr. John Adams of Boston. I call him the Atlas of American Independence. He it was who sustained the debate, and, by the force of his reasoning, demonstrated not only the justice, but the expediency of the measure." Now, at the very end of the long argument, it was John Adams who urged in Congress the case for freedom, just as another Adams — his older cousin, Samuel Adams — had first urged it in Boston, many years before.

After Adams's speech, a quick canvass made it clear that only nine states were strong for independence; and it was most desirable that an affirmative vote should show unanimity. Pennsylvania and South Carolina were opposed to independence. New York delegates said their instructions held them back and they would abstain from voting. The two Delaware delegates who were present, McKean and Read, were split, and Thomas McKean, the pro-independence delegate, sent at once for the absent Caesar Rodney, who was strong for independence. Before the day's session ended, Rutledge of South Carolina was prevailed upon to concede that his colony would fall into line if, for the sake of unity, Delaware and Pennsylvania supported independence.

The large, prosperous, central colony of Pennsylvania was the last stumbling block. Of her seven delegates, three were for independence; four opposed. After further arguments and exhortations, it was finally agreed that Morris and Dickinson, two opposed, would not officially attend the next day, and then the three for independence, Benjamin Franklin, John Morton, James Wilson, could outweigh the other two against. These two, Charles Humphreys and Thomas Willing, never signed the Declaration of Independence. In fact, because of changes soon afterward, several signatures on the Declaration are those of men who were not even present at the voting on July 2.

So passed July 1. The vote would be taken the next day.

July 2, 1776, dawned squally with showers. It had been raining, with thunderstorms, all night — a most disagreeable ride for a man on horseback. Yet Caesar Rodney, responding to McKean's summons, rode all that wet night to reach Philadelphia. Inside the hall in the morning, the atmosphere was tight with tension. When word came that Rodney was on his way, Delaware suddenly became very important. As the members reassembled after lunch, Rodney, mud-stained, soaked to the skin, exhausted, rode up on his dripping horse.

Then the voting began, colony by colony. Rodney brought Delaware's vote over to the side of independence. With South Carolina's decision for independence, Pennsylvania came into line. With New York still abstaining from the vote, twelve colonies voted for independence. There was no vote against it.

It had all taken a vast deal of "managing." But it was done at last: the final act of an idea first born in a room in Boston fifteen years before, Samuel Adams's great dream.

John's letter to Abigail told her that he felt sure July 2 would be "celebrated by succeeding generations as the great anniversary festival." He thought it ought to be commemorated "by a solemn act of devotion to God Almighty." It should "be solemnized with pomp and parade, with shows, games, sports, guns, bells, bonfires and illuminations, from one end of the continent to the other, from this time forward forevermore."

Adams had no time for rest or relaxation. More and more duties were heaped upon him, until, worn out by the hot summer months of constant and arduous labor, anxious about his family at

home, and wishing to confer with his constituents in his own har-
rassed state, he was able to leave Philadelphia at last on October
13.

He spent the next three months at home, returning to Congress
on February 1, 1777. By that time the British held Philadelphia
and Congress had to meet in Baltimore. Committee work now
obliged him to take part in the debates on currency, on the French
loan, on price regulation. In late October, 1777, he left Congress
and, though re-elected, he did not serve because he had also been
chosen as Commissioner to France.

With his ten-year-old son, John Quincy Adams, he sailed for
France in February, 1778, aboard the new twenty-four-gun frigate,
Boston. It is interesting now to note what a traveler had to take
with him on a sea voyage two hundred years ago. In addition
to their clothing, Mr. Adams and his son had their own bedding
and food for a six-week crossing. Their baggage included a
bushel of Indian meal (for making johnny cakes and hasty pud-
ding), a keg of rum, tea, chocolate, brown sugar, two bottles of
mustard, six chickens to provide eggs until they were themselves
eaten, two fat sheep, five bushels of corn, a barrel of apples, fourteen dozen eggs, wafers, pepper, two mattresses and bolsters —
among other things! Adams had three reams of paper, two account books, 25 quills (for use as pens), a bottle of home-made
ink, tobacco and a dozen clay pipes.

Though his long life had not yet reached its half way mark at
forty-three, John Adams had now done the work for which we
read about him here — the work that made him a Signer. This
man who once, as newly appointed congressman, had happily
anticipated the sights he would see on a journey between Boston
and Philadelphia, was now to undertake several trips to Europe.
He spent the war years in France as commissioner of treaties and
of peace, with journeys to Holland to negotiate loans. After
his first return to Braintree for an all-too-short reunion with his
family, Congress again appointed him commissioner to France
and, later, minister to Holland. On this second trip he took his
second son, Charles, as well as John Quincy, the elder. On the
first trip, John Quincy had done so well in school in Paris that his
father was encouraged to try the experiment with Charles. Abi-

gail stayed home and worked the farm. In 1784, however, Adams
sent for her and the two younger children. Until 1785, John Adams
served the new United States as diplomat in France.

After Cornwallis surrendered at Yorktown the war was practically won, but endless negotiations were still necessary to frame
the peace. By this time John Adams was, next to Benjamin Franklin, his young country's most experienced diplomat. It became
his heart's desire to be appointed America's first minister to the
Court of St. James.

He achieved his wish and from 1785 to 1788 represented the
United States in Great Britain. In February of 1789, when the
presidential electors voted George Washington first President of
the United States, they elected John Adams first Vice-President,
and after serving two terms he became the second President.
Adams commented on Washington's pleasant and friendly manner
during the inauguration, but added slyly that he knew very well
the old hero was delighted to lay down the burdens of his office.

Since the new White House was not yet finished, the President
and his family remained in Philadelphia during most of his term
but moved into the new (and still unfinished) White House late
in 1800. Abigail wrote a friend that she did not arrive till October 16 and added, "This house is twice as large as our meeting
house." Not a single room was yet completed, but six could be
made comfortable though thirteen fires had to be kept going.
Mrs. Adams found one comfort, however: the huge audience room
made a fine place to hang her washing!

At last the chunky little boy from Braintree had reached the
climax of a great career. His had been, on the whole, a happy life.

Although he suffered some severe illnesses, John Adams lived
in harmony with a loving family and many friends. Like all great
men in politics, he had his enemies, but even these — or some of
them — became more friendly in his old age. With all his intense
and lengthy working hours, he enjoyed periods of relaxation in
country walks at his beloved old Braintree farm and, later, in the
parks and gardens in France.

The active years flew by. Adams was growing old. When he
was eighty-three he lost his dear Abigail after fifty-four years of an
ideal partnership. Thomas Jefferson wrote him a consoling letter.
In fact, one of Adams's greatest pleasures in his latter years was

his correspondence with Thomas Jefferson. The two men had had serious differences when Jefferson, defeating Adams, became the third President of the United States; but that was now in the past. Jefferson also wrote to congratulate Adams upon the election of his son, John Quincy Adams, to be the sixth President of the United States. Corresponding with Jefferson became the old man's deepest satisfaction. "Every line from you exhilarates my spirits and gives me a glow of pleasure," he wrote Jefferson, adding, "I look back with rapture to those golden days when Virginia and Massachusetts lived and acted together like brothers."

Two cherished events of his last years were the visits of Hannah Quincy who had been a teen-age sweetheart over fifty years before, and of the Marquis de Lafayette whom he had known in wartime. Hannah Quincy was now Mrs. Ebenezer Storer and a widow, but the years fell away as she entered the room, and old Adams greeted her with a happy smile, saying, "What! Madam, shall we not go walk in Cupid's Grove together?" That was the name of the nearby lover's lane. Taken aback for the moment, the old lady replied, "Ah, sir, it would not be the first time that we have walked there."

And then, in 1824, the year which saw Adams's son nominated for President, the old General Lafayette returned with his own son to visit the United States. The Marquis was given a hero's procession in Washington, again in New York, and again in Boston. He was honored as the great French friend who had come, a young man, to help the cause of the thirteen colonies. Adams sent him an invitation, and from Boston the Marquis went to the Adams farm at Braintree. They sat and talked of their reminiscences, of the battles and glories of a half century gone. But the years had made their mark on each and, though delighted at meeting again, both were saddened by time's toll. Aware, too, that this would be their last meeting, each made the same comment afterwards: Adams said privately, "That is not the Lafayette I knew." The Frenchman said, "That was not the John Adams I knew."

One more summer: 1826 — the summer which began with great plans for the fiftieth anniversary celebration of American independence. The historic cities, most especially Boston, bustled with excitement. In June, a committee called upon John Adams, asking him to attend on the Fourth of July. What a thing to have the

Grand Old Man present and on view on this day! No one would ever forget it. But Adams regretted he could not undertake the carriage ride, and he couldn't sit still on a hard seat all that time in July heat. He dictated his message: the thirteen United States were "destined to date the periods of their birth and emancipation from the Fourth of July 1776."

As the time drew nearer, the days became hotter and Boston was in a fever of excitement over the approaching anniversary day. A half century had passed since those great events. Every one seemed to have gathered that day on the Common to hear the bands, to see the Ancient and Honorable Artillery Company and the Boston militia pass in review. Josiah Quincy, Senior, gave the oration. People were jammed together under a hot sun to hear him. He described the growth and progress of the country since that great day fifty years ago, when it cut the ties with England. He referred to "that ancient citizen of Boston, that patriarch of American independence." But the sole survivor of "New England's worthies" never knew what was being said, for out in the old farmhouse, with family and friends gathered about him, old John Adams was sleeping away his last morning on earth.

When he was conscious for a time, a servant by his bedside asked: "Do you know, sir, what day it is?" "O yes, it is the glorious Fourth of July," replied the dying man. "God bless it. God bless you all."

He fell into a coma but about noon revived for a few clear moments and murmured: "Thomas Jefferson survives." Then he became unconscious once more.

About six in the evening of that July 4, 1826, John Adams met "the great and solemn event" of death. He had written to Jefferson some time before that he was ready for it. Unknown to him, at beautiful Monticello, Thomas Jefferson had preceded his friend into history by a few hours.

It took almost a week for the word to spread throughout the country — a country that now extended west to the Mississippi and beyond. Astonishment grew into wonder, amazement, awe — that these two great figures in the cause of national freedom should have expired on the same day — and that day the fiftieth anniversary of the birth of the United States.

It seemed as if destiny had taken a hand in it.

Elbridge Gerry

Elbridge Gerry

July 17, 1744 — November 23, 1814

ELBRIDGE GERRY'S FATHER came from the village of Newton Abbot in Devonshire, a beautiful and balmy region in southwestern England. He left in 1730, about thirty years before the American colony where he settled began to have troubles with the mother country. Since Newton Abbot lies close to the sea in the mouth of the Teign river, Thomas Gerry grew up near the water. He arrived in New York as master of his own ship. He sailed on until, northeast of Boston, he found the place he wanted to live at Marblehead. It was a little point of land jutting out into salt water — the kind of locale where he could feel at home.

Before Thomas Gerry went on to Marblehead however, he met Elizabeth Greenleaf, a daughter of a wealthy Boston merchant, and promptly married her. They had twelve children, the third being their son, Elbridge. Settling permanently in Marblehead, Thomas built up a business in shipping, trading, and importing, in which he made a respectable fortune. He also became a militia officer, commanding the local fort.

His son Elbridge entered Harvard in 1758 at the age of thirteen, but this is not so astonishing as it seems now, for the Harvard of those days was not much more advanced than a modern preparatory school. Graduating four years later, he took a Master's degree and, about this time, began airing his views on the steadily mounting oppression the British Parliament was inflicting on the American colonies.

Though the young graduate wanted to study medicine after college, he gave up the idea and joined his father and two older brothers in the family business. The Gerrys exported, in their own fleet of vessels, shipments of dried codfish south to the Barbados and Spanish ports, from which their ships brought back Spanish goods to be sold in the colonies.

The fishermen and merchants of Marblehead lived on the

bounty of the ocean. It was principally a fishing town and stood next to Boston in the extent and value of its trade. Men and boys earned their living most of the year on or from the sea — a dangerous life that called for bold, adventurous men. Such men are lovers of liberty. Naturally, when controversy between Great Britain and the colonies began, the inhabitants of Marblehead were among the first to show attachment to their country's cause.

In May of 1772, Elbridge Gerry made a start in public life, which appealed to him more than work in the counting-house, by being elected representative to the General Court. On making the acquaintance of Samuel Adams, he was completely won over to the older man's political ideas; and, after two years of steady correspondence, Adams began to feel that in Gerry he had found a receptive mind and a willing worker against British tyranny.

When a circular letter sent out by Adams's Boston Committee of Correspondence brought about a town meeting in Marblehead on December 1, 1772, the Gerry family took a prominent part. Thomas Gerry was moderator, and his sons Elbridge and Thomas, Junior, were on the committee that drafted the resolutions adopted. To obtain unity of ideas and effort, local committees of correspondence were being organized throughout the colonies, and the Marblehead committee, chosen at this town meeting, included all three Gerrys. Unfortunately, two years later Gerry and the whole committee of correspondence resigned in disgust when the isolation hospital for smallpox, which Gerry and other prominent citizens had built and paid for, was burned down by an angry and ignorant mob. The incendiaries did not know how contagious smallpox was and resented isolation of patients.

When in the Spring of 1774 Great Britain closed Boston's harbor, Marblehead became the port of entry for shipments of provisions sent up from southern colonies to aid the harassed Massachusetts Bay Colony. For England's high-handed act had angered the other colonies and aroused their sympathy.

Massachusetts now set up its First Provincial Congress. This was an assembly of delegates from all the towns in Massachusetts. It convened, after Boston harbor was closed, at Salem in October, 1774, with Gerry as member from Marblehead. This first convention adjourned to Concord and assumed the form of a legislative assembly by choosing John Hancock president. It had no legal justification under any provision of King George's provincial charter. It was supported wholly by voluntary consent and approbation of the people in their first attempt to organize resistance to the British. Since it assembled without royal authority, the royal governor of the province was excluded. He had no connection with it and no knowledge of its deliberations, except what he learned by espionage. These angry patriots simply assumed authority over Massachusetts, thereby in effect deposing the governor and ignoring the royal charter. They had decided to meet highhandedness with the same kind of medicine.

"From the day of their first meeting the royal authority within the province of Massachusetts was forever at an end," wrote James T. Austin, Elbridge Gerry's biographer. The mere assembling of these distinguished citizens in provincial congress really was the revolution, for by this act the province threw off its allegiance to the Crown.

Gerry, re-elected in 1775, worked with John Hancock and Samuel Adams in making last preparations in that never-to-be-forgotten April of '75. The British wanted to get their hands on the rebel leaders, Adams and Hancock, and their spies had learned that the Americans had stores of ammunition which they also wanted to capture. On the eighteenth of April in '75, the night of Paul Revere's side, when Adams and Hancock were sleeping in Lexington, Elbridge Gerry was at the Menotomy Tavern on the road the British took to Lexington. He and two American colonels were in bed when a detachment of redcoats came down the road to search the house. All three escaped in their nightclothes and hid in a cornfield until the search was over. (Corn high enough to hide anyone in the month of April would have had to be last year's cornstalks the farmer had left standing.)

Gerry spent the rest of the year raising troops, procuring munitions and supplies for the provincial army, and collecting material for fortifications. His business connections and shipping activities made him an ideal man for the supply department in which he labored efficiently until he departed for Philadelphia, January 25, 1776, as delegate to the Second Continental Congress.

Massachusetts members of the First Continental Congress had been the two Adamses, Robert Treat Paine, Thomas Cushing, and James Bowdoin. When Bowdoin declined re-election, John

Hancock took his place; and when Cushing retired at the end of the year, Gerry succeeded him. The other three remained. Elbridge Gerry traveled to Philadelphia in company with John Adams, and they became friends.

A week after taking his seat in Congress, Gerry was appointed one of five members of the standing committee for superintending the Treasury. During the Spring of 1776, the question of independence steadily moved to top place in the deliberations of Congress. Mr. Gerry made several speeches in which, a colleague said, "he laid out his whole soul" and "poured out his reasons with an energy and fervour that spoke the honest convictions of his mind."

After the long debate on June 10, the question of independence was postponed until July 1 in order to give the assemblies of the middle colonies, who were holding back, an opportunity to take off their restrictions and let their delegates unite in the measure. In the interim, Congress proceeded with plans for confederation and foreign alliance.

An early believer in the separation of the colonies from the government of Great Britain, like all the representatives from the particularly aggrieved province of Massachusetts, Elbridge Gerry voted for independence when the roll was called in early July. Then, worn out from the arduous and constant work and nervous tension of the past few years, he hastened home and wrote the Adamses later that month to sign his name for him on the Declaration of Independence, when it was engrossed and ready for signatures. But they did not have to sign for him; he was back in Philadelphia and signed for himself on September 3. He was thirty-two at this time, one of the youngest of the Signers.

Elbridge Gerry was a slight, dapper little man, with a long nose, a rather stern expression, and an aristocratic air, but with pleasant manners that made him a favorite of the ladies. He apparently looked down his nose at the "common man," with whom he did not care to come in contact in public meetings — an attitude wholly different from that of Sam Adams. But a good many prominent Bostonians were like that; and, besides, not unusual to find in men of small stature a cocky attitude and a pronounced sense of personal dignity, compensating for their slight physique. As he grew older, this characteristic became so noticeable that

Gerry came to be considered a snob and was naturally not very popular.

Some of his other qualities also made him difficult: He changed his mind so often that it was not easy to count on his views. He lacked a sense of humor, which is deplorable and deadening in human relations. He was prone to be suspicious of other people's motives. There were some who felt that sometimes, through obstinacy, Gerry would "risk great things to secure small ones."

He was, however, industrious and conscientious both in business and in Congress. His integrity was never questioned and his attention to detail was helpful to all with whom he worked. He was always the gentleman, and this, too, was appreciated by his co-workers, for it is always easier to deal with persons of good manners.

Gerry's work in supplying the army was invaluable. As a private merchant, he was able to show his brothers how to route their ships and to tell them what the army needed. He sent instructions about the manufacture of tents and gunpowder. The Gerry brothers shipped fish to Spain for the account of the colonies and received army supplies in return. A Marblehead man, he took more interest in fisheries than other congressmen. As the war went on and older congressmen retired, Gerry remained as one of the most experienced.

At the age of forty-two, Elbridge Gerry married Ann Thompson, daughter of a New York merchant. This was ten years after Independence, when he no longer had to devote all his time and effort to work. He now retired from business with a very fair fortune invested in government securities and real estate. He bought the beautiful house and grounds in Cambridge, Massachusetts, now known as "Elmwood," where James Russell Lowell lived in later years. This fine estate had been confiscated from a Tory family.

In 1797, our second President, John Adams, sent Gerry with John Marshall and Charles Pinckney on a mission to France as, after the war, French-American relations were greatly strained. France demanded a cash payment from the United States and tried to force the Americans to pay a personal bribe. The Americans refused and the mission failed, but Gerry, still hoping for an agreement, remained. When he returned later, he found himself snubbed by the Federalists and praised by the Republicans.

Loyal as he was to his country and able as he was in business, Elbridge Gerry nevertheless lost friends through mistaken efforts and through his inconsistent opinions. Though several times defeated for the governorship of Massachusetts, he ran again in 1810. He was now sixty-five and still not popular, but since his opponent, Christopher Gore, was a man of "even stronger aristocratic traits," Gerry won. In 1812 he was elected Vice-President of the United States with James Madison as President and took his oath of office in his Cambridge home, May 4, 1813.

Though he was then in his seventieth year and rather frail, he joined happily in the social life of Washington. But he had not long to enjoy it. Driving to the Senate chamber on the morning of November 23, 1814, he was seized with a hemorrhage of the lungs. He died in a matter of minutes.

Gerry suffered many losses in his last dozen years of life, and though he had once had a considerable fortune, left large debts which consumed his entire estate save for the lovely house. Congress paid for his burial in the Congressional Cemetery.

His wife lived on until 1849, the last surviving widow of a Signer. Their daughter, Emily Louise, lived until 1894, the last surviving child of a Signer.

Though Gerry's personality did not draw warm friendships, he had a genuine devotion to his country. Dr. Rush considered him "a genuine friend to republican forms of government." Gerry himself declared, "I hold it to be the duty of every citizen, though he may have but one day to live, to devote that day to the good of his country."

Robert Treat Paine

Robt Treat Paine

March 11, 1731 — May 11, 1814

"THE OBJECTION MAKER," as Robert Treat Paine was later to be called in Congress, was born on Beacon Hill's School Street, Boston, March 11, 1731, son of the Reverend Thomas and Eunice

Treat Paine. He had many notable forebears as befits one born in Yankeeland's core and on the hallowed ground of her blueblood aristocrats. The first Paine in America was Thomas, who was a freeman of Plymouth Colony as early as 1659. An ancestor on the mother's side, Major Robert Treat, had been a governor of Connecticut colony. The Signer's father left the ministry to engage in the more financially rewarding mercantile business in Boston and Halifax, Nova Scotia. When Robert Treat Paine was born, he was carried down to the foot of Beacon Hill to be christened in Boston's Old South Church. By family tradition, he was expected to become a minister.

After winning high marks at Boston Latin School, the boy entered Harvard with the class of 1749, taught school for a short time after graduating, and then began to study theology. But since his health was frail, he sought a more robust life and went to sea, visiting the southern colonies, Spain, the Azores, and England, ending with a voyage on a whaler to Greenland.

Upon his return home, young Paine decided to pursue an earlier interest in law. He was admitted to the bar in 1757 and began practice in Portland, Maine, then a part of Massachusetts. A few years later he moved his office to Taunton, about thirty miles from Boston.

Paine was interested in the patriots' cause from the first. By the time of the Boston Massacre, March 1770, he was associate prosecuting attorney at the trial of the British soldiers who had fired upon American civilians. His argument on the basic question — whether the British Parliament had the right to quarter a standing army on a town in her American colony *without its consent* — sent his name throughout the other colonies, where eyes were eagerly turned upon all news from Boston. For what happened there could happen anywhere else in the colonies. How would the colony of Massachusetts accept this act of violence?

Now thirty-nine years of age, Robert Paine married Sally Cobb, the daughter of General David Cobb, lieutenant-governor of Massachusetts under the Royal Charter. Soon afterward, he was elected to the Provincial Assembly, where he served for several years. When the first call came for delegates of all the thirteen colonies to meet in Philadelphia in 1774, Robert Treat Paine was chosen one of the five from Massachusetts. His name was now known outside his own province, not only because of his Massacre trial speech, but because he represented the most important town in southern Massachusetts.

In the first Congress he was placed on committees for drafting the rules of debate, and for fasting and prayer. After the battle of Bunker Hill, June 17, 1775, Paine was made chairman of the committee charged with providing gunpowder for an army that had to be created quickly.

The next month, July, 1775, the colonies made their second and final appeal to the Crown for the preservation of goodwill. This was called the Olive Branch Petition and carried the signature of Robert Treat Paine. But, as Benjamin Franklin had thought, the Crown would not even consider it.

Re-elected to Congress in 1776, Paine, now forty-five years old, sat among the debaters on a declaration of independence. The Philadelphian, Dr. Rush, considered him "a firm, decided, and persevering patriot, and eminently useful in Congress, particularly upon committees, in which he was remarkable for his regular and punctual attendance." In conversation, he could be droll and amusing. Dr. Rush said, "His temper was amiable, and his speeches and conversation often facetious." But there was another side to Paine, for Dr. Rush also said that he "had a certain obliquity of understanding which prevented his seeing public objects in the same light in which they were seen by other people. He seldom proposed anything, but opposed nearly every measure that was proposed by other people, and hence he got the name of 'The Objection Maker' in Congress."

But, in spite of that, Paine had positive talents. He was one of the commission sent to negotiate a treaty with the upper New York State Indians. In 1777 he was elected attorney-general for Massachusetts. As the war came to an end, he was on the legislative committee which had to prepare a draft for a state constitution. And when the Tories fled, many of them to Canada, Paine helped to confiscate their estates. He also helped suppress Shays's Rebellion against the state of Massachusetts.

He continued to win honors. After he moved to Boston in 1780, he helped found the American Academy of Arts and Sciences. His life-long friend, Governor John Hancock, twice appointed him to the new Supreme Court of Massachusetts. Paine declined the first time, 1783, in order to retain his larger salary as attorney-general.

The second time, he accepted. Since Maine was still a part of Massachusetts in those days, Paine's work as judge required much travel into those then remote regions where life was severely regulated. At one time, he was arrested for traveling on Sunday! Once he was fined by a little cross-roads court for violating a law which he himself helped to frame years before.

After fourteen years he retired from the bench, since he was getting old and was bothered by increasing deafness. He died on May 11, 1814, at eighty-three, a ripe old age for those times. The man who had, when young, probably traveled farther than any other patriot "Father," was laid to rest in the Old Granary Burial Ground in Boston, along with other patriots and Signers, and near the very spot where he had been born and christened.

II

VIRGINIA

Th Jefferson

Richard Henry Lee

Benj. Harrison

Francis Lightfoot Lee

Th.s Nelson jr.

George Wythe

Carter Braxton

Thomas Jefferson

Th Jefferson

April 13, 1743 — July 4, 1826

THOMAS JEFFERSON IS UNIQUE among the Signers of the Declaration of Independence, for he did more than sign it. Jefferson also wrote it — and this was one of only three among all his achievements that he wished inscribed upon his tombstone. Any other man who had accomplished half as much as Jefferson would have wanted a great deal more in that inscription, for Jefferson's career was one of the most brilliant any man — of his own day or of modern days — has ever made for himself.

Twice President of the United States, Vice-President before that, Minister to France, Governor of Virginia, first Secretary of State, Jefferson was also a successful lawyer, a scholar, an inventor, a musician, a man of science, and a book collector — one of the three libraries he assembled for his own use became the basis for the present Library of Congress. (By his own secret marks of ownership, you can still distinguish the books that once were Jefferson's from the others in that great collection.) But to Jefferson all the distinguished posts he held were more or less tiresome tasks. It was his duty to undertake them and in that duty he did his brilliant best; but his heart was always with his books, his tools, his garden, and his fields at Monticello. If he could have had his own way, if he had not had so keen a sense of duty, if he had not always answered to his call, he would have spent a long, happy life as a country gentleman of intellectual tastes. He would never, in that case, have become world famous. But Thomas Jefferson wouldn't have minded that in the least. He once referred to the presidency as "a splendid misery."

Born into an old and wealthy Virginian family, Jefferson grew up on the estate of his father, Peter Jefferson, near Charlottesville, Albermarle County. This was a plantation of four hundred acres — small for those spacious days — which a friend had sold to

Peter Jefferson at possibly the lowest price ever paid for real estate anywhere. The price was a bowl of punch, and that land is still called "the Punchbowl Tract" in Albemarle County. It was, of course, only a part of Peter Jefferson's land holdings but it was the part where he built his house, to be near the friend who had "sold" it to him.

Thomas Jefferson was born here April 13, 1743. Peter Jefferson, who liked to name his lands for places in the Old World with which his family had been associated, had called his plantation "Shadwell," because that was the London parish in which his young wife had been baptized twenty-three years before. He called another plantation "Snowdon," after a mountain in Wales near which he thought his Welsh ancestors once had lived.

In addition to being born into a good family with plenty of money — a blessing by no means to be despised — Thomas Jefferson had two other advantages. He was born with iron health and lived a long life with almost no illness. Best of all, he was born with a fine mind which, by constant study all through a busy life, he kept improving to the very end.

Though his own tastes inclined him to a quiet home life, he gave the best years of his life to his country's service. Even when he had completed two terms in the presidency and could at last go home, Jefferson spent endless hours planning the new University of Virginia, designing the beautiful buildings that are still its pride, and supervising their erection. To this day, it is a custom at the university to refer to him always as "Mr. Jefferson." People still talk, a surprised visitor once remarked, "as if he were in the next room."

His aristocratic and luxurious background spared Jefferson many of the hardships and struggles other great men have sometimes had to endure. He was not a poor boy, fighting his own way from poverty to fame and fortune, like Benjamin Franklin. The young Jefferson, when he was still only a boy, inherited thousands of acres of land, with many slaves to farm it for him. In the end he owned large estates and several beautiful plantation houses — though Monticello was always the place he loved most. The young widow whom he married brought him a second fortune, equal to his own.

In colonial days there were no public schools in Virginia. The sons of poor people usually received no education — or none worth mentioning. Very wealthy families sometimes employed private tutors and later sent their sons to the great English universities. Other prosperous families often sent their children to small private schools kept by local parsons. Some of these clergymen did not have churches at all, but devoted themselves entirely to education.

As a boy, Thomas Jefferson was sent to a private school of this sort, kept by the Reverend Matthew Maury — probably the only American schoolteacher who educated three Presidents of the United States, for both James Madison and James Monroe also studied under him. Captain Meriwether Lewis, another of his pupils, was one of the two leaders of the Lewis and Clark Expedition.

From the Reverend Mr. Maury's school, the boy went on to the College of William and Mary, in Williamsburg, then the capital of Virginia, and after only two years there, to the law office of George Wythe in Williamsburg. Wythe, who also became a Signer of the Declaration that his pupil wrote, was one of the most distinguished lawyers of the day. Jefferson studied in his office for five years.

Young as he was, during this period he regularly made one of the group of four who dined together at the Palace of the Governor. Lieutenant-governor Francis Fauquier, then acting as governor, was, of course the host. Professor William Small, of the William and Mary faculty, and George Wythe himself were the others. Although these men were much older and were among the most prominent in Virginia, they made the young man from Albemarle County one of themselves. In spite of his youth, they recognized his brilliance.

When the five years of study in Wythe's law office were over, Jefferson was admitted to the bar and at once established a legal practice of his own. He had begun to make a success of it as the Revolution approached, but became so much involved in public affairs that he closed his law office, turned over his remaining cases to a friend, and never practiced law again.

Jefferson's public service had begun long before the Revolution. In 1770, he became county lieutenant of Albemarle County, the official in general charge of county affairs, including the militia.

He was county surveyor in 1773. A year later, as disputes with the British grew more serious, he was chosen for the Virginia Convention, which was to become the state legislature. Unable to attend, he nevertheless sent the members his *Summary View of the Rights of British America*. Not yet in favor of separation from the Mother Country, Thomas Jefferson nevertheless expressed in this paper many of the ideas he was to use, two years later, in the Declaration of Independence.

In 1772, he married Mrs. Martha Skelton, a young widow of twenty-three, to whom he remained intensely devoted throughout the ten years of their marriage. She was to die in 1782 after bearing numerous children, all of whom, except two daughters, Martha and Maria, died in infancy. Married in midwinter, which can be cold even in Virginia, Jefferson bore his bride away to their new house at Monticello which he had designed and built himself and for which he had especially leveled off the top of the "little mountain" on which it stood. He was to modify and refinish this beloved home, in one way or another, throughout the rest of his long life.

The midwinter snow was so deep that the bridal couple, unable to get up the steep slope of Monticello in their carriage, unhitched two of the horses and rode up. (Any Virginia girl of that period was perfectly familiar with horses.) When they reached their new home, however, their problems had not ended. The slaves, not expecting them in such weather, had all gone to bed; and, since the house was still unfinished, only one room was ready for them. Gaily they built a fire, and there is a legend that Jefferson played the violin for his bride.

Thomas Jefferson's services in the Second Continental Congress and his authorship of the Declaration of Independence have already been discussed in the opening chapter of this book. That trying period was made agonizing for Jefferson by the difficulty of getting news from his wife, who lay ill at Monticello. Postal service was slow and bad in those days and often he had no news from her for long periods. She died as the Revolution was drawing to a close.

After her death, Jefferson was appointed one of the Peace Commissioners to meet with the British in Paris; but Benjamin Franklin and the other commissioners, already on the scene, had finished negotiating the treaty before Jefferson could sail. He remained in America.

Jefferson did go to Paris in 1784, however, to assist Franklin and John Adams in arranging treaties of commerce; and when Franklin, first American Minister to France, wanted to return, Jefferson became our second Minister to France. Some one asked him one day whether he was replacing Dr. Franklin. Jefferson, a modest man, replied: "I succeed him. No one can take his place."

He remained in Paris until 1789, traveling widely in Europe and Great Britain, observing agriculture, industry, the lives of the people, inventions, and the fine arts. There has probably never been another American diplomat who knew so much about the country to which he was accredited.

During this period, Jefferson made the designs for the present Virginia State Capitol in Richmond, based largely on a reproduction of the Maison Carrée at Nîmes, and sent them home to guide the workmen. It is believed that these designs were the real start of the classical revival in American architecture.

Jefferson returned in 1789 to become Secretary of State in President Washington's first cabinet, a position that brought him into constant official association with Alexander Hamilton, Washington's Secretary of the Treasury. That meant inevitable friction and endless trouble. For — though both had brilliant minds and were devoted patriots — the two men's fundamental views of what the new American government should become were poles apart.

Hamilton, a West Indian immigrant of the humblest possible birth, was a Federalist. That meant he favored a government by "the wise and good," in other words, the wealthier, better educated upper classes, with a rigid restriction of the right to vote and a powerful central government. Jefferson, born a wealthy Virginian aristocrat, called himself a "republican." This did not mean that he belonged to the Republican Party as we know it. This party did not yet exist. We should call him a "democrat" (with a small "d") today. He favored government by almost all the people, or at least by all property holders. He also favored the utmost freedom in thought, speech, and religion, and complete freedom of the press. Hamilton favored restriction and control.

Jefferson at first tried to co-operate with him but did not succeed. Some years of bitter disagreement followed, which President Washington could not smooth over.

In July, 1794, Jefferson resigned as Secretary of State, though he remained in office until the end of the year. After that, weary of political life, he returned to Monticello, hoping to settle down at last to his plantation, his garden, his books, his music, his scientific studies. But when Washington left the presidency in 1797, Jefferson and Vice-President John Adams were both candidates. Jefferson did not really want the office and can hardly have been disappointed when John Adams won by three electoral votes. Jefferson thus became Vice-President, under the original provisions of the Constitution, whereby the candidate with the second highest number of electoral votes received the second highest office.

Very likely the coolness that developed in Adams's friendship for Jefferson dates from this election — which is a pity, considering how little Jefferson wanted the presidency. If so, the election of 1800, in which Adams lost entirely, did not strengthen whatever was left of their friendship. This was the only presidential election that has ever resulted in a tie, though Rutherford B. Hayes in 1876 won the presidency by the margin of one electoral vote and John F. Kennedy won by one tenth of a per cent of the popular vote.

In 1800, the Federalists had nominated John Adams for a second term as President and Thomas Pinckney for Vice-President — hoping that Adams would get a majority of the electoral votes and Pinckney would have the second largest vote, making him Vice-President. The Republicans nominated Jefferson for President and Aaron Burr for Vice-President, hoping for a similar distribution of the vote on their side. But when the electoral vote was counted, Jefferson and Burr had exactly seventy-three votes, Adams sixty-five, Pinckney sixty-four, while somebody had cast one vote for John Jay.

This situation made it necessary for the House of Representatives to choose between Jefferson and Burr. The count of the electoral vote had been announced February 11, 1801. It took thirty-six ballots before, on February 17, the deadlock was broken and Jefferson was elected, only for two weeks before the inauguration. Realizing the danger of such a situation, Congress immediately passed the Twelfth Amendment to the Constitution, providing for the present method of voting separately for President and Vice-President.

This defeat embittered John Adams more than ever. Intent on getting his own men into office despite Jefferson's success, he spent the last few hours of his administration busily signing commissions for judges and other high U. S. officials, to keep out the men Jefferson would have appointed. He is said to have kept on signing till about nine o'clock that night — till midnight, it is sometimes said. As a result, Jefferson, as President, had to deal with a great many hostile subordinates, instead of with men of his own choice.

After that, President Adams left the capital at once, not waiting for Jefferson's inauguration. From that day to this, no outgoing President has ever shown such rudeness to his successor. Yet the two men had been good friends and, when a few years had sweetened John Adams's disposition, became warm friends again. It must be said for President Adams that as he was only the second man who had ever been President, the now familiar ride of the outgoing and the incoming President to the Capitol together had not become an established custom.

Matters grew worse when Jefferson removed Adams's son from a government job and replaced him with another man. Jefferson explained later that he had merely made a new presidential appointment, not knowing that this would deprive the younger Adams of his office.

During his two terms as President, Thomas Jefferson practically transformed the United States, though the far-reaching effect of some of the things he did could not be fully realized until many years had passed. Unquestionably his most important achievement was the Louisiana Purchase, which extended the territory of the United States at least to the summit of the Rockies. (The exact boundaries of the Louisiana Purchase were not very clearly defined in that wild country.)

Actually, this meant extending American territory to the far Pacific. The United States already had a claim to the Columbia River Valley, beyond the mountains, for the river had first been entered by an American ship. Lewis and Clark, whom Jefferson sent out, ensured the American territorial claim and brought back so much information about the Great West, that the fur-trade and then white settlement swiftly followed.

Jefferson also fought the "Barbary pirates," small Mohammedan countries on the north coast of Africa that had been attacking American ships passing their coast. His success made the Eastern Mediterranean safe for American shipping and before long the Barbary pirates became helpless little nations no one feared any longer. His efforts to keep out of the Napoleonic wars in Europe succeeded so long as Jefferson himself was President, though we did eventually have to fight the War of 1812, which was directly related to the conflict overseas.

When the second term of his presidency ended in 1809, Jefferson was at last able to retire permanently to Monticello, as he had so long wished to do. But he never wholly ceased serving the public. During this period he created the new University of Virginia, made suggestions for its curriculum, served as a member of the Board of Trustees, became the new university's first Rector, and designed some of the beautiful buildings that are still the university's pride.

But Jefferson had devoted too much time to his country's service to give his own estates the attention they needed. He had been compelled to leave his rich plantations in the hands of overseers, and lands rarely prosper save in the hands of the owner himself. To make matters worse, the British had carried off thirty of his slaves. The various offices he had held paid salaries and some of them must have included expense accounts, but expenses were almost always larger than salary and expense account combined. Martha Jefferson once remarked that the vice-presidency was the only office her father ever held that paid the cost of holding it. In other words, the patriotic Jefferson had for years been paying for the privilege of placing his tremendous talents at his country's service.

Though Jefferson did his best to build up such estate as he had left, it was a difficult task, which had been postponed too long while he was in his country's service. The fame he had achieved added to his financial difficulties. Hundreds of people, from far and near, came calling. With the usual hospitality of the Southerner, Jefferson gave food and lodging to all comers — and they literally ate him out of house and home.

One consolation of these later years, however, was reconciliation with his old friend, John Adams. In the end the Yankee statesman forgot his defeat for a second term as President and forgave their political struggles. As for Jefferson, it is doubtful if he ever had any resentment toward Adams. After the reconciliation, they wrote each other lengthy letters for years, on all sorts of subjects — literature, art, politics, philosophy. Until the very end, the two elder statesmen found a continual delight in this correspondence.

When, on July 4, 1826, Adams lay dying at his Massachusetts farm, he was heard to murmur that Jefferson still lived. But Adams was wrong. Jefferson had died only a few hours earlier. For some days both he and the devoted Dr. Dunglison — who had lived at Monticello for a week to be sure he would be at hand when needed — had known there was no hope. But at seven o'clock on the evening of July 3, the physician heard the sick man murmur: "Is it the Fourth?" He replied: "It soon will be."

At eleven o'clock that night, the sick man asked again: "This is the Fourth?" Rather than disappoint him, Nicholas Trist, husband of a granddaughter, nodded affirmatively.

"Ah," murmured the dying man, and an expression came over his face that seemed to say, "Just as I wished." He did die on the Fourth, a little before one o'clock in the afternoon.

It was the fiftieth anniversary of the Declaration of Independence.

Richard Henry Lee

Richard Henry Lee

January 20, 1732 — June 19, 1794

JOHN ADAMS BELIEVED the Virginia Lees had produced more "men of merit" than any other family. Whether he was right or not, the Lees well deserved their reputation for brilliant service to their colony, to their state, and to the cause of Independence.

The first Lee to come to America was Richard, great-grand-father of the two Signers, who left his home at Stratford Laughton in Essex County, England, during the reign of Charles I. He made several voyages back to England afterward, each time re-turning with a number of followers to settle in the New World. Since he was granted a tract of land as "Head Rights" for each man he brought, he acquired vast land holdings. With these, he grew wealthy as a tobacco planter, and left his offspring "consider-able fortune, high standards of culture, morality, and a sense of public service." This first Richard Lee finally settled in North-umberland County in Virginia's "Northern Neck," between the Rappahanock and Potomac rivers.

His grandson, Thomas, married Hannah Ludwell, a daughter of Colonel Philip Ludwell of Green Spring, near Williamsburg, then capital of the colony. Ludwell had been a member of the King's Council, and the Ludwells as a family had become con-spicuous for public service. Thomas and Hannah Lee were the parents of the two Signers and of other sons and two daughters. It is interesting to note that Hannah Lee's mother was a Harrison, of the famous Harrison family which also produced a Signer and two later Presidents of the United States. High quality of char-acter marked both sides of the Lee family.

Richard Henry Lee was born on the family estate called Strat-ford, no doubt after the old home in England. He was educated by private tutors and, while still in his teens, was sent to England to round out his education at the academy of Wakefield, in York-shire. Before returning to America, young Lee spent some months traveling. By the time he was nineteen, he was home again, now a young man well read in Greek, Latin, and English literature, and possessed of an attractive, polite manner. His candor, charm, and complete lack of pride made him popular. He seems to have had everything required for success in public life.

Though his father had died during his absence, he did not at once make plans for his future. In fact, he never needed to think of living by a profession, since he was heir to rich plantations. He stayed at home, read, and studied by himself from the books in his father's fine library, while enjoying a congenial home life on his flourishing and beautiful Virginia estates. He made a special study of the laws of his own country, of the principles of civil law, and of history, especially that of England and her colonies. He was a thorough student, who, after reading a work, liked to write a digest or synopsis of its contents. In this way he learned a conciseness of style of which, in later life, he was esteemed to be a master.

It was only natural that Richard Henry Lee should follow his father and more distant ancestors into public life. He was about twenty-five when he was appointed justice of the peace for his county. Diligent in this office, which involved more important duties at the time than it would later, he was presently elected to the House of Burgesses, where his father had also served. Richard Henry Lee served in the House for thirty-three years.

At first, the shy young member was so concious of his youth that he was hesitant about standing up to speak before that august assembly of his elders. But with each attempt, the ordeal became easier, and he seems to have begun to enjoy public speaking by 1776, when he went to Philadelphia as one of Virginia's delegates to Congress. By that time he had acquired such "harmonious" gestures while speaking that one of his colleagues suggested that he practiced them before a mirror. However that may have been, young Richard Henry Lee was soon winning friends, admiration, and even the respect of his opponents.

In 1757, the year in which he began to hold public office, he also began married life. His bride was Anne Aylett, daughter of William Aylett of Westmoreland County. The young newlyweds resided at "Chantilly" — an estate near Stratford.

About a year after becoming a member of the House of Burgesses, young Lee made a very important speech in opposition to slavery. All Virginia planters had slaves to work in the fields. But as early as 1759, Lee saw the coming dangers and, in his speech, proposed that a duty be paid on the importation of slaves — a duty so heavy that it would "put an end to that iniquitous and disgraceful traffic within the colony of Virginia." He advised the House to give serious attention to the debate on this subject, as the consequence would "greatly affect posterity." Foresighted though he was, Richard Henry Lee could not then have imagined that a descendant of his uncle — who would be born at Stratford, his own birthplace — would grow up to be General Robert E.

Lee, leader of the Confederate Army, in a war caused by slavery just about a hundred years later.

By 1764, Lee was speaking against the parliamentary plan to tax the colonies. He wrote to a friend in England that "free possession of property, the right to be governed by laws made by our representatives, and the illegality of taxation without consent" were principles of the British Constitution. His firm stand places Richard Henry Lee in the front rank of the defenders of colonial rights.

When the House of Burgesses registered a protest against the Stamp Act, Lee was the committeeman chosen to draw up an address to the king, another to the Lords, and a remonstrance to the Commons. He was absent from the House on May 30, 1765, when Patrick Henry astonished the assembly by his proposal of five resolutions denouncing the Act. But Lee and Patrick Henry were in agreement, and the eloquence of both these orators caused Silas Deane of Connecticut to describe them as the Demosthenes (Henry) and Cicero (Lee) of America. Deane wrote: "God grant that they may not, like them, plead in vain for the liberties of their country."

In February, 1766, Lee formed a Westmoreland Association of citizens from his own county, who bound themselves not to import any British goods until the Stamp Act was repealed. This was the first of many boycotting measures the colonists tried in order to convince the British government of the seriousness of interfering with the colonists' rights and liberties.

Though the Stamp Act was repealed, matters grew worse. When the New York legislature was suspended in 1768, Lee wrote that this "hangs like a flaming sword over our heads." In that same year, he began to urge the colonies to set up inter-colonial correspondence, in order to unite their counsels. This was the start of what would eventually be a Congress of representatives from all the colonies — today, from all the states. In February of that same year, the Massachusetts House of Representatives adopted a circular letter prepared by Samuel Adams to be sent to assemblies of other colonies, suggesting *united* opposition to Great Britain by discussion and petition.

It was in 1768, too, that Lee's wife died, leaving him with four young children. The next year, he married a widow, Mrs. Anne

Pinckard. From this year until 1773, Lee was also engaged in shipping tobacco to his brother William in London. Both his brothers, William and Arthur, had gone to England to engage in mercantile enterprises, and during these years, Arthur's letters from London kept Richard well informed on British opinion.

Sometime during the 1760's, Lee had a bad accident. A gun exploded while he was hunting, and he lost all the fingers of one hand. Thereafter, he always wore a close-fitting black silk scarf around what was left of his hand, with an opening for the thumb.

In 1769, a new voice for liberalism came to the Virginia House of Burgesses when Thomas Jefferson was elected. Jefferson, Lee, and Patrick Henry were soon working cordially together for the American cause. It was these men who, in May, 1774, "cooked up" — as Jefferson said — a resolution to make the day when the port of Boston was to be closed, a day of "Fasting, Humiliation, and Prayer." Lee prepared a set of resolutions, which included a call for a general congress of all the colonies to secure their rights and liberty. But before the Virginia convention assembled and announced its demand for a general congress, Massachusetts had already sent out the call, naming Philadelphia as the place.

Of Virginia's seven delegates, the conservative Peyton Randolph, speaker of the House of Burgesses, was named first; Richard Henry Lee second. The other five in the first Congress were George Washington, Patrick Henry, Benjamin Harrison, Richard Bland, and Edmund Pendleton.

In Philadelphia, Lee now came in contact with kindred spirits from other colonies, especially the two Adamses of Massachusetts, the colony which had suffered the most marked British spite. A lifelong friendship began between him and Samuel Adams, while John Adams, though never a close friend, thought Lee "a masterly man." Silas Deane of Connecticut (who was later to suffer grave injustice at the instigation of Lee's brother Arthur) said that Lee was regarded as Patrick Henry's equal in eloquence. Lee was active on many committees in Congress — always in favor of strong measures, always against any weak remonstrances that lacked spirit. His speeches were polished, easy, and "inspired with more than mortal powers of embellishment," according to one admirer — the kind of oratory people like to listen to.

Lee was now forty-four, tall and slim, with reddish hair, bold striking features, a deep, melodious voice, and the commanding manner of the real aristocrat. Well-read not only in history, Latin, Greek, French, but also in politics and various branches of science, he was competent to discuss almost any topic of the day. Dr. Benjamin Rush observed of Lee: "I never knew so great an orator whose speeches were so short." They were also convincing. As Dr. Rush said: "He conceived his subject so clearly, and presented it so immediately to his hearers, that there appeared nothing more to be said about it."

Perhaps Richard Henry Lee had been thinking of an independent American union of states as early as November, 1775, when he agreed with John Adams that it was time the colonies adopted their own government. Samuel Adams had certainly believed that for a long time, and the idea was steadily being forced upon Americans by the stubborn attitude of the British. In March, 1776, Lee joined George Wythe, another Virginia Signer, in proposing a resolution that the king, rather than the ministry, was the "Author of our Miseries." Before long, Lee was advocating independence, not so much as an end in itself but rather as a "necessary prerequisite" to a foreign alliance. Others were coming to entertain the same views, but it was Lee's insistence which brought the Virginia convention to adopt, in May, 1776, its resolution favoring independence, foreign alliances, and a confederation. It was, therefore, appropriate to choose Lee to move these resolutions in Congress the next month.

He wrote them and on June 7, on the floor of Congress in Philadelphia, made the first formal declaration "that these United Colonies are and of right ought to be free and independent states."

Much as Lee was admired, he had adversaries, even among Virginians. Benjamin Harrison, Pendleton, and other conservatives of the "cold" party, were still trying to make themselves believe reconciliation was possible.

Having offered the resolution for independence, Lee did not remain in Philadelphia for the final vote on the Declaration, though he eventually returned to Congress to sign it. By this time he had devoted himself so whole-heartedly to the patriot cause for so many years that his private affairs were suffering, and his plantation needed the owner's personal attention. Lee also wanted to go back to Virginia to help form the new state that would replace the old colony. He left Philadelphia in the middle of June. That is probably why he was not appointed to the committee that drafted the Declaration of Independence.

Troubles now arising in foreign relations caused serious disputes in Congress and badly strained Lee's reputation as a statesman. To give a brief outline of this unfortunate affair we go back to the year before, when Silas Deane of Connecticut had been a delegate from his colony to the First Continental Congress. In March, 1776, Deane was selected to represent the colonies abroad. If war came, they would need foreign aid. In the following months, he secured eight shiploads of French military supplies, which arrived in time for the Saratoga campaign of 1777. He also sent over a large number of European military officers. Later, desiring to strengthen relations with France, Congress appointed a commission of three — adding Benjamin Franklin and Arthur Lee, a brother of Richard Henry, who was already in Europe — to continue the work originally undertaken by Deane alone. Franklin was the best choice, and Arthur Lee the worst choice, they made. The commissioners succeeded in signing treaties with France in February, 1778. Soon afterward, Congress called Silas Deane home.

Arthur Lee, an erratic and unreliable individual, had made grave accusations against Deane. He charged that he was dishonestly trying to get money for himself, because Deane and the French dramatist, Beaumarchais, who was also a businessman, requested payment for the supplies the French had turned over. Arthur Lee "supposed" these supplies had been a gift from the French government! During the ugly controversy that ensued, Richard Henry Lee vehemently took his brother's side. A rift, dividing Congress into two hostile factions, produced most unhappy difficulties in American foreign relations for at least two years. Arthur Lee was at fault; his brother in Congress in grave error. By his devoted service to the American cause, Silas Deane had lost so much that he lost faith in the cause; and being rewarded with ill will, suspicion, and slander, he left America entirely and spent his last years in exile. Long after all his accusers were dead, Congress tried to make it up, in 1842, by voting to give Deane's heirs the sum of $27,000, and by admitting that the original inspection of Deane's account, which had been made under Arthur

Lee's direction, was "erroneous and a gross injustice to Silas Deane." Deane had long since passed away, and so had the Lees, but Richard Henry, in standing up for his troublesome brother, lost stature as a statesman. Had he known the truth, he might have known much remorse.

In May, 1799, Lee resigned his seat in Congress. The next year he was elected to the Virginia House of Delegates. In 1784, once more elected to Congress, he was gratified at being chosen its president for a year. In 1787, though a Virginian, he favored the veto on slavery north of the Ohio river.

The American government had thus far operated under the Articles of Confederation, which had at length been formally adopted in 1781. Though these provided for a "perpetual union" of the states, they did not provide a strong central government. Congress was the whole government, but it had no way of collecting taxes or establishing a strong central government. But after his experience with King George, Lee was extremely suspicious of a too much centralization. He especially feared giving Congress power over "both purse and sword." Congress obviously had to have power over the sword — that is, it had to possess the right to make war. Hence Lee opposed giving it the right over the purse — that is, the right to tax — even the right to collect a five per cent tax on imports.

When it became clear to everybody that the government could not go on under the Articles of Confederation, a convention met in Philadelphia in 1787, with George Washington as president and with Benjamin Franklin and many other Signers as members. Richard Henry Lee was not among them, however. Though chosen as a Virginia delegate, he declined to serve.

Though called only to amend and improve the Articles of Confederation, the convention eventually cast them aside and prepared the Constitution of the United States, under which we live today. Even to this Lee objected, largely because it did not yet contain the first ten amendments, usually known as the Bill of Rights; but when the Constitution was adopted, he became one of the first two Senators from Virginia. The Bill of Rights, which was soon adopted, met most of his objections.

He had for some time been suffering from attacks of gout. By October, 1792, realizing that his health was broken, he resigned

as Senator and spent his remaining two years at Chantilly, where
he died June 19, 1794.

Benjamin Harrison

Benj Harrison

c. 1726 (day and month unknown) — April 24, 1791

Two of the signers, Benjamin Harrison and Carter Braxton, were
first cousins. Both these "founding fathers" belonged to the First
Families of Virginia.

The first Benjamin Harrison in America came to Virginia Colony
in the early 1630's — or at least before 1633. The Signer was the
fifth of the name in the direct line of descent. All these Harrisons
were important to their Colony, holding high offices in their province or sitting in the House of Burgesses. Benjamin, the Signer,
had a son, William Henry Harrison, who became President of the
United States. And he had a great-grandson, another Benjamin
Harrison, who also became President — a remarkable record for
any family, equaled only by the Adamses and Roosevelts.

Benjamin, the Signer, was born at "Berkeley," the family seat in
Charles City County, in 1726. He entered the College of William
and Mary but, while he was a student there, his father and two
sisters were killed by lightning. The nineteen-year-old Benjamin
had to leave without graduating, as the charge of the great estate
fell upon his young shoulders. Plummeted into a man's responsibilities while hardly more than a boy and needing a helpmeet badly,
he married his second cousin, Elizabeth Bassett.

Still in his early twenties, Benjamin Harrison was elected to the
House of Burgesses (as the Virginia legislature was called) and
served in it, sometimes as speaker, for twenty-six years, until it
was dissolved in 1774.

Harrison labored mightily as the head of a great estate, whose
duty it was to build up the property he had himself inherited, for
the benefit of his children. It was not an easy task, for in addition
to managing his plantation, growing tobacco and breeding horses,

he erected extensive mills, established a large shipyard, and built his own ships. Like Washington and Jefferson and all wealthy Virginians of his time, he owned slaves as a matter of course.

Since John Rolfe, husband of Pocahontas, had shipped the first experimental crop of tobacco to England in 1613, the tobacco trade had grown to the point where it was not only the chief income of the Maryland and Virginia colonies, but a source of great prosperity to the mother country. It is no wonder that these able planters and businessmen were incensed and offended when members of Parliament in faraway London began to enact laws for the colonists overseas, though they did not understand what life was like here nor how the tobacco business was run.

In 1764, Harrison sided with those who protested the Stamp Act. But, a man of conservative nature, he at first considered the extreme attitude of the radicals to be unwise. As the political storms broke with ever more frequency, however, Harrison stood for Virginia as a member of the Committee of Correspondence.

In August, 1774, the Virginia convention elected him delegate to the First Continental Congress. He was in Carpenter's Hall in Philadelphia on the opening day, when his brother-in-law, Peyton Randolph, was chosen first president of Congress. When Harrison first went to Philadelphia, he shared a house with Peyton Randolph and Colonel George Washington.

Washington, chosen by Congress to lead the new Continental Army, took command in Cambridge in June of 1775. The following September, Benjamin Harrison, Benjamin Franklin, and Thomas Lynch were the congressmen sent to Cambridge to confer with the general and with delegates from the New England states with regard to the support and regulation of the army. Soon after this conference, one of the first of the six small armed vessels that were the beginning of a United States Navy was named the *Harrison*.

Benjamin Harrison was a large, impressive-looking man. He stood six-feet four-inches tall and weighed two hundred forty pounds when he signed the Declaration of Independence at the age of fifty. In Congress, Harrison did not indulge in high-flown oratory. He preferred making short speeches in plain words which, it was said, often had more influence than the long and windy speeches of some of the others. He was among the first in advocating decisive and energetic action. Even critical John Adams observed that "these gentlemen of Virginia appear to be the most spirited and consistent." The tubby little Massachusetts patriot also recorded some unflattering opinions of Harrison.

This worked both ways of course, and Dr. Rush noted that though Harrison well understood "the forms of public business," he had strong state prejudices and was hostile to the leading men from the New England states. This is understandable when we read that Benjamin Harrison was an open, generous, vivacious and liberal host, enjoying the pleasures of dining with convivial company. Even then the warm Southern hospitality and the colder, more reserved New England frugality were at odds. Nevertheless, Harrison was a man of good humor and a master of repartee. Thomas Jefferson thought that he had made the "readiest and most successful remarks ever heard in Congress."

But John Adams was really impressed when Harrison said that he would have come on foot (from Virginia to Philadelphia) to be in Congress, rather than not come at all. For here was a loyal man who would set aside his own interests to help his country. Devoted to his own Virginia, he showed equal devotion later to the Union for whose establishment he had worked most diligently.

After the signing in early August, 1776, a new delegation from Virginia presented their credentials in Congress, their number reduced from the seven — who had signed the Declaration — to five. Harrison was not included. He left Philadelphia in late August and returned home. He had been away so long that ugly suspicions about him had begun to circulate and dissension had arisen in the Virginia delegation. Therefore, when the Virginia legislature convened that fall, Harrison demanded a hearing. The result showed his wisdom in not allowing malicious gossip to go unchallenged. The air was cleared, and that same month the Virginia legislators re-elected him to Congress, entering in their Journals the resolution that "the thanks of this House are justly due to the said Benjamin Harrison for the diligence, ability, and integrity with which he executed the important trust reposed in him as one of the delegates of his country in the General Congress."

Upon his return, Harrison was appointed to a committee to consider the establishment of a War Office. This was the beginning of an effort, heartily sponsored by Harrison, to free General Washington from the continual interference of "Congressmen who were supremely ignorant of military matters." By this action, Washington was no longer hampered in the direction of his armies in the field, as he had been before 1777, when he had to await orders from a congressional Board of War. While in Congress, Harrison was the man upon whom Washington depended for guiding the legislative measures that pertained to the army.

Harrison was the first member named for the Committee of Secret Correspondence, created in November, 1775. Later, he was appointed to the marine committee and to the Board of War and Ordnance. He thus had a share in establishing three of the great departments of the American government: State, War, and Navy.

As chairman, when Congress met as a committee of the whole, he usually presided over the momentous debates which determined the text of the Declaration of Independence. He presided, too, over the first debates concerning the Articles of Confederation. He was noted for his fairness, his ability to make decisions, both in Congress and in his own state's assemblies.

When the traitor Benedict Arnold captured Richmond in 1781, he made his headquarters at Westover, the plantation adjoining Harrison's Berkeley. At the time, Harrison himself was in charge of the state militia. The British, who destroyed so much property of American patriots, seized his house and burned his collection of paintings in the back yard.

After the war, Harrison was elected Governor of Virginia several times, and when his last governorship terminated, he was again elected to the House of Delegates, remaining a member until his death.

In the Spring of 1791, he suffered a severe attack of gout. But the day after his unanimous election to the legislature, he invited a party for dinner and happily received congratulations upon his popularity. The day passed pleasantly. During the night, however, he had a relapse and died the next day.

Over a period of two hundred and fifty years, from 1634 to 1889, when a Benjamin Harrison became the twenty-third President of the United States, the Harrison family of Berkeley furnished more men distinguished in public life, in an unbroken male line, than any other American family.

Francis Lightfoot Lee

Francis Lightfoot Lee

October 14, 1734 — January 11, 1797

THE TWO LEES OF VIRGINIA were the only two brothers among the Signers. Francis Lightfoot and his brother Richard Henry, older by two years, belonged to the fourth generation of Virginia Lees. All these wealthy Lees were owners of vast plantations, inherited and then enlarged by diligent sons. They lived pleasant lives as country gentlemen, many of whom, like Francis and his brother, interested themselves in politics.

Francis was born at the family plantation, Stratford, a lovely spot in Westmoreland County on the Potomac river, where his brother also was born. Both boys were educated by private tutors, as was the custom among families that could afford it. He was still a young man when he inherited from his father an estate in Loudon County where he lived for a long time. It was that county that he represented in the House of Burgesses from 1758 to 1768. While he was a member of the House, Francis did not hesitate to sign the protest against the hated Stamp Act.

In the Spring of 1769, Francis Lee married Rebecca Tayloe, and moved farther south to a plantation called "Menokin" in Richmond County. By this time, he already had some reputation as a man in public life, and his marriage brought him new connections in his wife's county, where he was again elected Burgess, serving during the critical period preceding the War of Independence.

Though Francis Lightfoot Lee was not so well known as his older brother Richard Henry, he attained great political influence, was perhaps as able, and was certainly the more ardent revolutionist. He took part in every measure of defiance to the government of Great Britain. Like his brother, he was shy about speaking in public, but unlike his brother, he never did become a good speaker. Nevertheless, he was one of Virginia's boldest spirits in taking a stand against the British.

In 1773, Francis became one of the committee who formed the Virginia Committee of Correspondence. Having signed the call for the Virginia convention of 1774, he became a member of the convention, too, the following Spring and was chosen as one of the Virginia delegates to the First Continental Congress. He was thereafter re-elected until 1779. He was forty-two when he signed the Declaration.

In Philadelphia, he was active on many committees in Congress, being especially eager to win free navigation of the Mississippi River for American citizens — something America did not secure for a long time. Had he been a man of political ambition, he could doubtless have remained longer in Congress, but he preferred quiet country life on his plantation. Though he did his part for his colony and for independence, he was not a leader in the revolution. He did not have the ambition for that.

After his period in Congress, Lee served in the Virginia state senate for a time, but the later years of his life were uneventful. In the winter of 1797, he passed away at the age of sixty-three at his home, Menokin.

Thomas Nelson

Thˢ Nelson jr.

December 26, 1738 — January 4, 1789

IN THE 1690's, from Penrith on the English side of the Scottish border, came one Thomas Nelson, called "Scotch Tom," to settle in Virginia. His chosen locality was to become Yorktown, where Cornwallis would surrender almost a century later.

Scotch Tom amassed a large fortune as a merchant and incidentally built the first custom house in the colonies. His son, William, who inherited the fortune, bought up large amounts of land and became even wealthier as a merchant and planter. He married Elizabeth Burwell, who bore him five sons. The eldest, named Thomas for his grandfather, was born the day after Christmas, 1738, into the most luxurious style of living in early colonial Virginia.

Since there was plenty of money, education was no problem. When he was fourteen, Thomas went to school at Hackney, England. At nineteen, he entered Christ's College, Cambridge, for three years.

His father, now President of the Council and acting Governor of Virginia, had also served as Presiding Judge of the General Court, and the esteem in which the father was held helped the son's career. While Thomas was still on the vessel bringing him home, before he had even landed, York County voters chose him to represent them in the House of Burgesses, though he was only twenty-three.

The next year, in 1762, Thomas married Lucy Grymes, a daughter of Colonel Philip Grymes of Middlesex County. Father William gave the happy young couple a fine big house, almost opposite his own. Here the young Nelsons lived a delightful social life, entertaining frequently, while Thomas rode out over his plantation daily to keep an eye on everything. He kept a pack of hounds on a farm near town and during the winter he and his friends and neighbors went dashing off on a foxhunt twice a week. It was the southern gentleman's ideal existence. But nothing stays ideal forever.

As the 1760's moved fatefully into the 1770's and as black clouds of war gathered on the horizon and the dreadful storm of revolution drew near, Thomas Nelson — for all his formative years in England — felt keenly the injustices imposed by King George III upon the American colonies. He was one of eighty-nine members who met at the Raleigh Tavern in Williamsburg, after the royal governor had dissolved the House of Burgesses, to protest this invasion of their rights and to plan a provincial congress to replace their dissolved House.

Nelson was a member of this first Virginia convention, which met on August 1, 1774, in Williamsburg and chose seven delegates to the First Continental Congress.

The second convention of the Virginia colony met the following Spring in the old church in Richmond. By that time, England's vengeance upon Massachusetts for the Boston Tea Party had aroused the sympathies of all the colonies, and Virginia's feelings were intense. The excitement in that March, 1775, convention in Richmond is revealed in the ringing words of Patrick Henry, when he prophesied: "The next gale that sweeps from the north will bring to our ears the clash of resounding arms."

He was right. The very next month, Paul Revere and William Dawes made their "midnight ride," and the "clash" Patrick Henry had predicted occurred at Lexington. There was no turning back after that.

Four months later, in July, 1775, there was a convention in Richmond, at which Patrick Henry was elected colonel of the First Virginia Regiment and Thomas Nelson colonel of the Second. The next month, Nelson and George Wythe were elected delegates to the Philadelphia Congress to take the places of Patrick Henry and George Washington, the latter being now commander in chief of the American Army. In mid-September, the new congressmen took their seats in the Second Continental Congress, the body that was to decide the great question of independence in the following July.

For most personal appraisals and first-hand descriptions of our founding fathers we are indebted, as we have seen, to Benjamin Rush and John Adams. Adams was not always kindly in his comments. He noted that "Nelson is a fat man — he is a speaker, and alert and lively for his weight." Dr. Rush's comment on Nelson is more sedate — and duller: "a respectable country gentleman, with excellent disposition in public and private life."

"He informed me," Rush added, "that he was the only person out of nine or ten Virginians that were sent with him to England for education that had taken part in the American Revolution. The rest were all Tories."

The emotional attitudes and political loyalties of Americans changed swiftly through 1774 and 1775. Before that, most of them had been loyal subjects of the king. But by 1776 Thomas Nelson was writing to a friend that it was absurd to suppose Americans could have "any affection for a people who are carrying on the most savage war against us." Lord Dunmore had ordered the burning of Norfolk, Virginia. No wonder Virginians were changing their minds!

During the early months of 1776, the members of the various provincial assemblies throughout the colonies were busy debating, arguing, endeavoring to foresee all aspects of the problem. On May 6, Virginia convention delegates took over authority from the king's government. A week later, Nelson moved for independence and, when the Virginia resolution for final separation from Britain was finally passed, Nelson rode off to Philadelphia carrying it to the Continental Congress.

Thomas Nelson was only thirty-eight when he signed the Declaration in early August, but he had felt the strain of these arduous years and in the following May he withdrew from Congress because of ill health. In August, when Virginia feared invasion by the approaching British fleet, which actually invaded Pennsylvania, he was appointed brigadier general and commander in chief of the state's forces.

When, in the Spring of 1778, Congress appealed for volunteer troops of light cavalry "to serve at their own expense," Nelson raised a company of about seventy emergency soldiers, who marched to Philadelphia. In August, after the enemy had withdrawn to New York, the company disbanded, but the thanks of Congress went to General Nelson and his volunteers for their patriotic effort. Nelson had also advanced large sums of money for other purposes.

The next year, again in Congress, Nelson was once more forced to retire because of illness. In June, 1780, when the Virginia assembly asked for $2,000,000 to help the Continental Treasury pay for the French fleet, Nelson himself tried to raise the money and on his own personal security did raise the larger part of the loan. Later, he was forced to redeem the security at a great sacrifice, and the government never compensated him for his loss. He also paid two whole regiments who refused to march south until they had received the back pay due them; and when Benedict Arnold led British troops into Virginia, Nelson's plantations were exposed to the traitor's raids.

Nelson was elected Governor of Virginia in June, 1781, and at the siege of Yorktown, it was he who commanded the Virginia militia. In his orders of the day for October 20, Washington expressed his deep appreciation to Nelson to whom, he said, "the highest praises are due" for activity and bravery.

Again poor health forced Governor Nelson to resign. Thereafter, having spent his fortune for his country, he lived very modestly in Hanover County until he died in 1789, at the early age of fifty-one. He was buried in an unmarked grave at Yorktown.

His courage, his zeal, and his generosity marked him as a man of "true religion" in the minds and memories of many who had known him and worked with him.

George Wythe

George Wythe

1726 (day and month unknown) — June 8, 1806

"ONE OF OUR BEST MEN," George Wythe, was born in 1726 on his father's prosperous plantation on Back River, Elizabeth City County, Virginia. His father, Thomas, was the grandson of Thomas Wythe, who came to Virginia from England about 1680. For three generations, the Wythes had increased their property in America and become prosperous. George Wythe's father was also a justice for the county and its delegates in the House of Burgesses for three terms.

His mother was Mary Walker Wythe, daughter of Quaker George Walker, reputed to have been a man of considerable learning. A firm believer in the education of women — an idea not generally accepted until more than a century later — he had given his daughter such excellent schooling that she was able to teach her son Latin, Greek, grammar, rhetoric, and logic. She began teaching the boy when he was three years old immediately after his father died. She must have been a devoted teacher, filled with ardent love for the subjects she presented to him; for though he was given very little formal education later, the boy pursued his studies eagerly in later life, spurred on by the incentive she had given him. On this foundation he was able to build a successful career and win a great reputation. He never ceased to study and in later life became known as a proficient scholar in Greek and Latin literature.

George was the middle one of three children, with a brother many years older than himself, who inherited the family estate, and a younger sister, Ann. When he was still a mere child, his widowed mother died, and after that no one seems to have taken any interest in the boy's further education. The lack of such a mother's care and advice must also have been a sore misfortune for the growing Ann. Later, she was to marry one Charles Sweeney, who was probably not a man of the same quality as the Walkers and Wythes, and probably not the type of person Mary Walker Wythe would have liked her daughter to marry. At any rate, Ann's grandson was to bring tragedy and death to his great-uncle George, the Signer.

In his teens, George Wythe entered the College of William and Mary, but his stay was very brief since he was a poor boy who had to earn a living. He soon left college to study law at the office of Stephen Dewey, a connection of the family. He was so successful in his studies that he was admitted to the bar at the age of twenty and began to practice in association with a prominent attorney, John Lewis, in Spottsylvania County. He soon fell in love with Lewis's sister, Ann, whom he married the following year. But death robbed the young lawyer of his bride in less than eight short months.

In that same year Wythe, now twenty-two, began his first service in public office as clerk of the Committee on Privileges and Elections in the House of Burgesses. His efficiency surprised his elders. Six years later Governor Dinwiddie appointed him Attorney General of the Colony, during the absence of Attorney General Peyton Randolph in England. After his friend Randolph returned, Wythe courteously resigned.

By this time he was twenty-nine and upon the death of his much older brother, the large family plantation, with its usual population of animals and slaves, became his responsibility. However, as he was representing Williamsburg in the House of Burgesses, he continued to reside there. This same year Wythe was married again, this time to Elizabeth Taliaferro of Williamsburg. They had one child who died in infancy.

He was admitted to the bar of the General Court when he was thirty-two. Serving in the House of Burgesses for ten years, he built up a brilliant career. In 1761, he was elected to the Board of Visitors of the College of William and Mary, his alma mater, and, though he had never had money enough to graduate, he joined the faculty eight years later — the first man to hold a chair of law in an American college.

As a teacher, George Wythe gave some of the most effective service of his useful career. He loved teaching. He loved to direct the studies of young men and he had some remarkable students, among them Thomas Jefferson, Henry Clay, James Monroe, John Marshall, and others who became governors, United States senators, congressmen, and state and federal judges. A pioneer in American jurisprudence, Wythe brought honor to the college.

George Wythe was a man of middle height with a good figure, and remarkable for his courteous manners. He dressed conservatively, with his long hair combed straight back and curled up at the neck.

The mid-1770's brought special troubles with the mother country for Virginia tobacco planters. Virginia and her great tobacco trade which made fortunes for her planters was also extremely profitable to the London businessmen who bought and sold tobacco. In fact tobacco was so important that, under Virginia law and with the approval of the Crown, the churches paid their ministers in tobacco, which was better than money, for if the price of tobacco rose the clergy made a profit. When Virginia commuted these salaries at a fixed monetary rate without royal consent there was trouble, for now the clergy would receive only cash and there would be no chance of profit. Law-suits followed, and the Virginians' troubles with tobacco made them very sympathetic with Boston's tea trouble and the closing of her port.

When war threatened in 1775, Wythe recommended that Virginians set up a full-time regular army instead of relying on a part-time citizen militia, as the colonies had always done. Upon the opening of hostilities, he himself volunteered for service as a soldier, but he was sent instead to the Continental Congress in Philadelphia, where he took his seat in September.

Following the hot debates, discussions, and arguments that swayed Congress in the spring and early summer of 1776, he voted in favor of Richard Henry Lee's resolution for independence, and signed the Declaration the following September. Two months later, in November, 1776, Wythe was appointed by the Virginia legislature to the committee to revise the laws for the new state. His former pupil, Thomas Jefferson, was also on this committee.

In 1777, George Wythe became speaker of Virginia's House of Delegates and next year was chosen one of the three judges of the new Chancery Court, a post he held for the rest of his life. During these decades, Chancellor Wythe earned the appellation of "the American Aristides," an allusion to an ancient Athenian with a high reputation for fairness, known in Athens as Aristides the Just. Wythe, too, was known to be "scrupulously impartial," erudite, and logical. Dr. Benjamin Rush considered him a "profound lawyer and able politician."

"I have seldom known a man possess more modesty," he wrote, "or a more dove-like simplicity and gentleness of manner."

Like all large land-owners, Wythe suffered great losses during the Revolution and his income as chancellor was most welcome. When he received that post in 1789, he terminated his connection with the college and moved to Virginia's new capital, Richmond.

His political theories agreed substantially with those of Jefferson and Madison. He favored a representative republicanism — the kind of government we have today. Opposed to slavery as were other eminent Virginians, he freed his own servants, though he was well aware that he would have to support them until they learned how to take care of themselves. And this led to tragedy.

In his will, Chancellor Wythe made his sister's grandson, George Wythe Sweeney, the principal beneficiary. But he also left legacies to provide for three of his freed slaves. After Wythe's death, the income from the rental of his Richmond house and from his bank stock was to be used to support "my freed woman, Lydia Broadnax, and my freedman Benjamin and freed boy Michael Brown." Later, when Benjamin died, Wythe provided that Michael was to have half the bank stock and his grand-nephew Sweeney the other half. But if Michael should die before coming of age, Sweeney was to have it all. Sweeney decided to hasten his legacy by getting rid of his uncle and of Michael Brown at the same time.

While the Chancellor was in court on May 25, 1806, young Sweeney came to the house and went to his great-uncle's room. Lydia, the cook, saw him at the desk reading the will, but she believed him when he said his uncle had told him to do so. Next morning he came to the kitchen, asked for coffee and toast, and explained he could not wait to breakfast with his uncle. He took the whole coffee-pot to the table while Lydia was making his toast, and poured himself a cup. Lydia saw him toss a little white paper in the open fire but thought nothing of it.

Sweeney had poured a cup of coffee for himself and had then dropped yellow arsenic into the coffee-pot, and burned the paper that had contained it.

After Sweeney had left the house, Chancellor Wythe appeared, took some coffee with his breakfast, and told Lydia to get some breakfast for herself and Michael. Lydia was taken very ill, seized with a violent cramp. The Chancellor and the mulatto boy, Michael, died.

No one had any doubt what had happened — least of all the Chancellor, who as a lawyer had a lifetime of dealing with crime. He lingered on in agony for two weeks but he was able to change his will in time to keep Sweeney from profiting by his crime. Watchers by his bedside heard him say: "I am murdered."

Sweeney was arrested and given a preliminary hearing before magistrates. They had no doubt of his guilt and held him for trial on six charges — the murder of Wythe, the murder of Michael Brown, and the forgery of checks. But the only murder witness was Lydia Broadnax, the Negro cook. And under Virginia law of that day, the testimony of a Negro could not be received against a white man. Though Sweeney could not be convicted of the murder of which every one knew he was guilty, he was brought to trial for forgery, and convicted. But he was granted a new trial and the district attorney decided not to prosecute. Again the rascal went free!

Wythe died in great agony, both of mind and body. He said of the grand-nephew who had poisoned him: "I shall die leaving him my forgiveness." But it was an anguish, too, for him to realize that law suits would follow and that large expenses were to be caused by his death. He died on June 8, 1806, at his home in Richmond.

Years later Wythe's ardent admirer and erstwhile student, Thomas Jefferson, made notes with the idea of writing a biography of George Wythe. But he did not live to complete it. He noted, however, that "no man ever left behind him a character more venerated than George Wythe, whose virtue," he said, "was pure, whose integrity inflexible, whose justice exact." He considered his old teacher, "the honor of his own, and model of future times."

Carter Braxton

Carter Braxton

September 10, 1736 — October 10, 1797

THOUGH MANY OF THE PATRIOTS who survived the war suffered heavily in loss of health or lands or fortune because of the time and energy they devoted to their country, Carter Braxton was among the most unfortunate of all. Born into one of the First Families of Virginia with an inherited background of wealth and culture, he suffered heavier losses than most other patriots just because he had so much to lose.

Carter Braxton was the son of a wealthy planter, a member of the House of Burgesses, whose estate lay at Newington, in King and Queen County, Virginia. His mother, Mary Carter Braxton, was from an equally proud and wealthy family, but her son never knew her, for she died soon after September 10, 1736, the day when he was born.

The boy was educated at the College of William and Mary. He was only nineteen when he married Judith Robinson, who died two years later, leaving him with two small daughters. Perhaps it was this sad experience that caused him to go to England for over two years. Some time after his return, he married Elizabeth Corbin, and in the same year he was appointed, at the age of twenty-five, to represent King William County in the House of Burgesses.

The unhappy 1760's were beginning; and in the disputes between Great Britain and her Virginia Colony, Braxton, though a conservative, took Virginia's side, never at this time dreaming of such an extreme notion as American independence.

In 1769, however, he joined Washington, Jefferson, and other prominent Virginians in resolutions supporting the sole right of the House of Burgesses to tax Virginia. He also represented his county in the conventions of the early 1770's, and, when the House of Burgesses was dissolved in 1774, became a member of the patriots' Committee of Safety.

Peyton Randolph, Virginia's most popular leader during the decade before the war, had been representing his colony in the First Continental Congress in Philadelphia. When, in October, 1775, he died suddenly, Carter Braxton became his successor. It was said that the Virginians were "so alarmed with the Idea of Independence that they have sent Mr. Braxton [to Congress] on Purpose to turn the Vote of that Colony, if any Question on that Subject should come before Congress."

Braxton took his seat on February 23, 1776, four months before Richard Henry Lee introduced his resolution for independence. Many minds had had to change in those months, and Braxton's was one of them. He was just under forty when he voted for Independence and signed the Declaration.

Dr. Benjamin Rush, who recorded so many comments about his colleagues in Congress — not all of them favorable — thought Braxton an agreeable and sensible speaker and an accomplished gentleman, but strongly prejudiced against New Englanders.

When discussions came up later as to the form of government the new American states should have, Braxton doubted the success of a democracy, and he advocated a more conservative form of government for Virginia. In those days democracy was considered the most extreme radicalism.

(National attitudes have changed much in the last two hundred years. It is amusing now to reflect that Russia would have nothing to do with so radical a country as the new United States. The Tsar would neither send a minister, nor receive one from us in the early days of the United States!)

Braxton's expressed doubts about democratic government may have been one reason why he was not reappointed to the Continental Congress, but he did continue to serve in the Virginia Assembly. Here, in 1785, he supported an act to establish religious freedom. The next year he moved to Richmond because his losses during the war had been on such a gigantic scale that he could not continue living on his elaborate country estate.

While he was still possessed of great wealth, Braxton had loaned £10,000 sterling to "our Suffering country." It was never paid back to him. He had been engaged in merchandizing and shipping throughout the war, but some of his vessels had been captured by the British, others had been lost in unfortunate enterprises.

Vast debts due him were worthless in the depreciated Continental currency. All these misfortunes left him bankrupt at the end of the war.

Weighed down by the endless litigation in which these financial troubles involved him, and by the hopelessness of recovering from his misfortunes, Carter Braxton died in Richmond at the age of sixty-one. He lived only long enough to see the first few years of the new nation for which he had sacrificed so much.

III

PENNSYLVANIA

Benj. Franklin

Robt Morris

Benjamin Rush

John Morton

Geo Clymer

Jas. Smith

Geo. Taylor

James Wilson

Geo. Ross

Benjamin Franklin

January 17, 1706 — April 17, 1790

OF ALL JOSIAH FRANKLIN's seventeen children, his youngest son, Benjamin, was, from early childhood, the most promising. He was born with something the others never had. Even as he was the "different" member of his family, so was his career different from those of all the other men chosen for the Second Continental Congress. Of the Signers of the Declaration of Independence, Benjamin Franklin was the oldest, being seventy at the time, and also the most famous, both in his own country and in Europe. Several of the Signers were exceedingly able and talented men, two became President of the United States; but Franklin was the one possessed of genius — a quality that cannot be achieved, something that, like lightning, strikes no one can tell where.

Benjamin Franklin's forebears were of lowly British stock: farmers and blacksmiths, of Ecton, Northamptonshire, a county in central England. His father, Josiah, was a dyer in Banbury, Oxfordshire, who already had a wife and three children when he decided to cross the ocean to the colony of Massachusetts. Having broken away from the Church of England and become a dissenter, at a time when that was difficult and even dangerous, he hoped that his work would prosper better and his life be more agreeable in the new land, where there were fewer restrictions than in the rigid, class-conscious Old World.

He was right. His favorite brother, Benjamin, also a dissenter, remained in England and had a hard time of it. But Josiah, settling in Boston and finding that a dyer was not needed there, became instead a busy maker and seller of soap and candles and, as a tallow-chandler, flourished to a ripe old age. His wife, however, did not survive the birth of their seventh child. Then Josiah married young Abiah Folger, only twenty-two, the daughter of Peter Folger of Nantucket, and by her had ten more children, the seventh of whom was Benjamin. Josiah was nearing fifty when Benjamin was born on the first Sunday in January, 1706. The Franklins were then living in a house on Milk Street, opposite the Old South Church, and the new baby was carried across the street and baptized there the same day.

Benjamin was, of course, the favorite nephew of the English uncle for whom he had been named. Eight years older than his brother in Boston, the lonely uncle, who had lost his wife and all nine children, began to write letters in verse to his nephew Benjamin when the child was only four years old. At seven, the boy was writing verses in answer. Two years later, Uncle Benjamin came to visit the Boston Franklins, and he was much pleased with his namesake, for there was something about young Benjamin that usually drew marked attention from older men. Perhaps it was because he learned so easily and grasped ideas so quickly — more easily than the average child of his years. He could read at a very early age.

When he was eight, his father sent him to the grammar school (now the Boston Latin School), where, in less than a year, he advanced from the middle of the class to the top. At first, his father thought to have him educated for the Church; but seeing how expensive a college education was and how poor ministers were, he took Benjamin from the grammar school and sent him to a school for writing and arithmetic kept by a schoolmaster named George Brownell. Though the boy did well in writing, he failed in arithmetic, and after he was ten his father kept him home to help in the business. From this time on, Benjamin Franklin taught himself.

For two years, his father tried to get him to learn the tallow-chandler's trade. But candle-making was one thing that did not interest young Benjamin. In summers he spent his free time in, or on, the water, which he loved; and, as the Franklins lived right on the shore in Boston harbor, he learned early to swim well and to handle boats. He was so adept at sailing that the other boys let him take charge, "especially in case of difficulty," as Franklin recorded when he wrote his autobiography. With all this, he grew strong, not above average height, but with a stocky, sturdy figure and powerful muscles.

Seeing that Benjamin was not enamored of candle-making and so fond of the water, his father was afraid his son might run away to sea, as one of his older sons had already done. It was not an uncommon thing in the days of the sailing ships for a son to go off to sea without consulting his parents. But Benjamin Franklin stayed ashore because, mindful of his love of books, his father turned him over to James Franklin, his older brother, to serve as an apprentice in James's new printing shop. After learning the trade in London, James had returned to set up a shop of his own in Boston. He was twenty-one and Benjamin was twelve when the apprenticeship agreement was made. The father paid James £12 for teaching Benjamin the "art of a printer" and providing the boy's lodging, meals, and necessities. The sturdy young apprentice, as quick with his hands as he was with his mind, was soon a skillful printer. The elder Franklin had done exactly the right thing, for eventually his son Benjamin made a fortune as head of his own printshop.

Boston was then a small provincial town with a number of other printers, and the Franklin brothers, who were not burdened with orders, had to do all sorts of odd jobs, printing pamphlets and ballads (which young Benjamin began to write) and even designs on linen, silk, and calico. After his young brother had been in his shop for a year, James was engaged to print a newspaper, the *Boston Gazette*. He had printed forty numbers when the job was given to another printer, whereupon James started his own competing newspaper, the *New England Courant*.

An example of Benjamin's early wisdom was his recognition of the value of his own time. He liked people — if they were not boring — and made friends easily. He liked certain games and boating; he was an expert swimmer. But he never had any use for loafing around taverns, drinking, or gambling. At fifteen, he couldn't get enough time to read. With any money he could save he bought books, and when he finished these books, he sold them to buy others. He read history, travel, fiction, science, and biography — Plutarch's *Lives,* essays by Defoe, Cotton Mather, and Locke. By himself, he now mastered the arithmetic he had failed a few years before. He read to learn, not just to pass the time. He studied prose style, argument, and discussion. When he came upon a volume of the *Spectator,* he was delighted. This, he decided, was a style he wished to emulate; and he went about it cleverly, choosing one essay for study, jotting down the hints contained in each sentence, then rewriting it himself to compare his own work with the original.

Benjamin Franklin had a goal. While still young, he had considered the kind of man he wanted to be. He felt he must refine his taste constantly, and this led him to copy the literary masters. Like most adolescents, he loved to take part in serious discussion, but after reading Plato's accounts of Socrates, he "gave up the disputatious habits" he had formed when engaged in discussion, and assumed a manner more persuasive, agreeable, and modest in argument. Aiming constantly to improve his mind, he also considered his manners. All these were useful and most desirable achievements for a boy who was to become in later life his country's ablest diplomat.

Realizing that he needed time and money for making himself the kind of person he wanted to be, young Benjamin went to the printing house early in the mornings, stayed late on week-days, and went back on Sundays, in order to be alone to read and study. Wanting a little money to buy books (we must remember that there were no public libraries), he conceived the idea of asking his brother to give him half the money that his board cost and let him feed himself. Then he saved money by not eating meat. He found he could save half of the amount his brother paid him by making a meal of a biscuit or a slice of bread and some raisins. This gave him three advantages: he could have his light snacks alone in the office while the others went out for their meals and thereby have time to study; he discovered that he had a clearer head after one of his light meals than after a hearty one; he had more money to buy books and so feed his hunger for knowledge.

With a mind so inquisitive and acquisitive came a disposition to experiment. He liked to invent new things and new ways of doing things. Combining kite-flying with swimming, he gave himself a glorious experience one day by holding to the string of his kite while the wind pulled him across the pond. What strange experiments might not this young boy try in the future!

As printer's apprentice, his brother's newspaper brought him in touch with local affairs, current events, contemporary ideas. The *New England Courant* first appeared during a smallpox epidemic in the hot summer of 1721. Some doctors upheld the new idea of inoculation — a kind of early vaccination — while others denounced it as a "doubtful and dangerous practice."

When James Franklin invited his friends, through his newspaper, to send in short pieces to enliven the news, young Benjamin accepted the general invitation without telling his brother. He decided to submit a short "epistle" twice a month, hoping it would appear among the letters to the editor. But, because he knew his brother would not use anything written by his fifteen-year-old apprentice, he signed his pieces "Mrs. Silence Dogood." Slipping his papers under the printing-house door at night, the unknown correspondent soon had the pleasure of seeing himself in print. In his first contribution, he started out by describing the writer as a widow and gave a short and entirely imaginary account of her life. This and later Dogood letters entertained and amused the readers of the *New England Courant*.

Then James Franklin made the mistake of printing a fictitious letter from Newport, in which was a sarcastic jibe at the royal governor of Massachusetts. James found himself clapped in jail for ridiculing the authorities and, during his forced absence, young Benjamin had to print and edit the paper himself.

In time the real author of the Dogood articles was discovered, and James became intensely jealous when he found that the writer who had been so highly praised was really his younger brother. Resentfully, he now accused young Benjamin of being vain, which was most unfair. Benjamin Franklin may have had his faults, but vanity was never one of them. Inevitably, with all this ill feeling, an uncomfortable atmosphere crept into the printing office. Probably neither brother quite understood what was really wrong. The truth was that Benjamin was outgrowing his position and would soon be ready for bigger things. James had already reached his limits.

Presently young Benjamin was in more trouble. Having ventured upon what he later called "indiscreet disputations" about religion, he found himself denounced as "an infidel or atheist."

Strict, narrow-minded, and Puritanical, many people of eastern Massachusetts of those days were quick to form suspicions of other people's religious beliefs. This was ironical, since their own fathers had come to the New World seeking for themselves the very religious freedom which their descendants now refused to others. It had not been very many years since the more fanatical Puritans had hanged innocent women, calling them witches. One trouble was that Benjamin had not been a steady attendant at church because he wanted the time for study. His father, of course, disapproved, and apparently others made it their business to disapprove also. Benjamin Franklin later recorded in his autobiography that he believed in God, but he could not believe that God was as narrow-minded as many of the New England preachers.

Troubled by this petty public criticism and gossip, and by his uncomfortable relations with his jealous brother, and with his father who sided with James, the seventeen-year-old Benjamin decided it was time to seek broader horizons. Borrowing a little money from a boyhood friend, he secretly boarded a sloop for New York. Fearing his father would prevent him, he did not tell his family. This was to be a permanent break — with family, home town, and familiar ways.

Becalmed off Block Island, the sailing vessel took three days to reach New York, at that time a smaller city than Boston, though less provincial. Calling on the town's only printer, William Bradford, Benjamin was told that a new hand was not needed. However, the printer's son, Andrew Bradford, in Philadelphia, might be able to use him.

Benjamin arrived in the Quaker City on a sunny September morning, tired, hungry, and dirty. The first thing he needed was food. Inquiring of a passing boy who was carrying bread, he learned where to find the baker. Unaware of the differences in the price of bread between Boston and Philadelphia, he simply asked for three pennyworth and was surprised to be given "three great puffy" rolls. With one under each arm while nibbling the third, he walked on up the street. As he passed a house where a young girl was standing at the door, she watched him go by, amused because he looked "most awkward" and ridiculous. He found this out some years later when this same girl, Deborah Read, became his wife.

Following many "cleaned-dressed people" all walking in one direction, he came to the Quaker Meeting-house. Every one else went inside. So did he and, during the quiet service, fell asleep. Out in the street again afterward, he inquired of a young Quaker where to find lodging. The next day, making himself as neat as he could, he went to see Andrew Bradford, the printer. This was the beginning of Franklin's Philadelphia career.

It was not easy at the start. Though Bradford welcomed the teen-age runaway, he could not offer steady work, and for some time Benjamin was a "journeyman" printer, working at odd jobs of printing wherever he could find them. Eventually, he rented a room in the house of Mr. Read — the house where the girl stood on the stoop that first Sunday morning. Even as journeyman printer he soon began to earn more money than he ever had earned in Boston.

In Philadelphia that first winter, Benjamin made friends and enjoyed his new freedom. He liked the Quakers and their tolerant views of their fellow men. It was a great relief not to be under the domination of his older brother and the criticism of his father. Though he probably did not realize it yet, he already had a more active brain, more wit, imagination, common sense, and industry than any one of his relatives. In the spring, he visited his family in Boston and told them about his life in Philadelphia.

Seeing his young son dressed in a good new suit, wearing a watch in his pocket, with more money than he himself had ever accumulated in Boston, Josiah Franklin gave up all hope that Benjamin would ever work again with James and consented to his return to Philadelphia. This eased Benjamin's mind, of course, for he was still a minor. His father could have forced him to come home.

By this time Benjamin Franklin had grown to be a well-built, vigorous young man, about five-feet nine- or ten-inches tall, with a large head (which accommodated a good brain), and strong, deft hands. His hair was light brown, his eyes gray, and his regard steady and honest. His unfailing sense of humor was revealed by a humorous mouth and easy smile. He could be quick and prompt to act, but his speech was hesitant and slow. He was at his best in small groups of chosen friends in the clubs he formed, or others which he joined.

Evenings spent in discussions, listening to and criticizing poems written by each other, sharing their opinions on the books they read, Sunday walks in the beautiful countryside around Philadelphia — these were the pleasant ways in which Benjamin and his young friends, mostly clerks, used their free time. Generous and disposed always to help others, young Franklin more than once had the unpleasant experience of loaning his hard-earned money to "friends" who never repaid him. He believed too easily in the word of people who, having nothing else to give, airily gave promises and forgot them.

It was this trusting disposition that presently left Franklin stranded in London whither he had sailed relying on the promises of no less a personage than Sir William Keith, royal governor of Pennsylvania. Sir William had been impressed by a letter that Benjamin had written to his own brother-in-law, who was master of a sloop that operated between Boston and Delaware. Sir William took the trouble of looking up the young man, liked him, and made elaborate plans for setting him up in a printing shop of his own. He was to go to London to select the stock he would need, and Sir William would advance the necessary credit.

This offer came when Benjamin, now eighteen, was courting Deborah Read, whose parents wanted the marriage delayed until his return. With his friend, James Ralph, Benjamin boarded a ship for London. Until the last moment, he was expecting Sir William's promised letters of credit and of introduction. They did not come. Then he hoped to find them on his arrival in London. But Sir William's promises were but air. The papers never came, and once more Benjamin Franklin found himself in a strange city with no friends and little money. He had, however, his trade and his will to work. He soon found his chance in the printing house of Samuel Close.

He also had on his hands James Ralph, who now proved to be less than a friend. Ten years older than Benjamin, he had left behind a wife and baby and now declared he was not going to return to them. Nor did he even try to support himself, but proceeded to live on Benjamin's earnings, borrowing steadily while planning to be a poet, then an actor, then an editor of a weekly paper "like the *Spectator*." Their ways parted when Ralph went to Berkshire to be a schoolmaster, leaving only an unpaid debt. Benjamin was well rid of a knave.

For a year and a half, the young printer lived in London during one of its most brilliant periods. At the beginning of manhood, Franklin was eager to drink in the advantages of this center of luxury, fashion, and wit. A poor young American printer of twenty had no way of meeting the great writers and artists there — Lord Chesterfield, Fielding, Defoe, Swift, and a refugee from Paris named Voltaire; but he had his own intellectual interests which led him to good reading, and he made good use of his time. He soon moved to a larger printing-house, and among the printers, his strength and speed distinguished him. At this time he published his first pamphlet: *"A Dissertation on Liberty and Necessity, Pleasure and Pain."* A printer friend suggested they travel through Europe as journeymen printers together, but Benjamin's thoughts were turning toward home. He sailed for America in July, 1726.

With plenty of time for reflection during the long voyage, Benjamin drew up a plan for his future conduct in life. His first aim, he decided, was to be extremely frugal, pay his debts and save money "for some time." Second, he must "endeavor to speak truth in every instance, to give nobody expectations that are not likely to be answered," (was he thinking of Sir William's vain promises?), "but aim at sincerity in every word and action; the most amiable excellence in a rational being." Third, he must apply himself industriously "to whatever business I take in hand, and not divert my mind from my business by any foolish project of growing suddenly rich; for industry and patience are the surest means of plenty." Fourth, he decided "to speak ill of no man whatever, not even in a matter of truth; but rather by some means excuse the faults I hear charged upon others, and upon proper occasions speak all the good I know of everybody." In his autobiography, the old Franklin wrote that he followed these resolutions, on the whole, "quite through to old age."

Upon his return, Franklin first kept store for his friend, Thomas Denham, a Quaker merchant whom he had met on the homeward voyage. Denham set up the store with stock he had brought from England. But after some months, Franklin returned to his own trade and became foreman for the printer Samuel Keimer.

Through his twenties, Benjamin Franklin's advancement was rapid. Keimer employed him to print paper money for New Jersey, and for this work Benjamin contrived the first copperplate press in the country. The New Jersey Assembly liked his work and they liked him. It was he — not Keimer — whom the assemblymen invited to their houses while the printers were working in Burlington,

New Jersey. Franklin was now making friends for life. Older men were attracted by his innate charm and simplicity of manner, his conversation, and his marked ability. Success came swiftly now. Within four years Benjamin Franklin was his own master, the proprietor of a printshop, and the best printer in America.

Always, somehow, he found time to write, and now he began writing articles, which he signed "Busy-Body," for the *American Weekly Mercury*. Before long, he was planning a newspaper, the *Pennsylvania Gazette*, which he started with the issue of October 2, 1729. For many issues he was the writer as well as the printer; and after two years, as the *Gazette* became profitable, he became part owner of other *Gazettes* in South Carolina and Rhode Island.

An alert man of business, he was also deeply interested in public welfare, in good companionship, and in stimulating talk. He brought together a group called "The Junto," for Friday evening meetings to discuss civic improvements and the improvement of their own knowledge. Under his leadership, the Junto was a gathering of tradesmen and artisans for pleasure as well as for serious debate. It was a kind of brotherhood, whose members promoted each other's interests and businesses. At first they met in a tavern, sometimes in their homes. Young people always like to organize social groups, but few last as long as Franklin held the Junto together. It continued to meet for thirty years.

While he had been away in England, he had written only one letter to Deborah Read. As the months passed into a year and longer, still with no further word, she concluded he had forgotten her and married a potter named Rogers. But she was unhappy with him and learning, too late, that he already had a wife, she parted from him. Rogers ran away to the West Indies, leaving many debts. Finally the report came of his death. In 1730, when Benjamin Franklin was twenty-four, he "took her to wife" as he noted in his autobiography.

He set up a shop in a part of his house where his wife helped in selling books and stationery. Wanting more income, and needing more work for his active brain, the budding philosopher began writing the famous *Poor Richard's Almanac*. The first issue appeared in December, 1732, and a new annual number was forthcoming for many years thereafter. *Poor Richard* was translated into French when Franklin achieved international fame, and his amusing nuggets of wisdom have afforded entertaining reading now for over two hundred years.

There seemed to be no limit to the intellectual curiosity of this man. He studied languages by himself till he could read books in Italian, French, and Spanish. He enlarged his shop to offer all kinds of goods that he could sell through advertisements in his own *Gazette*. The business broadened until Franklin became a general trader; he even operated a kind of employment agency, offering for sale (again through his paper) the unexpired time of indentured servants.

Ever eager for more books, he conceived the idea of what we call today a lending library, an idea which he suggested to the Junto. They agreed, and Franklin worked out the details: fifty subscribers paid for membership, and the Library Company was formed. It is still operating in Philadelphia!

Concerned about the town's fire protection, Franklin formed the first volunteer fire company in December, 1736. He also helped establish the "City Watch," thus providing better police protection for the city.

As the years passed, Franklin's reputation as a helpful citizen increased and put him into various offices. He was appointed clerk of the Pennsylvania Assembly and, the next year, postmaster for Philadelphia.

Working with the newspapers and trade of other colonies, Franklin's affairs brought him in touch with ideas in other colonies. He was about thirty-seven when he conceived a kind of intercolonial Junto. This resulted in his founding of the American Philosophical Society. It, too, is still operating in Philadelphia.

Busy at his work six days a week and studying with his friends evenings and Sundays, Franklin had, by the age of forty, made enough money to be able to indulge in some leisure. But to a man of his lively mind, leisure did not mean idleness. It meant time for new ideas, and a very big new idea soon came his way.

Visiting Boston in 1746, Franklin met "a Dr. Spence, who was lately come from Scotland, and showed me some electrical experiments." Electricity interested Franklin so much that he soon wanted to make his own experiments. When the doctor visited Philadelphia, Franklin bought Spence's apparatus and was soon engrossed in experiments.

Some of those experiments were more dangerous than Franklin quite realized. When he drew lightning from a cloud with his electrical kite, he escaped injury, but he was really playing with fire. Later he did receive a severe shock when he tried to kill a turkey by "electrical fire." He described his experiments in pamphlets and articles, one of which — his account of his electrical kite — was read before the Royal Society in London. In November, 1753, the Society awarded him a gold medal for his scientific observations on electricity and some time later made him a member. Already known as printer, publicist, philanthropist, philosopher, tradesman, journalist, Franklin was now becoming famous as a scientist and inventor. In the six years from the time he first saw those experiments in Boston until he flew his electrical kite in Philadelphia, he made fundamental contributions to the scientific use of electricity. One of the most important of these was the lightning rod. He put the first one ever used on his own house, "fixed to the top of my chimney." He always refused to patent his lightning rod, though every one knew he had invented it and it was often called the "Franklin rod."

One writer says that Franklin "found electricity a curiosity and left it a science." To the public, who knew nothing of these strange things, he seemed to be a magician. To scientific men, who did know, he appeared to be a master; and though he had never attended college, both Harvard and Yale gave him the honorary degree of Master of Arts.

Never ambitious for fame, and wise in the knowledge of human nature, Franklin well knew that petty people — even among scientists — easily become jealous of another's success. He was careful not to stir them up by emphasizing his inventions. Himself free of jealousy and of vanity, he would not risk raising envious emotions in others if he could help it. With all his ability, he was a modest man.

At the age of forty-two, Franklin retired from business, turning the management of the printing-house over to his partner, David Hall. The firm, known as Franklin and Hall for many years, continued to bring its founder a steady income.

As time went on, Franklin, now free from business, was drawn more and more into public affairs.

His public interest, like his intellectual interest, blossomed out in every direction. Though he was given so little formal education as a boy, he was the man who proposed and helped organize the Pennsylvania Academy because he felt that his province should have a college. He also helped to organize the Pennsylvania Hospital, the first fire insurance company, the first voyage — or one of the first voyages — for Arctic exploration.

On the other side of the Atlantic wars were going on. England and Spain were at odds over British smuggling in Spanish America. England and France were at odds over Austrian affairs. Here, the English and French were both stirring up the Indians and, as a result, Pennsylvania, like other colonies, suffered from Indian trouble.

In the late 1740's raiding privateers — both French and Spanish — came dangerously close to Philadelphia, entering the bay and plundering two plantations just below New Castle, Delaware. They captured a ship and murdered the captain. Franklin, concerned for the safety of the city itself, called meetings to organize self-defense, and wrote and published pamphlets to awaken the people to their danger. But it was difficult to persuade the large Quaker population — all pacifists — to organize military defense.

Franklin's career as a public official began with his election to the assembly — the Pennsylvania state legislature. His remarkable career in diplomacy began with his mission to Carlisle to make a treaty with the Indians.

Franklin liked and respected the Indians, regarding the tribes and their customs with kindly curiosity. He had a real admiration for the Iroquois Confederacy. If the Six Nations of "ignorant savages" were able to form a successful union, the colonists, he thought, ought to be able to do it, too. Franklin had had this idea long before the Revolution.

As representative in the assembly, Franklin had sounded his first warning to the British governor on England's crude disregard for her American colonies in getting rid of her felons by shipping them to America. He proposed sending American rattlesnakes back to England and trading them for the British convicts, saying that the rattlesnakes were better! In spite of this criticism, however, the British government appointed him Deputy Postmaster-General two years later, thus giving him prestige as an officer of the Crown. In reorganizing and improving the postal

service, he traveled through the New England colonies, and
through Maryland and Virginia; he visited post offices, acquainted
himself with the local postmasters, studied their various problems,
road conditions, and the fords and ferries the mail carriers had to
use. He instituted the Dead Letter Office. By improving the speed
and safety of the mails, he caused an increase in their use and
thus provided easier communications which helped to draw the
colonies closer together. No one had done so much to improve
the mails as Franklin.

As early as 1751, Benjamin Franklin outlined a plan for the
union of the colonies; and, as a defense against Indians, he proposed an intercolonial council on Indian Affairs. Though the
colonies' resistance to the king would not grow serious for another
decade, Franklin was already looking forward to a larger and ever-
growing America. The population had increased greatly in the
hundred and thirty years since the first settlers came to Virginia
and Massachusetts. It was reasonable to conclude that the spread
of the American frontier and colonial growth could not long be
regulated from distant London. It would have to be controlled
by Americans who were there and understood American conditions.

In 1755 the frontier was not far from Philadelphia. Less than
a hundred miles away, Indian raiding parties from the Ohio
slipped through Pennsylvania's dark forests, scalping and killing
settlers in the "back country." Franklin himself visited the frontier, and when the Assembly resolved to send commissioners to
London to explain these problems, Franklin was chosen to go as
agent of Pennsylvania, with a petition to the Crown.

For safety's sake, Britain and France being at war, it was necessary for the small packets to sail in a convoy. As the convoy approached European shores, the packet Franklin was on was chased
several times by French privateers. But the ship escaped each
time and, three and a half months after leaving Philadelphia, he
reached London on July 27, 1757, little thinking that London was
to be his home for several years to come.

After being abroad for five years, he returned to America with
an honorary degree from St. Andrew's University in Scotland.
After that, he was always known as Dr. Franklin. But little more
than a year later, he was back in London, the official voice for

the colonies in England. He wrote a pamphlet on the value of the American colonies to the Empire. When he attended the coronation of George III in October, 1760, Franklin regarded him as a generous and virtuous young king, but he learned better five years later when the king's government imposed the outrageous Stamp Act. Franklin's enemies blamed him for allowing it to be passed at all! "I took every step in my power to prevent the passing of the Stamp Act," he wrote; and he added that he might as well have "hindered the sun's setting." Nevertheless, after the Act had passed the House of Commons and the House of Lords and had received the king's assent, Franklin thought it wiser to submit to it temporarily, while working for its repeal.

Nobody could have worked harder than Dr. Franklin to explain the American attitude on the Stamp Act to the British, who seemed unable to grasp the viewpoint of the colonists and were angered by the Americans' outcry against the Act. During the following months, Franklin received much news from home about American opposition; and when he was summoned to the House of Commons for questioning, he had the answers on the end of his tongue. No question could surprise him. He attempted no eloquent speech, but simply replied to anything the members asked, clearly, unhesitatingly, and brilliantly. The House of Commons was the most influential audience he had ever faced.

The *Examination* — the report of what Franklin said — was published in London, in five American cities, and later in Strasbourg, France. And when the Stamp Act was repealed the next year, Franklin was the hero of the jubilant colonists.

The reason for all taxes is that the government needs money. Great Britain had been carrying on wars — in part for the defense of the colonies — and the wars had to be paid for. Feeling that American colonists were growing rich and owed something for British protection, Parliament passed the act requiring a stamp on every legal paper, on marriage licenses, on newspapers, advertisements, office appointments, college degrees, liquor licenses. The last three required expensive stamps. Commodities were also taxed. The stamp for a pack of cards was to cost a shilling; a pair of dice, two shillings; and many other commodities were similarly taxed.

It was impossible to enforce this act, especially in the back woods. Dr. Franklin explained to the House of Commons that it might cost four or five times the price of the stamp for a backwoods man to travel the distance to the tax office where the stamp was obtainable. The colonists had no objection to helping pay for their own defense. The taxes they had imposed themselves were already heavy because of wars, even as were those of the British. But Franklin explained that the colonists should be represented in any vote that imposed *internal* taxes on the colonies.

During these periods of ticklish diplomacy when, as one writer says, Franklin was walking on eggs, he nevertheless enjoyed London life. He had many friends among scientists, writers, economists, with whom he could converse on his many different interests. He enjoyed the sophisticated, urbane society of an ancient city. The Royal Society became a kind of club house for him. Artists wanted to paint his portrait. Priestley, the discoverer of oxygen, was his friend. Life in London was much more stimulating than it had been in provincial Philadelphia for a mind such as his. He wrote timely articles for British newspapers. He traveled to other countries, and enjoyed finding presents to send to his wife and his daughter Sally. His wife was his best correspondent during all those years of separation, but in 1774 she died of a stroke. Some time passed before Franklin even heard of it; it took weeks for news to cross the ocean.

When, long after they had happened, Franklin heard about the Boston Massacre (1770), the Boston Tea Party (1773), and the establishment of Committees of Correspondence, he knew that England and her colonies were drifting apart. And, after the stubborn Lord North became the king's prime minister in 1770, he lost all hope of reconciliation. To help the British understand, Dr. Franklin, in 1774, published in London an article explaining all the trouble. He called it "On the Rise and Progress of the Differences between Great Britain and Her American Colonies." But it was too late.

The First Continental Congress was called together in Philadelphia.

Through all these troubled times in his own country, Franklin was kept busy in London until, disappointed and disgusted, having lost all hope that Lord North's disastrous ministry could be overthrown, he sailed for home. The last news from the colonies he had read with eyes filled with tears. It was only too plain that war was coming nearer.

Arriving in Philadelphia early in May, 1775, he learned that the battles of Lexington and Concord had been fought the month before. The very next day, Dr. Franklin was chosen by the Assembly as one of Pennsylvania's members to the Second Continental Congress, which was to meet within four days to carry further the dispute with Great Britain.

Franklin was the oldest, as well as the most famous, member of that most famous Congress. He was seventy when he signed the Declaration of Independence, and was chosen as one of three commissioners to the Court of France who were expected to secure French aid against the British. In the autumn of 1776, Dr. Franklin again crossed the Atlantic to play his part, now on the international stage, to persuade France to acknowledge the American colonies as an independent nation. The new country needed French soldiers, arms, and money.

It was a perilous voyage. Had the American armed sloop *Reprisal*, on which he traveled, been captured, Franklin would surely have been hanged for high treason, or perhaps beheaded. Yet the indomitable traveler took two grandsons with him: Temple Franklin, almost seventeen, the son of Franklin's Tory son, William, and the seven-year-old Benjamin F. Bache, the son of Franklin's daughter Sally.

The sage from Philadelphia was greeted by the French with an outburst of enthusiasm. Having lived thirty years in the society of scientists, scholars, politicians, clergymen, merchants and men of fashion, Dr. Franklin was no backwoods philosopher. He was at ease anywhere. His manner was urbane. He could speak French, though not always correctly. But he retained his simple dress — almost Quakerish, though he was not a Quaker. The French were charmed to see the stocky figure in the long brown coat, wearing the fur cap he had brought along to keep his head warm on the cold November voyage. His spectacles were the only ones to be seen in Paris. His long hair, straight and gray, was a contrast to the powdered wigs of fashion. The very plainness of his appearance made him conspicuous in a Parisian salon of Louis XIV's reign, when men dressed in lace-trimmed silks and satins of all colors. The Parisians regarded him as a kind of hero, "a combination of Voltaire and Rousseau, in a plain American package."

Soon it became the fashion to have a medal or an engraving of his likeness on every French mantelpiece. He wrote his daughter Sally that his portrait was appearing on the lids of snuffboxes, even tiny ones in finger-rings "and the numbers sold are incredible." These and other busts and prints "have made your father's face as well known as that of the moon," he told her.

Dr. Franklin was the perfect diplomat. His country profited by the French passion for this plain but brilliant American. The ladies, in whose salons he was quite the rage, adored him. In the spring, Louis XIV received him in the great palace at Versailles. Even here, where the other envoys wore formal court dress as prescribed by the chamberlain, Franklin appeared without wig or sword, in his dark brown velvet, his own gray hair hanging loose, spectacles on nose, white stockings, and a white hat tucked under his arm — the plainest and most conspicuous figure present and, among the envoys, the most eminent.

Franklin's last years in France, as the Revolution drew to its close, were taken up mainly with peace negotiations and, after the war, with peace treaties. He enjoyed his life in France and the warm friendships he made there. But he was growing old, becoming infirm and uncomfortable and plagued with "the stone" (kidney or gallstones). He was almost eighty when he made plans to leave. Several of his French friends begged him to stay and spend the rest of his life with them.

To save him from a rough carriage journey, which would have been painful to him, he was furnished with a royal litter swung between two Spanish mules to carry him from his home in Passy, a suburb of Paris, to his ship at Le Havre. This last voyage home in midsummer proved the most pleasant and cheerful of all his eight Atlantic crossings, partly because his two grandsons were with him.

Nine days before he landed in Philadelphia, a ship preceding his carried the news of his coming, and his home town prepared a great welcome for her most famous citizen. Dr. Franklin's landing was announced by a boom of cannon at the Market Street wharf — the very wharf where, as a runaway from Boston, he had first set foot in the city over fifty years before. Bells rang as he moved up the four blocks to Franklin Court, his house which the British had plundered, where his daughter and grandchildren, those he had never seen, now lived.

The reception continued for a week. People gave him the next day to rest from his voyage and see his family, then began calling in droves, representatives from all the various activities with which Benjamin Franklin had had to do. Members of the Constitutional Society called and saluted Dr. Franklin as the "father of our free and excellent constitution." Less than a month after his return, he was voted President of Pennsylvania, or Governor, as we should say today.

Having spent almost thirty years in Europe on public business, he had had no time to attend to his private interests. But he was more fortunate than Jefferson, who was ruined by his public services. Franklin found his estate more than tripled in value since the war. Money was due him for service as agent in Europe from colonies as far away as Georgia, and he obtained a right "to take up three thousand acres of Georgia land." He had a large tract on the Ohio River, and several properties in Philadelphia. The old man now amused himself by improving these city properties, building houses and designing gardens with gravel walks and flowering shrubs, perhaps remembering the charming gardens of England and France.

Now he was old and his memories went back to friends of other years. Looking through his son-in-law's papers, he discovered a letter written to him in 1775 and never forwarded. It was from Mrs. Polly Hewson. She had been the little daughter of the lady in whose house he had taken rooms when he was a young stranger in London, over sixty years earlier! He answered the eleven-year-old letter:

> The companions of my youth are indeed almost all departed, but I find agreeable society among their children and grandchildren. I have public business enough to preserve me from ennui, and private amusement besides in conversation, books, my garden, and cribbage. . . . Cards we sometimes play here, in long winter evenings; but it is as they play at chess, not for money, but for honour or the pleasure of beating one another. . . . I have indeed now and then a little compunction in reflecting that I spend time so idly; but another reflection comes to relieve me, whispering: "You know that the soul is immortal; why then should you be such

a niggard of a little time, when you have a whole eternity before you?" So, being easily convinced and, like other reasonable creatures, satisfied with a small reason when it is in favor of doing what I have a mind to, I shuffle the cards again and begin another game.

But games and time were soon to end for this lovable old philosopher and "friend to mankind." Tormented by "the stone," he now had to be given opium to relieve the pain. This caused him to lose appetite until "little remains of me but a skeleton covered with skin," he wrote his sister, Mrs. Jane Mecom. He spent most of the last year in his bedroom. Pain seemed to have no effect on his memory or wit, or even on his cheerfulness. He continued to do a little work: he composed the inscription for the corner-stone of the Library Company's new building. He listened to his nine-year-old granddaughter Deborah, who came to him every day to recite her next day's lesson from the Webster spelling-book. He answered letters with his usual grace and wit.

After Thomas Jefferson returned from France and was on his way from Virginia to New York to take up his new duties as President Washington's Secretary of State, he stopped in Philadelphia to call "on the venerable and beloved Franklin," whom he found in bed. It was to Jefferson that Franklin wrote his last letter, just nine days before he died on April 17, 1790, at the age of eighty-four.

The *Pennsylvania Gazette* announced his death on a black-bordered page. The funeral cortège, forming at the State House, was made impressive by the presence of Pennsylvania's leading men in all fields. Twenty thousand people were estimated to have followed or watched the funeral. Muffled bells tolled, and in the harbor flags flew at half-mast. James Madison moved that the House of Representatives wear mourning for one month. The National Assembly in Paris wore mourning for three days.

Benjamin Franklin seemed to have been one individual in whom there was a harmonious combination of many men, his life and works had touched so many people in different walks of life.

His grave is in the churchyard of Christ Church in Philadelphia beside that of his wife, Deborah. When it was too late, he expressed the wish to see Boston again, perhaps to rest his bones there, but he could no longer undertake the journey.

Robert Morris

Robt Morris

January 31, 1734 — May 8, 1806

WITHOUT ROBERT MORRIS, financier of the American Revolution as well as Signer of the Declaration of Independence, General George Washington could not have held his army together and history would tell a different story of America's fate.

Morris was another of the Signers not born in the colonies. He came, instead, from Liverpool, England, where he was born January 31, 1734, the son of Robert Morris, an iron worker. His mother, Elizabeth Murphet Morris, died young, and when his father came to America, he left the boy under the care of his grandmother Murphet. Only after he had become well established as an American tobacco importer, did the father send for young Robert, who arrived in Oxford, Maryland, on the Eastern Shore of Chesapeake Bay, when he was about twelve or thirteen.

For a time, Robert was tutored by the Reverend William Gordon, who had himself come to America as an indentured servant, until one day he told his father he had learned "all that the master could teach me." Deciding that his son was right, the elder Morris sent him to the leading school-master in Philadelphia, but after a year the boy's formal education came to an end, and he was placed in the counting-house of Charles Willing, one of the city's most important business men. This sudden curtailment of his education may have been due to the father's early death in an accident.

When he entered business life at fifteen, Robert Morris was a tall, strong boy with a round fair face under a thatch of sandy red hair. Good-humored, with a pleasant personality, he was also a diligent and conscientious worker, whose industry, integrity, and common sense won him the high respect of his employers.

With its own ships and its own banking business, the Willing firm was engaged in importing British goods and exporting American goods. Much of the firm's trade was with the British colonies in the West Indies, and young Morris asked permission to go on one of their ships to visit the "Sugar Islands," as they were called. The older Willing, who had taken on young Morris, had died; and the son, Thomas Willing, only three years older than Morris, was now head of the firm. Morris was given the responsibility of selling the ship and cargo in Jamaica, a job which he accomplished successfully.

While he was in the West Indies on a second voyage, a merchant of Jamaica invited Morris to become his partner. The decision was to be made by Morris himself, as the merchant had already written to Thomas Willing about it, and Willing had replied that he held Morris "in great esteem" and hoped to see him "advantageously engaged anywhere." Robert Morris pondered the offer. A partnership looked attractive. But he finally declined it and decided to stay with the House of Willing.

While he was returning, however, his business career very nearly ended for good. The brig on which he was traveling was captured by French privateers, who robbed the passengers of everything. But Morris, the captain, and the American crew escaped and managed to reach the shore of Cuba. Here they wandered through fields and forests, half-starved, until they finally reached Havana, a city ruined by the French three years before.

They had saved their lives, but they had lost their money and baggage and were stranded. One day Morris, seeing a man trying unsuccessfully to make his watch run, suggested that he might be able to repair it. He did, and this first customer not only paid the stranded American boy, but sent him other customers who wanted repair work done. In this way, Morris managed to buy food and necessities until an American vessel arrived and took him home.

Thomas Willing, delighted by his safe return, offered him a partnership not long afterward, when Robert Morris was only twenty-two. The firm became Willing, Morris & Company, later Willing & Morris. Though he had been in America only about a decade, Robert Morris had already achieved remarkable success as a businessman. To be a partner in one of the most important Philadelphia firms was a very real achievement. For Philadelphia, until 1830 the largest city in the country, was naturally the largest business center and also a busy port, with ships constantly sailing in and out. The merchant aristocracy, of which Morris now became a part, could boast of the greatest prosperity and gayest society in all America, even though it was established in a sober Quaker city.

Prosperous though they were, however, the merchants and ship-owners were soon to find themselves in serious trouble. After the French and Indian War (1754–1763), the British government, in an effort to "regulate trade," began to pass laws that seriously hampered colonial businessmen. At first these may have been mere emergency measures, but the British government found these so-called "regulatory acts" so profitable that they were kept permanently. Most annoying of all was the law that required ships returning home with cargoes from Europe and Africa to stop in an English port on the way. This round-about route meant needlessly long voyages, cost time and money, and encouraged smuggling to escape English import duties. Customs officials, knowing that smuggling was going on, began annoying investigations of merchants and shipping, and British naval vessels began prowling about to enforce the revenue acts.

Though the firm of Willing & Morris, with its huge foreign shipments, remained above reproach, all this governmental interference made trouble for them. Any financial or other business difficulty worried the senior partner, Willing, a timorous man who became very gloomy and pessimistic at such times. But Robert Morris rose to meet these problems with such optimism and determination that, as time went on, Willing, with ever-increasing trust, began to place greater responsibilities upon his partner. The two were great friends as well as partners. Finally, when Willing was elected Mayor of Philadelphia in 1763, at the end of the French and Indian War, Morris took over management of the business alone and remained the active head for almost twenty years.

When Parliament passed the Stamp Act, twenty-nine-year-old Morris took part in a meeting in Davenport's Tavern, at which four hundred Philadelphia merchants, including Willing & Morris, signed the Non-Importation Resolutions. Though this was a serious blow to their business, it seemed a patriotic duty to resist British encroachments on American rights. The next year, Morris entered public life as Warden of the Port of Philadelphia.

An eligible young bachelor, a wealthy and successful merchant, a dashing man-about-town, Morris was invited everywhere. The most elegant social events were the Assembly dances, managed by Willing for some years, to which only Philadelphia's elect were invited. When thirty-five-year-old Robert Morris met the charming nineteen-year-old Mary White at one of these balls, his bachelor days were soon to end. Though he had no "family," he had achieved a position in society by his own ability and personal charm. Mary's father consented, and the wedding took place in Christ Church under crystal chandeliers sparkling with candles.

Mary Morris was to prove her husband's greatest blessing, the perfect partner. She was the gracious hostess for Robert Morris's generous hospitality in their fine house on Front Street, facing the river in Philadelphia, and later at "The Hills," their three-hundred-acre estate overlooking the Schuylkill River, eight miles from Lancaster, Pennsylvania. Here, in the years to come, they would entertain the most important Americans and Frenchmen of revolutionary times, General Washington and the Marquis de La-fayette among them. When prosperity fled from Morris at last and he was betrayed by the jealousies of lesser men, Mary stood by him. Apparently the only real fault in this able and generous man was his too easy trust in his associates. A man of integrity himself, he did not suspect others of jealous machinations and treachery.

The Stamp Act had been passed and then repealed a few years before Morris's marriage. Within a few years, still graver events were taking place. In the early summer of 1774, Paul Revere rode to Philadelphia with news of the closing of the Port of Boston and of Parliament's action in quartering British troops upon Boston's citizens. Philadelphia's businessmen closed their offices on the first of June in sympathy with the Bostonians. Flags on the river boats were lowered to half-mast. The bells of Christ Church and other churches were muffled and tolled mournfully. On June 18, a meeting in the Pennsylvania State House, over which Thomas Willing presided, passed a resolution declaring that the Boston Port Act was unconstitutional and that the cause of Massachusetts was a common cause to all the colonies. The meeting further decided that a Continental Congress ought to be called. The

Committee of Correspondence soon had messengers riding swiftly from colony to colony.

In September, 1774, the delegates to the First Continental Congress met at City Tavern in Philadelphia and walked to Carpenter's Hall to begin their deliberations. The colonies were pulling themselves together. "Meatless days" were ordered. Companies of infantry, artillery, and cavalry had to be formed, outfitted, trained. Pennsylvania's newly appointed Committee of Safety — with Benjamin Franklin as chairman, Robert Morris as vice-chairman — met every morning at six o'clock. Their tasks were heavy: They must devise plans for the fortification of the Delaware river, which still lay open to attack, organize militia, issue bills of credit, purchase arms and ammunition, create defenses for the city and port of Philadelphia, and raise funds. And who could know better than Morris, long-experienced businessman and ship-owner, how to manage all these practical matters?

Morris's successful labors for defense led to his appointment to the Second Continental Congress, November 3, 1775. He was immediately detailed to find two swift sailing vessels to carry dispatches and two weeks later was put on a committee on naval armaments. Early in 1776 he was on the committee that drew up instructions to Silas Deane, American envoy to France, then put on the "ways and means" committee to help raise funds, and on another to fortify seaports.

Meantime, Willing & Morris imported supplies for the army and at times did banking for Congress. Like any other businessmen, they charged commissions for their services. This led his enemies to accuse Morris of what would today be called "conflict of interest." But his fellow-congressmen, who knew all about it, had every confidence in him. John Adams remarked that Morris "no doubt pursues mercantile ends," but thought him "an excellent Member of our Body," a man with "an honest Heart."

Robert Morris worked hard at his duties in Congress, and at the same time he and gracious Mary Morris were hospitable and lavish hosts to many of the congressmen and others who had occasion to visit Philadelphia. In July of 1776, however, Morris was not in favor of independence. He was one of Pennsylvania's "moderates." Voting against Independence on July 1, he did not attend the following day when the "violents" voted Independence, since he considered the vote premature. Benjamin Rush later explained Morris's stand. Morris, he wrote, "was opposed to the *time* (not to the *act*) of the Declaration of Independence, but he yielded to no man in his exertions to support it, and a year after it took place he publickly acknowledged on the floor of Congress that he had been mistaken in his former opinion as to its time, and said that it would have been better for our country had it been declared sooner."

Morris had no hesitancy in signing the Declaration the next month, and he always worked for the American cause, living his belief that it was "the duty of every individual to act his part in whatever station his country may call him to in hours of difficulty, danger, and distress." This, he said, was the only thing a gentleman could do.

When the struggle grew desperate the following winter, and Congress was slow in supplying food and money for the army, it was to Robert Morris that General Washington appealed — and not in vain. On Christmas night, when Washington crossed the Delaware and captured over a thousand Hessian soldiers, the British suffered their first stinging defeat. Back of all the fighting and planning was Robert Morris, working day and night to raise the funds to pay the soldiers, to procure food, clothing, and ammunition. General Washington never forgot how he had relied on the faithful financier.

On committees that dealt with commerce, supplies, and foreign affairs, Morris was a most valuable man. Often he served as banker and middleman. If he made large profits, he took great risks. Timid merchants considered him "bold and enterprising," his own self-confidence inspired confidence in those who dealt with him. This was a period when Morris was popular.

When, in the autumn of 1777, the British occupied Philadelphia and Congress had to move, Morris stayed in the city with (British) General Howe's permission. This must have been galling itself, aside from the appalling difficulty under which he then had to work. He had sent Mrs. Morris with the children to Maryland to stay with her step-sister, Mrs. Hall. "Having got my family and books removed to a place of safety," he wrote, "my mind is more at ease, and my time is now given up to the public, although I have many thousand pounds' worth of effects here without any prospect of saving them."

In March, 1778, he signed the Articles of Confederation on behalf of his state, and retired from Congress at the end of his term, November 1. But five days later he was elected to the Pennsylvania State Assembly.

In January, 1779, the editor and writer, Thomas Paine — who was not a businessman and not without a temper — attacked Morris and Silas Deane in the newspapers, charging them with handling "private commercial enterprises" while holding public office. Since everyone knew that Morris was director of the firm of Willing & Morris and that the firm was carrying on its legitimate business, this had little effect. Paine's accusation was petty, ignorant, and absurd. But it showed that the wealthy, clever, and successful Robert Morris was drawing envious eyes upon himself. A later member of Congress, Henry Laurens, even charged Willing & Morris with fraudulent transactions. Morris thereupon invited examination of the firm's books by a congressional committee. Their opinion was that Morris had "acted with fidelity and integrity and an honorable zeal for the happiness of his country."

But all this had been bad publicity. Though Morris was cleared, ugly rumors had spread. His political opponents, especially the ones who were not rich and consequently were jealous of his wealth, continued to criticize him. With his popularity weakened, Morris was defeated at the polls in November, 1779. The next year, however, he was again elected to the Assembly.

The year of 1780 saw the American cause at its lowest point. The Treasury was empty. Credit was gone. "Paper money was not worth the cost of printing it." The condition of the army was deplorable, and there were two serious mutinies. Though Morris had warned Congress for years against currency inflation, nothing was done to head it off. When prices sky-rocketed and Congress, having exhausted its own resources, could not meet the soldiers' demands, it had to turn to the man who had never yet failed his country. It appointed Morris Superintendent of Finance. Never has anyone since held such a position. On his shoulders, Congress placed all the responsibility for America's finances.

The task that now confronted Robert Morris was herculean. He was the only man on the continent who could possibly have pulled order out of such financial chaos as now existed. He received many letters from generals, congressmen, and financiers, expressing their enthusiasm over his appointment and the deep satisfaction and renewed hope that his acceptance had given them.

The financial wizard became the nation's banker and pulled his country through its financial doldrums. Yet his salary as Superintendent of Finance was only $6000 a year. Of his private fortune he had given a million dollars for the Yorktown campaign, and half a million for mustering out the army.

But envious tongues wagged. Acrimonious and ignorant critics of Morris, observing his sumptuous hospitality, were not bright enough to realize how much it contributed to the profit of the country. His enemies, not understanding the intricacies of high finance, sneered at what they called Morris's "financial sleight-of-hand." They did not credit him with the enormous risks he had taken, or the tremendous services he had performed. Often, when the credit of the nation was almost gone, it was Robert Morris's signature alone — which stood for business integrity, stability, and commercial honor — that made it possible to borrow money for the public cause.

After years of struggling because the states, unwilling to accept their obligations, let him down by not paying their required revenue, Morris despaired at last. He resigned January 27, 1783, saying, "To increase our debts, while the prospect of paying them diminishes does not consist with my ideas of integrity. I must therefore quit a situation which becomes utterly insupportable."

Then Morris was violently abused in the press. Ingratitude is universal, and if a man allows himself to be imposed upon, there are always those who want to go on imposing upon him. As there was no one else who could even undertake the work, Morris consented to stay in office until the army was paid and demobilized. John Adams succeeded in obtaining a loan in the Netherlands which carried Morris through until he was free from his grave responsibility in September, 1784, and free from what had always been a thankless task. A few men, General Washington among them, understood what the financier had accomplished and were grateful.

Unfortunately, Robert Morris, like many another, was caught up in the epidemic of land fever that swept the country after the war. Many rich men who wanted to be richer still began land speculation. Investigating carefully before purchasing, Morris traveled through inhabited Pennsylvania, Virginia, and Georgia, buying lands and forming partnerships to buy more lands. He bought lands also in western New York State. With a partner he acquired a large part of the site on which our present city of Washington, D.C. now stands. Then a swampy wilderness, ten years later it was to become the site of the capital city. But unfortunately, Morris could not hold his purchase as long as that.

Then, as usual, the unforeseen happened. The Napoleonic Wars paralyzed Europe and cut off much of the immigration to America. As it was the immigrants who bought land, when their numbers diminished, so did the sales of land — and land values, too.

Rich as he was, Robert Morris had borrowed to make many of his larger land purchases. Now, when he had to meet taxes and interest on his loans, he did not have the money. And when he tried to sell some of his properties to meet these costs, he could not raise enough money from sales. Thus the great financier lost everything. His beautiful town house, his other city properties, and, eventually, his beloved estate The Hills, all had to go. When the crash came, he had been in the process of building a marble mansion in Philadelphia, designed by the French architect L'Enfant, who had run up more expenses than Morris had intended.

Retreating to The Hills, he was arrested by a *small* creditor. The great financial wizard of wartime was taken to the Prune Street debtors' prison where he was confined for three and a half years. How could a man, imprisoned, pay off his debts?

Now he knew who his friends were. George Washington went to the prison to dine with his unfortunate friend. Mary Morris proved staunch and true. The erstwhile gracious hostess, accustomed to elegant and rich surroundings, was her husband's support in these years of poverty and disgrace. She lived on an annuity from the Holland Land Company obtained for her by Gouverneur Morris (no relation), and this supported Robert Morris when he was released August 26, 1801, under the federal bankruptcy law. The prison, on Walnut and Prune (Locust) streets was a large stone building, neat, well-kept, and considered an ornament to the city. But, ironically enough, while confined for debt and thereby denied the chance of earning money to pay his debts, Morris had to pay a high price for the rent of his room! Courageously, he remarked, "a man that cannot bear and face misfortune should never run risks, but I have been too adventurous and therefore it is a duty to meet my fate with fortitude." His comfort came from his wife and his loving sons and daughters.

Morris was sixty-six when he was released, a penniless man, dependent upon his sons and his wife's annuity for subsistence. He tried several times to find something to do to earn money. He went to Washington by stagecoach to confer with President Thomas Jefferson and enjoyed a bit of social life such as he had been used to in bygone days. He dined with the President, and visited the ex-President, George Washington, at Mount Vernon.

During his last years, the Morrises lived modestly in a small house on Twelfth Street, the house in which he died on the eighth of May, 1806, aged seventy-two. He was buried in the family vault in Christ Church graveyard.

For years his will was sought, but not until 1939 was it discovered — with the wills of six other Signers — in a forgotten vault near the furnaces in the cellar of the Philadelphia City Hall. In his last testament this wise and shrewd man left a message "to the inhabitants of the United States of America," prepared about the time when he retired as Superintendent of Finance. Stressing the need for a sound economy, he wrote: "How soon we may be plunged into another, a longer or more expensive contest, is known only to Him from whom no secrets are hidden, but . . . the only moral surety for peace is a state of constant preparation for hostilities."

Benjamin Rush

Benjamin Rush

January 4, 1746 — April 19, 1813

DR. BENJAMIN RUSH was the best known physician practicing in America during the Revolutionary period. He was born on a farm in the community of Byberry, near Philadelphia, the day before Christmas, 1745 (old style), which would be January 4, 1746, by our modern (new style) calendar. His father, John Rush, was descended from the first American John Rush, who had once been a soldier in Cromwell's army, and had come to Pennsylvania from Oxfordshire, England, in 1683. When Benjamin was five, his father died at the early age of thirty-eight, and his mother, Susanna Harvey Hall Rush, now twice widowed, kept a grocery store to earn a living and provide education for her children.

At the age of eight, Benjamin was sent to a country school at Nottingham, taught by his uncle, the Reverend Dr. Samuel Finley. West Nottingham Academy was later situated in the country at Colora, about two miles south of where it was in Rush's day, and a memorial arch was placed there to commemorate its two alumni who became Signers of the Declaration of Independence: Richard Stockton and Benjamin Rush.

Seven years later, at fifteen, Benjamin Rush entered the junior class in the College of New Jersey (now Princeton) and received his B.A. degree in 1760. He had been advised by friends and by the head of the college, the Reverend Dr. Samuel Davies, to study law. But the young graduate consulted his old teacher, Dr. Finley, who insisted that the law was not the profession for him. Rush ought to study medicine. Accordingly, he became the pupil of Dr. John Redman, then Philadelphia's leading physician. He lived in his teacher's house for four years, studying medicine under his direction, with only eleven days absence the whole time. He also attended lectures at the College of Philadelphia.

Finishing this study in July, 1766, Rush again took his former teacher's advice and sailed off in August to continue medical study at the University of Edinburgh, whose medical faculty was then the most celebrated in the world. While in the Scottish city, Rush met the Reverend Dr. John Witherspoon.

Dr. Witherspoon had been invited to come to America to be President of the College of New Jersey in 1766. But he had declined because of his wife's fear of crossing the ocean. Richard Stockton had presented the invitation. In another decade, these three men would all be together in Philadelphia and all three would sign the Declaration of Independence!

The next summer, 1767, Benjamin Rush visited the Wither-spoons at Paisley. The young twenty-two-year-old medical student must have described his own ocean crossing and persuaded Mrs. Witherspoon that it was not to be feared. At any rate, when in 1768 Princeton sent Dr. Witherspoon a second invitation to be-come President, he accepted, and the Witherspoons sailed for the New World.

Medicine was not the only subject that interested Benjamin Rush while abroad. He studied French with a tutor, and Italian and Spanish by himself, until he was able to read in all three lan-guages. Then, upon graduating at Edinburgh, Rush went to Lon-don to train in St. Thomas's Hospital, and to attend lectures on medicine. Another Philadephian, Benjamin Franklin, had been in London since 1764 as agent for the Province. Young Rush at once wrote Franklin asking for letters of introduction. The older man re-sponded generously, and with these letters, the young doctor's introduction to English life was most agreeable.

After visiting Paris, Benjamin Rush returned home to be-gin his medical career. Two months later, he was given the professorship of chemistry at the College of Philadelphia — the first man to hold such a chair in any of the colonies — while at the same time he opened a doctor's office. For some time most of his practice was among the poor; and though his office, which he called his "shop," was soon filled with patients, he treated many of them without charge. Others he visited, walking through all the streets and alleys of the city, sometimes climbing ladders to reach the upper rooms. But within five years his practice grew to the point where he was making a good income, in spite of his generosity to the poor.

Rush was one of those rare persons who knew the value of using every bit of his time. In spare moments, he began to jot down notes on his observations, ideas, and conclusions until, before long, he had enough material to write articles and essays. His first publication was the first American textbook on "A Syl-labus of a Course of Lectures on Chemistry." In 1773, his news-paper articles on behalf of the colonists' cause brought him into public affairs, and he also became a member of the American Philosophical Society, which still exists in Philadelphia.

In September, 1774, Rush and some of the other Sons of Liberty, rode a few miles out from Philadelphia to meet the first congressional delegates who were coming down from New England. He now had an opportunity to become acquainted with the great patriot leaders who came from the other colonies to attend the First Continental Congress — such men as Samuel Adams, Thomas Jefferson, and Thomas Paine. As he listened to their views, the young doctor became more and more inflamed with the colonists' indignation against mother England.

In January, 1776, he married Miss Julia Stockton, the eldest daughter of Richard Stockton of Princeton, another Signer. He had admired Julia ever since she was fourteen years old.

The following June, Dr. Rush was elected to the Provincial Conference. As a member of this body, he at once took his stand for independence. A month later he was sent to the Second Continental Congress. He was only thirty when he signed the Declaration.

When George Washington received his appointment as commander in chief, Dr. Rush attended the party given in his honor. Later, he offered his services to the patriot cause and in April, 1777, was appointed surgeon-general of the armies of the Middle Department. Investigating the army medical service, he found it in such poor condition that he protested to General Washington, accusing Dr. William Shippen, another important Philadelphia physician, of bad administration. Washington referred the matter to Congress, which decided in Shippen's favor, whereupon young Dr. Rush angrily resigned. Not long afterward, General Washington met his discouraging defeats at Brandywine and Germantown — not far from Philadelphia — and Rush took this opportunity to raise questions as to Washington's ability as a commander. It is a sorry thing to have to report that Rush even wrote an anonymous letter to Governor Patrick Henry of Virginia, urging that Washington be replaced by either General Gates or General Conway. Had this been done, the Americans would surely have lost the war, but the iniquitous plot to get rid of Washington — the so-called Conway Cabal — soon collapsed, leaving Washington still in a command that only he could fill.

Governor Henry sent the letter on to Washington who, recognizing the handwriting, accused Rush of personal disloyalty. This contretemps ended Rush's military career, of course.

Clever, industrious, studious, and socially agreeable though he was, Benjamin Rush had some less admirable traits, as this regrettable incident shows. He could never believe or admit that he might have a wrong opinion; and as he kept no records of his cases or opinions, it was easy for him to forget that he had ever been wrong. He did not examine facts and was often therefore in the center of professional jealousies and arguments. He had an able, versatile, but not a critical mind.

John Adams, with whom he had a friendly correspondence for years, described Rush as being "an elegant, ingenious body, a sprightly, pretty fellow." But, Adams added, "too much of a talker to be a deep thinker; elegant, not great."

Two years after the opening of the new University of the State of Pennsylvania in 1778, Rush began to lecture there. Three years later, he went on the staff of the Pennsylvania Hospital, where he remained for the rest of his life, and in 1786 he established the first free dispensary in America.

Interested in social reforms, Dr. Rush condemned capital punishment and worked to improve education for girls. He argued against overemphasis on classical training, that is, on Latin and Greek, and advised more training for children in science and utilitarian subjects. After urging in the newspapers the acceptance of the new Federal Constitution, he was elected to the Pennsylvania Convention, in which he and James Wilson, another Pennsylvania Signer, led the movement for its adoption.

Dr. Rush was also treasurer of the United States Mint from 1797 to 1813.

When the College of Philadelphia merged with the University of the State of Pennsylvania to become the University of Pennsylvania in 1791, Dr. Rush became professor of medical theory and clinical practice, and this is probably where he achieved his greatest distinction. His students adored him. His classes became very popular and increased enormously in size. He thus probably contributed more than any other man to making Philadelphia the main center for medical training in America during the first half of the nineteenth century.

Unfortunately — since he was more given to ideas than facts, and a doctor, like any scientific man, is always up against facts — Dr. Rush came to believe that all diseases and physical ailments were practically the same, and therefore one cure sufficed for all. Thinking as he did, Dr. Rush saw diagnosis and treatment as simple matters. All he had to do, he thought, was administer his "cure," which was the bleeding and purging of the patient. Dr. Rush was even willing to remove as much as four-fifths of the body's blood. The average doctor of the period, when giving a treatment by bleeding, rarely took more than ten ounces, for bleeding a sick man could be dangerous. George Washington's last illness was laryngitis, caused by exposure to rain and cold; but it is now believed that he would have recovered had he not been weakened by the amount of blood taken by the physicians who were trying to cure him. Other medical men proclaimed Rush's "system" fanciful, declaring that he carried bleeding to dangerous extremes. During the yellow fever epidemic of 1793, he became involved in another serious medical controversy, thus making many new enemies among medical men. But, by this time, he was America's most widely known physician, for he had had a great deal of publicity, and he remained influential.

There were times, however, when Dr. Rush's cures were effective. During the Lewis and Clark Expedition, when Thomas Jefferson was President, the two leaders kept journals recording everything. From these Journals we learn that they carried with them some of "Dr. Rush's pills," which they administered freely, and with excellent results when all their men were exhausted after crossing the Rockies.

At the age of sixty-eight, after only a few days' illness, Dr. Benjamin Rush passed away after a busy, full life. He was buried in Christ's Church graveyard, in Philadelphia.

John Morton

John Morton

c.1724 — April, 1777

THE FIRST AMERICAN of John Morton's line was his great-grandfather, Morten Mortenson, who sailed from Gothenburg, Sweden, in 1654, a member of the Tenth Swedish Expedition, and settled along the banks of the Delaware River, not far from Philadelphia. The Signer's father was another John Morton, who married Mary Archer when he was very young and died before his child was born, some time in 1724, though the exact date is unknown. Mary Morton then married again, and John's step-father, John Sketchley, took a fond interest in the boy.

Sketchley was a surveyor who had come from England and was a man of some education. He taught his step-son at home, instructing him in the common branches and also in surveying. John had a quick mind and an industrious nature. He studied, helped in surveying, and worked on the home farm.

He was thirty before he married Ann Justis, a young woman who also descended from early Swedish settlers in Delaware.

Interested in public welfare and affairs, John Morton was elected to the Provincial Assembly from Chester County in 1756 while he was still in his early thirties, was re-elected for the next ten years, and was appointed speaker of this assembly in 1775. He also served as justice of the peace and as high sheriff. Though he had no formal legal training, Morton was appointed President Judge of the Court of General Sessions and Common Pleas and in 1774 he became an Associate Judge of the Supreme Court of Pennsylvania.

In 1765, Judge Morton was one of the four Pennsylvania delegates to the Stamp Act Congress. He was definitely not one of the Pennsylvania moderates but stood boldly for freedom in a province where opinion had long been divided.

Though Morton made no spectacular contributions to the cause of independence, he felt strongly about the patriot cause. So little is really known about him that it is interesting to read passages from a letter he wrote to Thomas Powell, a merchant in London and a friend to whom Morton felt able to speak freely. As early as June 8, 1775, Morton was writing that "we are really preparing for the worst that can happen, viz. a Civil War. We have nearly 2000 Troops now under Arms in this City, and very well disciplined. I suppose the Province will raise 20,000 effective Men determined to support the Noble Cause of Liberty." Congress had turned out in a body on June 8 to see soldiers drilling and Morton had been impressed by the spectacle.

He pointed out that General Gage was now so closely besieged in Boston that he "cannot penetrate 500 Yards into the Country, were he supported by all the troops now in England." The letter concludes: "You have declared the New England people Rebels, and the other Provinces Aiders and Abettors. This is putting the Halter about our Necks, and we may as well die by the Sword as be hang'd like Rebels. This has made the People desperate." This gives an idea of the determination with which Congress was meeting its problems.

A delegate to the Continental Congress from 1774 until early 1777, Morton cast one of the votes which placed Pennsylvania on the side of independence by a majority of one.

Morton served on many committees in Congress. He was chairman of the committee for the adoption of the Articles of Confederation, though these were not finally adopted until after his death, in the Spring of 1777.

Soon after the battle of Lexington, Morton had been offered a colonelcy of Pennsylvania volunteers, but he declined because of his other duties.

A man of strong character, Judge Morton was modest about his self-made career, but men discovered that his judgment was sound, his social manner pleasant.

Morton was buried in St. Paul's Churchyard in Chester County, the county in which he first entered public life.

George Clymer

March 16, 1739 — January 24, 1813

GEORGE CLYMER'S GRANDFATHER, Richard Clymer, came to America from Bristol, England. His son Christopher married a Philadelphia girl named Deborah Fitzwater, and these were the short-lived parents of the Signer. Both died the year after George was born, and the little boy's uncle, William Coleman, a prosperous merchant and a friend of Benjamin Franklin, became his guardian.

George grew up in the home of his aunt and uncle in Philadelphia, where he made good use of the large library his uncle had collected. His uncle seems to have provided the boy with a good schooling because when George was old enough to start work, he was prepared to enter his uncle's business as a clerk. He proved to be so diligent and competent that he was made a partner in the firm. Later on, William Coleman left the business to his nephew who, in his turn, became a well-known and successful Philadelphia merchant.

When George Clymer was twenty-six he married Elizabeth, daughter of Reese Meredith, another important merchant. He now enlarged his activities by working in association with other merchants. Taking his father-in-law and brother-in-law into partnership, he established the firm of Meredith and Clymer.

From early years, Clymer was an ardent patriot. Men engaged in the importation of goods from England and her West Indian colonies were, of course, among the first to feel the restrictions of British taxation. Included in this group were those southern planters who were sending cotton and tobacco back to England.

George Clymer attended all the first meetings of those men who were offended by Britain's insensitive high-handedness, and he also became a captain of volunteers in General Cadwalader's brigade. In 1773, there was a "Philadelphia Tea Party," very much like the Boston Tea Party, which forced the resignation of merchants who had been appointed by the British to sell tea. Clymer was chairman of the "Party." Like so many of the Signers, he became a member of the Council of Safety. This was a first step into a public career. Clymer, however, who was of a modest, retiring nature, never sought public honors. But as his diligence and faithfulness became known, he was repeatedly chosen for office, and he was elected to the Independence Congress.

With the New Jersey Signer Richard Stockton, Clymer was sent in September, 1776, to inspect the northern army at Ticonderoga. He also advocated broader powers for General Washington. In 1777, when the British drove Congress and the colonial government out of Philadelphia, Clymer went to Baltimore with Signers Robert Morris and George Walton as a committee for congressional business.

When he was re-elected to Congress in 1777, George Clymer was assigned to the Board of War and the Treasury Board. He was also on the local committee for the protection of Philadelphia. Here, his duties were so arduous that he was forced to take a rest, but by July he was back at work as one of the commissioners to investigate and remedy the food shortage in Washington's army. Then, in the autumn, he became commissioner of prisoners, his duty being to receive Hessian prisoners and send to Allentown all those who were able to travel.

After the British victory at the Brandywine, some of the British took the trouble to detour in order to raid Clymer's house. His family, fortunately, had left, but the raiders destroyed all his furniture, and seized whatever supplies they could use. The redcoats had a special hatred for the men who had signed the Declaration of Independence, and they found out from local Tories where Clymer lived.

In the winter of 1777, Clymer was sent to Fort Pitt with two other commissioners to investigate the Indian disorders that the British had instigated. He rode through Pennsylvania's dark forests all the way to the frontier fort at Pittsburgh. In Congress again, for the third time, he worked steadily on committees, then retired to Princeton to educate his children.

In the first Congress after the Revolution, Clymer supported his old friend, George Washington, as President, and later supported the economic policy of another old friend of the stirring days of '76 — Thomas Jefferson. President Washington appointed Clymer to serve in two commissions, after which he retired from national affairs. He was then fifty-seven, and he had spent over twenty years in the service of his country.

George Clymer now took a leading part in the development of his own community, serving as the first president of the Philadelphia bank, first president of the Academy of Fine Arts, and vice-president of the Philadelphia Agricultural Society. These honorary offices he was still holding when he died in 1813.

In Congress, Clymer had not been one of the orators. He had spoken only briefly, very seldom, but always to the point. One fine thing was said of him that can be said of very few people, he "was never heard to speak ill of any one."

James Smith

Jas. Smith;

c.1719 — July 11, 1806

OF THE THIRTEEN COLONIES, Pennsylvania had the largest number of representatives in the "Declaration" Congress. With such well-known men as Benjamin Franklin, Robert Morris, and Dr. Benjamin Rush among her nine congressmen of the Revolution, it is not surprising that some of the others are known today only because their signatures are on the revered document.

One of these lesser-known men is James Smith, who was born in northern Ireland about 1719, the second son of a large family. His father, John, persuaded to come to America by James's uncles who had already settled in the new country, migrated when James was about ten or twelve. The family settled near the other Smiths in beautiful Chester County in southeastern Pennsylvania.

John soon became a successful farmer in this fine agricultural region and sent young James to the school in nearby Philadelphia that was taught by the Reverend Francis Alison.

In those early days in America, when congregations were not large enough to be able to pay their pastors an adequate salary, nor to require all of a pastor's time, it was common for a minister to "keep school." In most communities, he was the best educated man and so the man best equipped for teaching.

Thus James had the opportunity to study Latin and Greek, some knowledge of which was essential to any educated gentleman. He also studied surveying. Afterwards, he read law in the office of his brother George in Lancaster.

Admitted to the bar when he was about twenty-six, he moved to Cumberland County, near Shippensburg. At first he earned his living by surveying and practiced law when a chance offered. But after four or five years in this scantily populated region, almost on the frontier, he moved back east forty or fifty miles and settled in York, Pennsylvania, where he lived for the rest of his life. Until 1769, he was the only resident lawyer in town.

Even so, little legal business came his way during his first years there, and in order to earn a better living, he started to operate an iron furnace. Unfortunately, instead of making anything, he lost £5000 before he sold out seven years later, having employed two incompetent managers, who simply let the business fail. One, said Smith, was a knave, and the other a fool.

When he was forty-one or thereabout, he married Eleanor Armor, the daughter of John Armor of New Castle, Delaware.

Through the 1760's, the colonists' dissatisfaction and unhappiness under the ever-tightening rule of the mother country was spreading, and Smith became a leader in his part of the country. In 1774, he attended a provincial conference at which he read an article he had written, "Essay on the Constitutional Power of Great Britain over the Colonies in America." In this he urged an end to import of British goods and promoted the idea of a general congress of the thirteen colonies, where colonial grievances could be discussed and shared. Several thoughtful men in different parts of the colonies were now getting this same idea. Encouraged by this conference, James Smith raised a volunteer company in York in 1774 and was selected captain.

This company grew into a battalion later on, and Smith was given the honorary title of Colonel, though he turned over the active command to younger men. Having been appointed delegate to the provincial convention in Philadelphia in January, 1775, he was busy helping to draft the resolutions for independence and recommending improvement of provincial defenses.

James Smith sat in the constitutional convention of June, 1776, and was made a member of the committee to draft a new frame of government, which he had been advocating for some time. On July 20, in the first week of this convention, he was elected to Congress. As this was after the great Fourth, Smith was too late to vote for independence. But he was on hand to sign the Declaration. Re-elected in December, 1777, he served one year longer, but declined re-election thereafter. While Congress met in York, Pennsylvania, the meetings of the Board of War were held in Smith's law office.

After retiring from Congress, James Smith held few political posts. He served one term in the assembly, and for a few months he was Judge of the Pennsylvania High Court of Errors and Appeals. In 1782 he was brigadier general of the militia and counselor for the Pennsylvania-Connecticut Wyoming Valley controversy.

Again, in 1785, Smith was elected to Congress by the assembly, but he declined because of age. He was about sixty-five at this time.

James Smith had a sharp wit and a lively manner. He was a good conversationalist, equipped with a fund of amusing anecdotes. He made good company and thus attracted to himself many friends. It was remarked that he had a most surprising memory. There were some who regarded him as rather an eccentric, but this might be said of any real individualist.

A fire destroyed Smith's office and all his papers in 1805. But for this we might now know more about his life and work. The next year, he passed away on the eleventh of July, at the ripe old age of eighty-six. He was buried in the graveyard of the English Presbyterian Church.

George Taylor

c. 1716 — February 23, 1781

LESS SEEMS TO BE KNOWN about George Taylor than any of the other Signers. He is believed to have been born in northern Ireland about 1716 and to have had some education before he arrived in Pennsylvania at about the age of twenty. We first hear of him in Chester County, where he became clerk in the Warwick Furnace and Coventry Forge. Later he became the manager.

In 1742 Taylor married a widow, Mrs. Anne Taylor Savage. When he was about thirty-eight, he moved to neighboring Bucks County, Pennsylvania, where he and a partner leased an iron furnace. This was his main business interest for the rest of his life, though after 1763 he lived in the town of Easton, where his political life began.

The next year, the ironmaster was elected to the Provincial Assembly, and he was re-elected for the following five years. Taylor was strongly opposed to the royal government, and when the Stamp Act was passed, he was on the committee that drew up instructions for Pennsylvania delegates to the Stamp Act Congress.

There is then no record of Taylor's appearing in politics for about four years, when he returns to the scene as chairman of a meeting of the important men of his county, called to protest the British order closing Boston harbor. Here, he spoke in favor of an intercolonial Congress and was one of six men named as a Committee of Correspondence. He attended the convention in Philadelphia in January, 1775.

The next July, Taylor was chosen colonel of the Bucks County militia; and, though he never saw active service, he retained the title.

In October, he was sent to the assembly again, served on many committees, and helped draft instructions for the delegates to the Continental Congress in November. Though he was a member of the second Committee of Safety from that same autumn to the following July, he rarely attended. After the great Fourth, George Taylor was appointed delegate to the Second Continental Congress to replace one of several Pennsylvanians who had refused to approve the Declaration of Independence. Taylor approved it, but as it was July 20 when he was sent to Philadelphia, he was not there for the voting. He was there for the signing, however.

After that, he took no further part in Congress other than to represent it, along with George Walton, at a conference with Indians at Easton, in January, 1777. Leaving Congress soon afterward, he was elected to the new Supreme Council of Pennsylvania, but served only six weeks because of illness. Soon after, he retired from all public affairs.

George Taylor was called a "moderate radical." He was a man of limited, provincial outlook, who never became absorbed in the broad, far-reaching questions of that great moment when a nation was being born. He probably had had only a little education, not enough to make him wish to follow it up in his own reading. His heart was not in politics, and this no doubt explains why so little is known about him. There was not much to know.

His wife died in 1768, and he himself passed away thirteen years later, at the age of sixty-five.

James Wilson

James Wilson

September 14, 1742 — August 21, 1798

AT THE AGE OF TWENTY-THREE, James Wilson was a newcomer to American shores, having arrived as late as 1765, the Stamp Act year, from Scotland.

He had studied at the University of St. Andrews for about two years, went to the University of Glasgow for a time, and then attended the University of Edinburgh. One does not know now why he moved from university to university, but he appears to have acquired considerable learning, a broad outlook, and rather more social polish than some of the other lesser known patriots who met together in Philadelphia in 1776.

However, when Wilson left Edinburgh University in 1765, he still had no degree. He began to study accounting, dropped it almost at once, and took ship for America, already equipped with a better education than most immigrants of the time. He carried with him letters of introduction to some prominent Pennsylvanians, among whom was Dr. Richard Peters, secretary of the Provincial Council, Episcopal rector in Philadelphia, and trustee of the College of Philadelphia. Through this contact, James Wilson secured a position as Latin tutor in the college in February of 1766, almost as soon as he arrived, and in May his petition for an honorary M.A. degree was granted. He was on his way up.

Though he always kept his scholarly interests, Wilson soon saw that advancement in America would not come through teaching. The law seemed to be the best and quickest way to power and position, and that was what he wanted most—that and wealth. A few months later, aided by his new influential friends, Wilson succeeded in entering the office of John Dickinson to read law. He applied himself to his legal studies for about two years and was admitted to the bar in November, 1767. The next summer, he began to practice law in Reading, Pennsylvania. This was near "Birdsboro," the home of Miss Rachel Bird, a young lady whom Wilson had met in Philadelphia.

His practice among the German farmers, who were the forebears of the people now known as the Pennsylvania Dutch, was lucrative indeed and as settlements spread westward, Wilson moved to Carlisle to practice among the Scotch-Irish settlers. His practice built up steadily until Wilson had the largest practice in the local bar. He was soon a rich man, thus achieving one of his great desires.

Then James Wilson bought a farm. Most properties in that sparsely settled region were farms, and even town lots were large enough to keep a few cattle, enough to supply milk for the family. He bought some livestock and a slave, and he married Miss Bird.

By this time, Wilson was handling almost half the cases tried in the county court and practicing in seven other counties as well. A man of unfailing energy, he was the go-getter of the region. Sometimes his work required trips to New Jersey and New York, over what seemed in those days considerable distances. During six of these busy years he even found time to lecture on English literature at the College of Philadelphia. Most of his law practice dealt with land disputes. Brought thus in touch with land titles, he was soon speculating in land himself and borrowing money to do so.

James Wilson was an early believer in the colonies' cause. In less than ten years after his arrival in America, he entered public life as a member of the Pennsylvania provincial meeting of July, 1774, and was asked to head the Committee of Correspondence at Carlisle. The next month, his pamphlet, "Considerations on the Nature and Extent of the Legislative Authority of the British Parliament," was published. In this he maintained that Parliament had no constitutional right to make laws for the colonies. This was an advanced position to take in 1774 and not many Pennsylvanians held it, but Wilson had already been arguing his points for four years. Of course, this was the opinion of the Adamses and Hancock of Massachusetts. His pamphlet was distributed among the first Continental Congressmen when they met and it made a considerable impression. Wilson was elected to the first Provincial Congress where, in January, 1775, he declared it was *possible* that the British Parliament *could* pass an *unconstitutional* act. But when he introduced a resolution declaring the Boston Port Act to be unconstitutional, it was not adopted.

The following May, Wilson was made colonel of the Fourth Battalion of Cumberland County, but he never saw active service because three days later he was elected to the forever famous Second Continental Congress. Assigned to serve on various committees, he attended faithfully for two years, though he found committee work burdensome. He was also on the Board of War.

On the question of independence — the question which steadily increased in importance, provoking more and more thought and discussion through 1775 and the first half of 1776 until the great decision in July — James Wilson, though favoring independence himself, was heedful of the wishes of his constituents, and, as we have seen, Pennsylvanians were seriously divided on that subject. Many thought a complete break with the mother country would be dangerous, perhaps disastrous, and they feared such an extreme move. Wilson, therefore, opposed Richard Henry Lee's resolution in June, 1776, arguing that a few individuals in Congress should not commit the whole province of Pennsylvania to such a step. It should be a decision of the people themselves. With three other congressmen, he thus succeeded in getting a three-week delay on the vote in order to ascertain the feeling of the Pennsylvanians. This debate on the Lee resolution occurred behind closed doors on the same day. When the debate ended, six states, including Pennsylvania, voted in the negative; seven states, affirmative. The matter was postponed to June 10, two days later. On June 11, a committee of five, with Thomas Jefferson as chairman, was chosen to prepare a Declaration.

Meanwhile, debates were hot and constant. The Independents had to use all their persuasive powers to win the luke-warm members to their side.

Wilson's stand, however, had caused a tempest of criticism. It looked to some as if he had gone back on his original views. He was so bitterly abused that twenty-two of his fellow congressmen felt it necessary to come to his defense. But on July 2, Wilson was one of three out of the seven Pennsylvania delegates who voted for independence. This was not to be the only storm of criticism he would have to face; others were to come in the future.

Dr. Benjamin Rush, to whom we are indebted for reporting his impressions of so many of the congressmen of 1776, regarded Wilson as an eminent lawyer, an enlightened statesman, a profound and accurate scholar. Wilson, he said, "spoke often in Congress and his eloquence was of the most commanding kind. He reasoned, declaimed, and persuaded according to circumstances with equal effect. His mind, while he spoke, was a blaze of light. Not a word ever fell from his lips out of time, or out of place, nor could a word be taken from or added to his speeches without injuring them. He rendered great and essential services to his country in every stage of the Revolution."

Wilson's personal appearance made his eloquence even more impressive. He stood six feet tall, with a large frame and erect bearing, and all his fiery energy went into his declamations. Though his voice was not melodious, it was powerful, and his blue eyes gleamed through heavy spectacles rimmed in metal.

The next storm that blew about him came when he fought the new constitution of Pennsylvania, which he thought "the most detestable that ever was formed." Even his close friend, Arthur St. Clair, considered Wilson "perhaps too warm" on the subject. His seat in Congress became precarious and he knew it. He was, in fact, removed in 1777 but reinstated after about two weeks because a successor could not be found. He continued to oppose the Pennsylvania constitution until he was finally removed from Congress September 14, 1777. Feeling ran so high that he could not feel comfortable in his own state and spent the winter in Annapolis; then he settled in Philadelphia.

Arrived at middle-age, the former frontier lawyer handling land disputes became a corporation counsel. The former congressman became a counselor for Loyalists, the former Whig became a leader of the Republicans, the former Scotch-Presbyterian became an Episcopalian. Wilson did not, however, change in his desire for wealth and love of speculation. Because he engaged in privateering — unlawful today but perfectly proper in those times — and various enterprises for making a quick dollar, some of his fellow citizens came to distrust him. When, in 1779, a food shortage developed in Philadelphia and there were riots in the streets against profiteers and Tories, Wilson found it necessary to barricade his house to defend himself and some of his friends against attack. A few were killed and wounded on both sides, but Wilson was rescued by the First City Troop and went into hiding for some days. In that same year, the French government appointed Wilson advocate general for France in maritime and commercial causes in the United States.

With the return of the conservatives to power in 1782, James Wilson was elected to Congress once more from 1785 to 1787. Through the 1780's, with his business and public interests taking up more of his time, he dropped his law practice. But he was legal adviser to Robert Morris, the Revolution's great financier, in the formation of the Bank of Pennsylvania and in drawing plans for the purchase of army supplies. In 1781, Congress chose Wilson as one of the original directors of the Bank of North America. In the Spring of 1782, General Washington paid Wilson 100 guineas for receiving Washington's nephew as a student in his law office. Later that year, Wilson defended Pennsylvania's claims against Connecticut's charter claims to the Wyoming Valley lands in Pennsylvania.

In May, 1784, James Wilson was one of eight Pennsylvania delegates to the Philadelphia convention to adopt a constitution for the United States, held in Independence Hall with George Washington as President. Only six of the thirty-nine members had been Signers of the Declaration of Independence: Benjamin Franklin, James Wilson, Robert Morris, and George Clymer of Pennsylvania; Robert Sherman of Connecticut; George Read of Delaware. The total number was small "but the quality was excellent." Students of constitutional history consider this "to have been as wise and capable a deliberative body as ever assembled in this country, perhaps the wisest."

Three years after the end of the war, in 1786, James Wilson's wife died, leaving him with six children. Seven years later, at the age of fifty-one, he married nineteen-year-old Hannah Gray of Boston. Four years later his speculations caught up with him, and he had to move to Burlington, New Jersey, to avoid arrest for debt.

Wilson was keenly disappointed in not being given a high office in the new federal government established under the Constitution. He had been mentioned as a candidate for Chief Justice, and even went so far as to suggest himself to President Washington who appointed him Associate Justice in September, 1789. That winter Wilson gave a law course at the College of Philadelphia.

More deeply involved than ever before, Wilson turned again from public interests to land speculation in 1792 and 1793, and, like most speculators, did not know when to stop. He involved the Holland Land Company in unwise purchases of hundreds of thousands of acres of land in Pennsylvania and New York. In the end, Wilson's own personal speculations ended disastrously, wiping out all of his accumulations, and led to his confinement for a time in a debtors' prison.

By 1798, when Wilson was fifty-six years old, he was in severe mental distress. He had too many worries. He wrote a friend, "I have been haunted — like a wild beast." In those days Supreme Court justices did not spend all their time in Washington, and Wilson arranged to be sent on a southern circuit of the United States Circuit Court of Appeals, and went to North Carolina to visit a friend. But his truly brilliant mind now lost its hold and gradually his lucid moments came at ever increasing intervals. He died that year at the home of his friend, of what was called a nervous fever. One hundred and eight years later, in 1906, his body was moved from North Carolina and re-interred in Christ Church, Philadelphia.

At last, the Signer had returned to the city where he had given the best of his life and work.

George Ross

May 10, 1730 — July 14, 1779

GEORGE ROSS WAS a Pennsylvania Signer with a persuasive manner, a liking for pleasantry and mild joking. He appeared always to be in good humor. He was born at New Castle, Delaware, on May 10, 1730, the eldest son of the Reverend George Ross and his second wife, Catherine Van Gezel Ross. The Reverend George had graduated at the University of Edinburgh and prepared for the Presbyterian ministry. But while engaged in theological study he came to feel that his church was censorious and hypocritical, and he took orders instead in the Church of England, came to America as a missionary, and became rector of Immanuel Church in New Castle, Delaware, where he remained for many years.

His son George, one of twelve children by his two wives, was given a classical education, studying Latin and Greek in addition to the three R's. Later, he read law in the office of his older stepbrother, John, in Philadelphia. At the age of twenty, he was admitted to the bar and opened his own office in Lancaster, Pennsylvania. The good humor, wit, and eloquence which Dr. Rush perceived in George Ross twenty-five years later in Congress, together with his ability, brought him a large practice.

Among his first clients was beautiful young Anne Lawler, whom he soon married. At twenty-one, with a good practice, a beautiful wife, an attractive personality, a cordial manner, a love of dining and wining among congenial companions, George Ross was on his way up.

He served twelve years as Crown Prosecutor (he would be called District Attorney today) in Carlisle, Pennsylvania, adding a political career to a legal one when he won election to the Provincial Assembly. During his seven years' service there, Ross became much interested in the steadily mounting disputes with the royal governor and stood boldly for the assembly and its rights. Gradually gaining political influence, he was elected to the Provincial Conference in Philadelphia in July, 1774, and was in the Pennsylvania delegation to the First Continental Congress in the same year.

At this time, Ross was still regarded as a Tory. But as tension with Parliament increased, he joined the Whigs in 1775, serving both in the assembly and on the Pennsylvania Committee of Safety.

Though he had been a Pennsylvania delegate to the First Continental Congress in 1774, Ross was not chosen as delegate to the Second Congress until the debates were over, the vote had been taken, and the Declaration of Independence had been adopted. He took his seat on August 2, 1776, when the new official copy of the Declaration, now engrossed, was ready for signing. He signed the "immortal instrument" on that day.

In those times a man might hold more than one high office at once. During his first two terms in Congress, Ross was also a member of the Pennsylvania Assembly, and in 1776 he was a colonel in the army while still serving as congressman. In that significant year, Ross, who had become much interested in Indian Affairs, helped negotiate a treaty with the northwestern Indians of Pennsylvania. He was also vice-president of the Pennsylvania constitutional convention of 1776, in which he helped to draw up the declaration of rights.

George Ross was elected to Congress three times. In 1777, the authorities of Lancaster County paid him a well-earned compliment by awarding him £150 as a testimonial "of their sense of his attendance on public business to his great private loss and of their appreciation of his conduct." But Ross declined to accept it. He said that it was "the duty of every man, especially of a representative of the people, to contribute to the welfare of his country without expecting pecuniary rewards." Ill health forced him to resign in January of that year.

Ross was at first in favor of the constitution establishing the new state government, but by 1779 he began to feel, as did other lawyers, that it was already time for a revision. In March, 1779, he was commissioned judge of the admiralty court in Pennsylvania. He became involved in a controversy between Congress and the new state of Pennsylvania — a controversy which dragged on for more than thirty years. But not for George Ross. He died, suddenly, four months later on a hot July day, from a severe attack of gout. He was only forty-nine.

He kept his good humor to the very end. On his deathbed, oppressed by midsummer's heat, he calmly observed that he was about to go on a "long journey to a cool place, where there would be most excellent wines." He might have added, "and no more gout!"

IV

NEW JERSEY

Jno Witherspoon

Rich.d Stockton

Fras. Hopkinson

John Hart

Abra Clark

John Witherspoon

February 5, 1723 — November 15, 1794

ONE OF THE BEST educated among the Signers, John Witherspoon was a late comer to the colonies, having arrived in response to an invitation to become President of Princeton (then called the College of New Jersey) only seven years before the Declaration of Independence.

He was the son of the Reverend James and Anne Walker Witherspoon of Yester, near Edinburgh. In the early eighteenth century the clergy were the best educated men in Scotland, and the Reverend Mr. Witherspoon was no exception. He sent his son John to the first-rate preparatory school at Haddington, where he was prepared for the University of Edinburgh at fourteen. A precocious boy, endowed with a good mind and diligent in study, he was soon the best in his class. An important feature of Scottish university life outside of classrooms was the existence of literary clubs, which were common among the students and the professional men of Edinburgh. His activity in these societies made Witherspoon proficient in debate, which is valuable training for an alert mind, for clearness of expression, and for public speaking. Long years after, no doubt remembering the literary clubs of his youth, Witherspoon encouraged two famous literary societies at Princeton: Whig Hall and Clio Hall.

After his four-year classical course, John Witherspoon entered the divinity school, and by the time he was twenty had both a Master of Arts degree and a degree in divinity. In the autumn of 1743, he became Presbyterian minister of the parish of Beith, where he remained for twelve years.

Shortly after going to Beith, he married Elizabeth Montgomery, daughter of Robert Montgomery, of Craighouse, Ayrshire, a dis-

tant kinsman of the Earl of Eglinton, who had appointed Witherspoon to the parish.

After entering the ministry, the young preacher became engaged in a dispute between two factions in the church — the
Popular Party and the Moderate Party. Witherspoon was active
on the side of the conservative orthodox, or Popular, party, who
were opposed to what they considered the religious decadence
of the Moderate Party. While he was still at Beith, he published
an essay on *Justification*, a little book which had a wide sale in
Great Britain and among the English-speaking churches of the
continent as well as in the American colonies. The year of his
transfer to a church in Paisley, he published a more pretentious
book on *Regeneration*.

With this, Witherspoon won a high reputation as a theological
writer and as the foremost man of his party in the Church of
Scotland. In 1764, the University of St. Andrews conferred upon
him a degree of doctor of divinity as a mark of his leadership and
ability. Increased reputation brought him invitations to preach
on special occasions, one of which was the anniversary of the
Society for Propagating Christian Knowledge. The foremost place
for such work was, at that time, the American colonies, where
one could work among the Indians.

The Scotch society had, some twenty years before, sent money
for the purchase of books for the library of the new College of
New Jersey, and had granted an appropriation for the education
of two young Indians. It was to Scotland, then, that two Americans went in the mid-1760's to raise funds for the much needed
new "seminary of learning" in the middle colonies.

The two Americans who visited Scotland in the interests of the
New Jersey College were the Reverend Samuel Davies, later president of the college, and Gilbert Tennent. Dr. Davies was much
impressed by Witherspoon's new little book, *Ecclesiastical Charac-
teristics*, considering the humor of it equal to Dean Swift's. It was
popular enough to require several printings. The far-reaching result of Witherspoon's rising publicity was a call for him to come
to America and accept the presidency of the College of New
Jersey.

The first letter of invitation was presented to him by Richard

Stockton, who was to be another New Jersey Signer nine years later. But Mrs. Witherspoon, fearing the ocean crossing, was very rude to Stockton, and her husband was forced to decline. Later, Mrs. Witherspoon regretted her bad manners and apologized, explaining that she had been ill at the time. When, not very long afterward, another American and future Signer, Dr. Benjamin Rush, who was in Scotland studying medicine, tried his persuasions, he succeeded in overcoming the lady's objections. Thereupon, the Reverend Dr. Witherspoon said he would accept if another invitation were forthcoming. The second invitation duly arrived, and in August of 1768, the Witherspoons entered upon the American scene.

From the beginning, Dr. Witherspoon was charmed with America and with the Americans. He was greatly impressed by the pleasant countryside, the fertility of the land — so far beyond that of his native Scotland — and by the many opportunities for future work and growth. The Scottish minister became a whole-hearted American.

Under his able administration, things began to change at Princeton. The new president introduced the study of history, oratory, French, and philosophy, together with the Scottish system of lectures. The college student body, faculty, and endowments increased. His students adored him. More and more came to Princeton until, less than ten years later, all these advances were destroyed by British invaders.

At first, Witherspoon thought that ministers should avoid becoming embroiled in political questions. But the treatment by the king and Parliament of their American colonies caused him to stand with his patriot friends. Though he refrained from touching upon controversial political ideas in his sermons, he wrote essays, arguments, and opinions on these matters, which were widely read. In Scotland he was now labeled a rebel and traitor.

The president of Princeton consented to act on committees of correspondence and to attend the provincial conventions called by the American patriots in their endeavor to organize resistance to British pressures. All the time he was involved with politics and the administration of the college, Dr. Witherspoon continued preparing long sermons for Sundays. In those days sermons lasted for hours and there were two a day — morning and afternoon. When John Adams spent Sunday in Princeton on his first journey to Philadelphia in 1774, he wrote home that he listened to Dr. Witherspoon all day and noted in his diary that Witherspoon was "as high a son of liberty as any man in America."

On June 22, 1776, Witherspoon himself was chosen as a delegate to the Second Continental Congress, the only minister among those "founding fathers" of a new nation. He arrived in Philadelphia just as Congress was getting ready to vote on Richard Henry Lee's resolution for independence. On July 1 came the greatest of the debates, when John Adams summed up the arguments for independence for the new members from New Jersey. The next day, Witherspoon stood up and spoke in favor of adopting the resolution without delay.

When one of the delegates who held back objected that times were not yet *ripe* for a declaration of independence, Dr. Witherspoon replied that, in his opinion, the country "was not only ripe for the measure but in danger of rotting for the want of it." His emphatic stand no doubt helped some of the waverers to vote for the Declaration on the Fourth.

John Witherspoon was fifty-three when he signed the Declaration and he had been an American for only seven of those years; but, with some intermissions, he served in Congress until November, 1782. He worked on more than a hundred committees, including two very important ones: the Board of War, and the Committee on Secret Correspondence. He debated on the Articles of Confederation, helped the new government form its foreign alliances, and helped in drawing up instructions for the American peace commissioners. Recognizing the dangers of inflation, he wrote an *Essay on Money* and fought against an issue of a large amount of paper money.

When the British drew near Princeton in November, 1776, the college could not carry on, and Dr. Witherspoon had to announce on the twenty-ninth that classes must be suspended. A week later, when the British arrived, they took over Nassau Hall and most of the private houses in the town, and Witherspoon had to flee for his life. In January, he wrote from Baltimore in a letter to his son: "We carried nothing away of all our effects but what could be carried upon one team. Benjamin Hawkins drove your mother in the old chair and I rode the sorrel mare and made John Graham drive the four young colts."

In little less than a month, however, General Washington drove the British out at the Battle of Princeton. College work was not resumed until the following August.

After the war, Dr. Witherspoon worked hard to rebuild the college, but Princeton did not recover from the war's disastrous effects in his lifetime. Twice in those intervening years, he returned to the state legislature. He was moderator of the first American General Assembly in May, 1789. In that year, his wife died.

Less than two years later, when he was sixty-eight, Witherspoon married Mrs. Ann Dill, a twenty-four-year-old widow. The marriage naturally caused much comment. But he was lonely and trying to find a little happiness in his last years. He had lost so much, and his beloved college was poor. The British had burned his own fine library, and the college's two thousand books were scattered everywhere. He had undertaken a trip earlier in the 1780's to England to raise funds for the college, but this was a foolish decision on the part of the trustees. No one was inclined to give money for an American college. His errand was without success. Moreover, he suffered a bad accident. During a storm at sea, he was thrown against the side of the vessel and received a blow which injured one eye. Some years later, the other eye was bruised by a fall from a horse while he was riding over land which he had bought in Vermont.

Blind the last two years of his life, Dr. Witherspoon lived on his farm "Tusculum," about a mile outside Princeton, enjoying the outdoors and gardening as long as he was able. He died there at the age of seventy-one and was buried in the President's Lot at Princeton.

He had been a powerful speaker and preacher. Someone said that his eloquence made one's blood "shiver along the arteries." But his voice was rather harsh and he spoke with a broad Scottish burr. John Adams said he could understand Witherspoon better after having conversed with him and hearing him speak in Congress. It is said that he coined the word "Americanism" in an article he wrote on the differences between English speech in the United States and Great Britain.

Richard Stockton

October 1, 1730 — February 28, 1781

THE FIRST AMERICAN Richard Stockton, the Signer's great-grand-father, came from England — probably in the 1650's — and settled in Flushing, Long Island, New York. Forty years later, in 1696, the next Richard, the Signer's grandfather, moved to New Jersey and acquired a large parcel of land, which included the spot where Princeton is now. On this land he built his house, called "Morven," now the property of the state of New Jersey. His son, John, became a presiding judge of the Court of Common Pleas in Somerset County. All this, of course, was while the colonies were under royal government. John Stockton was also a patron of the College of New Jersey at Newark, and he was influential in having the college moved to Princeton. John married Abigail Phillips, and these were the parents of the Signer, Richard Stockton, born at Princeton, October 1, 1730.

The boy was sent to school to the Reverend Dr. Samuel Finley, director of the West Nottingham Academy, after which he entered the College of New Jersey, graduating in 1748. He then studied law in the office of David Ogden, of Newark.

When he was twenty-two, he married Annis Boudinot. Their first child, Julia, was to grow up and marry Dr. Benjamin Rush, a Pennsylvania Signer.

Some years later, Richard Stockton was licensed as an attorney, and after that his advancement at the bar was rapid. In ten years he built up a practice so large that by 1766 a trustee of the college, the Reverend Dr. John Rodgers, was saying that Stockton was at the head of his profession in the colony. Dr. Rodgers also considered him a gentleman of learning and a man of probity.

Absorbed by his legal work, Stockton did not pay much attention to politics at first. As late as 1764 — the year before the infuriating Stamp Act — Stockton was writing to his friend and pupil, Joseph Reed, that "the publick is generally unthankful, and

I never will become a Servant of it, till I am convinced that by neglecting my own affairs I am doing more acceptable Service to God and Man."

It was not long, however, before "publick" affairs convinced him. First, as a trustee of his beloved alma mater, he was asked by the board to offer the presidency of the College of New Jersey to the Reverend John Witherspoon of Paisley, Scotland. This meant a trip abroad.

After his return, Richard Stockton entered politics the next year by being appointed to the council, remaining until the royal government came to an end. In 1774, he was commissioned a Justice of the Supreme Court. He spent much time making improvements at Morven, his grandfather's home, which he had inherited. It was a large estate where he bred horses and cattle, and collected books and works of art. Ever attached to his college, he was one of its financial advisers. He believed great changes for the better would be achieved when colleges sent "into the lower House of Assembly men of more foresight and understanding than they can now boast of."

On the differences that were fast forming between the colonies and the mother country, Stockton at first took a moderate stand. In 1764, he suggested that some able Americans be elected to Parliament. Of course, this representation where the laws were made was just what Americans wanted, but narrow-mindedness prevailed. The next year, when the Stamp Act was passed, Stockton held that the British Parliament had no authority over the colonies. Nine years later, he sent Lord Dartmouth a paper entitled, "An Expedient for the Settlement of the American Disputes," warning him that immediate measures would have to be taken or there would be an "obstinate, awful and tremendous war."

Elected to Congress June 22, 1776, Stockton arrived with his New Jersey colleagues to take his seat six days later in Philadelphia's Independence Hall just as the closing debate on Lee's resolution for independence was going on.

John Adams reported the scene in a letter. In many previous debates on the subject of independence, Adams wrote, the New Jersey delegates had voted against it. New Jersey constituents had been informed and had sent a new set of delegates "on pur-

pose to vote for Independence." Judge Stockton and Dr. Witherspoon were appearing for the first time. Chief Justice Stockton
asked to have the whole question discussed. Though it had been
gone over time and again, the newcomers did not wish to state
their opinions until they could hear other members speak. Hearing that Judge Stockton in particular was so eager to hear other
delegates' views, many began to say, "Let the Gentlemen be
gratifi'd," whereupon all eyes turned upon John Adams. One delegate said, "Come Mr. Adams you have had the subject at heart
longer than any of us, and you must recapitulate the arguments."

John Adams then made a speech that deeply impressed Stockton, who later reported to his friends at home: "The man to whom
the country is most indebted for the great measure of Independence is Mr. John Adams of Boston." On the day of the vote, all
five Jerseymen voted for independence.

When, in September, he was chosen first Chief Justice of his
new state, he declined, preferring to remain in Congress. At the
end of the month, he was appointed, with George Clymer of
Pennsylvania, on a committee to visit the northern army. From
Saratoga he wrote, toward the end of October, that the New Jersey soldiers were "marching with cheerfulness, but great part of
the men barefooted and barelegged. . . . There is not a single
shoe or stocking to be had in this part of the world, or I would
ride a hundred miles through the woods and purchase them with
my own money." While absent on this errand, Stockton was
appointed in late November as one of a committee to consider
ways to reinforce General Washington and to hinder the progress of
the British army.

Before Stockton could return to Princeton, the British had invaded New Jersey, where Morven, his family estate, lay in their
line of march. He hurried his family to safety in the home of a
friend. But on the night of November 30, he himself and his
friend were captured by Tories and cast into jail in Perth Amboy.
Here he was exposed to bitter cold weather, then removed to
prison in New York, where he was badly treated. Congress tried
to have him exchanged, but his health was already seriously affected.

After his release, Stockton was able to give only occasional
counsel to his country. His beautiful estate had been used as

military headquarters by the British, who had then destroyed it,
burning his library — one of the best in the country — his furniture, his clothes, and his writings. Reduced to the point where he
had to ask help from friends, Stockton, overwhelmed by losses
and deteriorating health, passed away in Princeton on February
28, 1781, at fifty-one.

The following October Cornwallis surrendered at Yorktown,
and how Stockton would have rejoiced, could he have known.

His widow, Mrs. Stockton, wrote a poem celebrating the capture of Lord Cornwallis and sent it to General Washington. He
wrote her a letter of thanks. Later, when he rode through Trenton on his way to New York for his inauguration as first President of a new nation, the young ladies of Trenton threw flowers
in his path, and sang Mrs. Stockton's composition,
"Welcome, Mighty Chief, Once More!"

Francis Hopkinson

Fras Hopkinson

October 2, 1737 — May 9, 1791

IN A LETTER to his wife, John Adams described Francis Hopkinson
as:

> . . . one of your pretty, little, curious, ingenious men. His
> head is not bigger than a large apple. I have not met with
> anything in natural history more amusing and entertaining than
> his personal appearance, yet he is genteel and well bred, and
> is very social.

This delightful, dainty little man, whose small features harmo-
nized with his short stature and general appearance, was a gentleman of many attainments. The small head contained a lively and
curious brain, as was shown by his animated countenance, by
his fluent speech and quick motions, and by what he achieved, as
lawyer, statesman, musician, and author. Like Thomas Jefferson
and Benjamin Franklin, he was interested in scientific invention.

Possessed of a curious mind, he was interested in many subjects, and being "very social," he was undoubtedly a most entertaining conversationalist.

Though Signer Hopkinson represented New Jersey, he was born in Philadelphia in 1737. His father, Thomas Hopkinson, was an Englishman who came to America in 1731 and settled in Philadelphia. About five years after his arrival in the New World, Thomas married Mary Johnson, daughter of Baldwin Johnson, who had distinguished family connections in England. The next year Francis was born, the first of eight children. In the prime of life, Thomas died. Left with eight children to raise, the mother, realizing that her eldest son Francis was the most brilliant, made special sacrifices in order to give him a superior education.

When the Academy of Philadelphia opened in 1751, Francis, at fourteen, was the first pupil to enroll. Six years later, he received the first diploma granted by the College of Philadelphia. At the age of seventeen, he began to study the harpsichord and showed his musical talent by being able to play in public three years later. He loved music, composed tunes, and his song, *My Days Have Been So Wondrous Free,* and his publication, in 1763, of a collection of Psalm Tunes mark him as our first American composer.

After graduating from college, young Hopkinson studied law under Benjamin Chew, attorney-general of the province; and in 1761, at the age of twenty-four, he was admitted to practice before the Supreme Court of Pennsylvania. He was hardly more than a boy when he began to display literary, as well as musical, leanings. Many of his poems appeared in the *American Magazine.* This small, young man was intelligent, quick of mind, and versatile in his accomplishments.

In 1766, the year the Stamp Act was repealed, Francis Hopkinson went to England to visit the land of his fathers, and to seek a government appointment through the influence of relatives there. He was sent off with a public expression of respect and affection by the board of trustees of his college. In England, he was entertained at Hartlebury Castle by the Bishop of Worcester, who was his mother's cousin. While in London, he visited the artist Benjamin West, from whom he may have received some instruction in drawing and painting. At any rate, he was fond of drawing crayon portraits in his later years. Lord North, a relative by marriage, tried to help Hopkinson attain a preferment, but even he was unable to do so; such offices in America were by this time being reserved for those who had lost their jobs when the Stamp Act was repealed. Hopkinson returned home after about a year without the appointment he had hoped for.

Soon after his return, his thoughts must have turned to romance, for he married Ann Borden on September 1, 1768. She was the daughter of Colonel Joseph Borden, the leading citizen of Bordentown, New Jersey.

Francis Hopkinson then settled in his wife's town and opened a shop to sell drygoods imported from England. The mercantile and importing business did not fully satisfy him, apparently, because after a few years, he went to New Castle, Delaware, as collector of customs. But this lasted only about a year and a half; the work was even less satisfactory. He returned, then, to Bordentown to practice law, for which he had been trained; and in this work, he rose rapidly.

In 1774, Hopkinson was appointed member of the Governor's Council; and from this, two years later, he was elected to the Continental Congress of 1776. His speeches, marked by his special gift for satire, were most influential in arousing the feelings of the people.

Throughout all these years, however, he had amused himself with his music and writing. Essays and verses from his pen were to be read in the *Pennsylvania Magazine,* and when he published a piece called *A Pretty Story,* in which he presented the grievances of the colonists, he found himself launched upon a long career as a political satirist.

It was the latter part of June, 1776, when Francis Hopkinson arrived in Philadelphia, his native city, to represent New Jersey in Congress. He was thirty-nine when he signed the Declaration of Independence.

He now began to hold various offices of considerable responsibility. He served as chairman of the Continental Navy Board for two years. Following this, he held the office of treasurer of loans. In 1779, he became Judge of the Admiralty for Pennsylvania, and ten years later a United States District Judge, a position he held for the rest of his life.

But the successful always have their enemies, especially in wartime. The British had marked him as a prominent rebel. During their occupation of Philadelphia, the Hessians plundered his Bordentown house, and his family barely escaped. Because of a quarrel with the Treasury Board, a quarrel instigated not by himself but by an enemy or enemies, Francis Hopkinson suffered the embarrassment of an impeachment trial and resigned his position as treasurer of loans. But he was acquitted, and so cleared.

During the war he wrote much of the time, turning out pamphlets encouraging the Americans, deriding the British, and excoriating all Tories. In 1777, he protested brutality to noncombatants in *A Letter to Lord Howe* and in *A Letter Written by a Foreigner,* he satirized the character of John Bull. Some of his most effective writing appeared in verse which he called "political ballads." In the best known of these, a humorous piece called "The Ballad of the Kegs," he celebrated the early use of mines in warfare. In 1781, he composed a dramatic allegorical cantata, words and music, called "The Temple of Minerva," which celebrated the French alliance with our new nation. This dapper, clever little man even directed its performance.

Acquaintances observed that Hopkinson had a very animated countenance, that he was fluent in speech and quick in motion. He no doubt bubbled with enthusiasm for all his many interests — artistic, political, and scientific. He was the happy kind of creature who found it delightful just to be alive, with so many fascinating interests around him. This attractive and winning quality is probably what led to John Adams's amusing remarks.

There seemed to be no end to things that caught his interest. He is said to have designed the seals for the American Philosophical Society and for the University of the State of Pennsylvania, which was founded in 1778. He designed the Great Seal of New Jersey. Hopkinson amused himself, too, by inventing such little articles as a shaded candlestick and an improved quill or "pick" for the harpsichord. He took an active interest in his church, too, and was known for his kindly disposition.

Some of his best essays and social satires were written after the war when two new magazines, the *Columbian Magazine* and the *American Museum*, were glad to publish everything he wrote for them. They republished most of his earlier pieces, which shows that he had achieved a certain reputation as an author. In 1788, he published a volume called *Seven Songs*, which contained his best lyrical poetry, and which gave him the distinction of being the first American composer to publish a "book of music."

On May 9, 1791, at the age of fifty-four, he died suddenly of apoplexy. It is interesting to know that he imparted his love of music to his son, Joseph, who became the finest harpsichord player of his day in the new America, and was the author of *Hail Columbia*.

John Hart

John Hart

c. 1711 — May 11, 1779

"HONEST JOHN HART," as his neighbors called him, was born in Stonington, Connecticut, but his parents, Edward and Martha Hart, moved to Hopewell, New Jersey, when John was only a year or so old. Though the year of his birth is uncertain, it was probably 1711.

Edward Hart, the father, had commanded a volunteer corps called the New Jersey Blues in the French-Canadian wars. At home, however, he was a farmer; and the vicinity of Hopewell is still beautiful, fertile country, better for farming than Connecticut.

Naturally, young John was raised to work on the farm with his father. Though this meant that he had very little schooling, he nevertheless grew rich enough in that excellent farming country to acquire, as he grew older, many acres of land for himself. Over the years, by diligence and good character, he won a reputation as "the most considerable man in his community."

When he was about twenty-nine, John Hart married Deborah Scudder of Ewing, New Jersey. His public life began when he was chosen justice of the peace. After that, in 1761, he was elected to the assembly and was re-elected until the assembly was dissolved in 1771, as matters grew ever more stormy in the colonies.

Hart opposed the Stamp Act in 1765. Three years later, he favored sending a message to the king bluntly saying that the right to tax the colonies lay with the colonies only — and not with Great Britain.

In 1775, he was appointed to the local Committee of Safety and the Committee of Correspondence, also serving as Judge of the Court of Common Pleas. Then he was elected to the First Provincial Congress of New Jersey. From this he went on to the scene of national politics in June, 1776, when the Provincial Congress elected him one of New Jersey's delegates to the Second Continental Congress, which in turn chose him as its vice-president.

We have Dr. Benjamin Rush's report that John Hart was "a plain, honest, well meaning Jersey farmer, with little education, but with good sense and virtue eno' [enough] to discover and pursue the true interests of his country." Hart was probably about sixty-five when he signed the Declaration of Independence.

In the autumn following the Declaration, the British invaded New Jersey. Since Hart's farm and mills lay in the path of the destroying armies, all his property was ruined by the Hessians. He himself had to hide in the area around the Sourland mountains, while British sympathizers hunted for him. He was exhausted by privation and, as if all this were not enough, he was further saddened by the death of his wife. These things took their toll of his health.

After the American victories at Trenton and Princeton, John Hart returned to find that the spot where his home had been was left in desolation. He tried to build up his farm again but there was not much left for him. Trying still to serve where he could, he became chairman of the Council of Safety for a while, until ill health forced him to retire in the autumn of 1778. The next Spring, he died.

Eighty-six years later, at the end of the Civil War, the New Jersey legislature erected a monument to his memory in Hopewell, in honor of their patriot father's services to his state and to his country.

Abraham Clark

Abra Clark

February 15, 1726 — September 15, 1794

As EARLY AS 1675, a shipwright named Richard Clark was living in Southold, Long Island. He moved about three years later to Elizabethtown, New Jersey. His grandson, Thomas, a charter alderman and magistrate of the town, inherited from his father and grandfather the family farm between Rahway and Elizabeth, and here his only son, Abraham, was born. In after years, he was nicknamed "Congress Abraham" to distinguish him from other Abraham Clarks in the vicinity.

He was a frail child, consequently pampered by his family, and as a growing youth he was considered too slight for heavy farm work. He seems to have had little formal education as a child, but he was a born student and was probably taught at home. His liking for mathematics led him to study surveying. As an aid in this, he equipped himself to settle land disputes and to transfer property titles by studying a little law on the side. He rarely — perhaps never — charged for legal services, and there is a strong suspicion he was never admitted to the bar. But he enjoyed giving free whatever his slight knowledge of law permitted, and he enjoyed, it is said, the title he thus acquired: "The Poor Man's Counsellor." Whatever his legal status may have been, a good many people were glad to get his advice.

When he was about twenty-three, Abraham Clark married a girl named Sarah Hatfield, who came from a family the Clarks had known for more than a generation. The newly-married pair went to live in Abraham's father's house near Elizabeth. Eventually, they had a family of ten children.

About the time of his marriage, Abraham Clark was given two offices under the Crown. He became Clerk of the Colonial Assembly and also High Sheriff of Essex County.

This was his start in public life. His integrity had been early recognized during his first work with the poor, who had found they could trust him. By 1774, Clark was an avowed Whig, identified with the patriot cause, and soon became a bold advocate of independence. When Committees of Safety began to spring up throughout the colonies, Clark was placed on New Jersey's committee, later becoming its secretary.

In May, 1775, Clark was elected to the Provincial Congress of New Jersey. Since he was already supporting a break with Great Britain, he was by this body appointed to the Second Continental Congress on June 22, 1776.

Abraham Clark was much impressed by the men he met in Congress. Himself a man of few words, he was enthralled by the orators in Congress. On July Fourth, he wrote from Philadelphia to his own local people: "Our Congress is an August Assembly — and can they support the Declaration now on the Anvil, they will be the Greatest Assembly on Earth." Aware, however, of the great danger in which the colonies had now placed themselves, he added: "We can die but once. . . . We are now embarked on a most tempestuous sea. . . . It is gone so far that we must now be a free independent State or a Conquered Country."

Knowing law as he did, Clark was well aware of the penalties for treason which, under British law, all the Founding Fathers incurred when they put their signatures to the Declaration. To have been a Signer is a proud title now, but Abraham Clark wrote a friend: "As to my title, I know not yet whether it will be honourable or dishonourable; the issue of the war must settle it. Perhaps our Congress will be exalted on a high gallows." That is exactly what would have happened, too, if the British had won — unless the victors had preferred to behead them.

Though he was much of the time "in want of health" there was no absenteeism in Clark's record in Congress. He was a most energetic member, and the Library of Congress still contains many reports in his handwriting on many different subjects that concerned the patriots of 1776. But devoted to his duty though he was, he never wanted to go to Congress. As he wrote his friend, James Caldwell, he would have preferred to remain in New Jersey, where he thought he would have been of more service to his own province.

Elected to Congress in spite of his own desires, Abraham

Clark won the approval and respect of those with whom he worked, even as he had proved his worth in his own colony. He served on committees, wrote many reports, and was always present to vote. He was very active in keeping people of doubtful loyalty from being elected, and he labored mightily to gather the supplies that General Washington's army so badly needed. He opposed "commutation of pay" for army officers — that is, commuting retired officers' pay to a lump sum — and to the unlimited issue of paper money, thus acquiring numerous enemies in politics. But nothing affected his industry or his influence. Three times he was re-elected to Congress while giving interim service in the New Jersey legislature, and he was, in 1786, a delegate to the Annapolis Convention, which met to discuss interstate commerce. Chosen a representative of his state to the Philadelphia Convention that framed the great Federal Constitution in 1787, he was unable to attend because of ill health.

When the British forces landed on Staten Island, they were only a few miles across the water from Clark's New Jersey home — too near for comfort. Luckily, his estate escaped destruction at the hands of the British, but Clark had so neglected his private business affairs while on his country's service, that he nevertheless lost heavily from the Revolution. Two of his soldier sons were captured and confined on a British prison-ship. Clark knew so much of the cruelty and oppression of Great Britain that his hatred did not end, even with the treaty of peace.

He was a man of average height, slender, with dark hair and heavy eyebrows, moderate in all his desires, "very temperate," with no special ambition for wealth, and in manner reserved and thoughtful.

On September 15, 1794, he was out in one of his fields watching a bridge being built when suddenly he suffered a sunstroke. Realizing his danger, he stepped into his chaise and drove himself home. Two hours later, he died.

V

NEW YORK

Phil. Livingston

Lewis Morris

W Floyd

Fran.ᵗ Lewis

Philip Livingston,
of Livingston Manor

Phil. Livingston

January 15, 1716 — June 12, 1778

PHILIP LIVINGSTON, one of the most distinguished, aristocratic, and wealthy of the Signers, was born in Albany, New York. By the time the decision for independence was made in Philadelphia, he was sixty and had already enjoyed almost a lifetime of distinction and wealth. He came by some of these blessings through inheritance, but being capable and energetic, he increased upon his gifts.

The first American Livingston was Philip's grandfather, Robert, who came to America in 1673 and settled in Albany. He had previously lived in Rotterdam, where he had been taken by his father who, as a Presbyterian minister in Scotland, had been banished for not conforming to the English church. Robert Livingston married Alida Schuyler, widow of a Van Rensselaer — two important names in the early Dutch settlement in New York. He received grants of large land holdings and, as the busy years passed by, he purchased more, so that by 1686, only thirteen years after his arrival, he was privileged to exercise his own jurisdiction as lord of his manor in the British colony of New York. His 160,000 acre estate extended north from Dutchess County about fourteen miles, along the east bank of the Hudson River — a glorious country. Robert's fifth son, Philip, became the second lord of the manor and was married to Catherine Van Brugh of Albany. These were the parents of Philip, the Signer who, born into all this wealth and feudal privilege, grew up on a princely scale uncommon in the colonies of early America.

The youthful Livingston took his A.B. at Yale in 1737. Nine years later when another Signer-to-be of New York, Lewis Morris, received his Yale A.B., these two were among the fewer than twenty men in the whole New York province who had a college education.

After graduation, Philip Livingston became an importer in New York City. When he was twenty-four, he married Christine Ten Broeck of Albany, and they began house-keeping in a fine house on Duke Street, New York City, while maintaining a country-seat in an ideal spot on Brooklyn Heights, overlooking the harbor. By the time he was forty, Philip Livingston had earned an excellent reputation. The British governor of the province, Sir Charles Hardy, wrote that "among the considerable merchants in this city no one is more esteemed for energy, promptness, and public spirit than Philip Livingston."

As he grew older, he became much concerned with civic affairs. Regretting the lack of an educational establishment in New York province (Massachusetts, Connecticut, and Virginia already had their colleges), Livingston was one of the first to advocate the founding of King's College, now Columbia University, and he contributed heavily to its support. He was only thirty when he set aside a sum to establish at Yale a professorship of divinity which still bears his name. He was interested in all kinds of public enterprises. He helped organize the New York Society Library; was president for a time of the newly formed St. Andrew's Society, the earliest benevolent institution in the city; and collaborated in 1768 in organizing the New York Chamber of Commerce. When the New York hospital was incorporated in 1771, he was a member of the first board of governors.

Civic interests eventually carried Philip Livingston into politics. He served on the Board of Aldermen for nine years. In 1758 he was elected to the assembly, where he came to disagree with the financial policy of the administrators of the Crown. In 1764, he helped to write the address of the assembly to the British lieutenant-governor, asking his aid in securing the rights of His Majesty's subjects everywhere, to be taxed only with their own consent. Though he deplored the rioting of the Sons of Liberty when the Stamp Act came into force the next year, he joined the lawyers and merchants in their protests and helped draft the protest to the House of Lords as a New York delegate to the Stamp Act Congress.

Livingston served on the Committee of Fifty-One, which

named the New York delegates to the First Continental Congress, and was himself one of the five selected. When he attended the Philadelphia sessions, he was very conservative, bearing in mind the terrible cost to colonial merchants that would follow a disruption of normal trade with the mother country. John Adams found Livingston unwilling even to listen to the ideas and proposals of the extreme patriots. Of course, many worthy Americans (who were, after all, transplanted Englishmen and subjects of the king) found it difficult to take a stand against the Crown. John Adams considered Philip Livingston a "downright, straightforward man" but a "great, rough, rapid mortal" with whom "there is no holding any conversation. He blusters away; says if England should turn us adrift, we should instantly go to civil wars among ourselves."

From reading the Adams chapters, we recall that the New England delegates, eager to meet the New York delegates in order to learn how they thought and where they stood on these vital questions, stopped over in New York on their way to Philadelphia. Some went to dine with Mr. Livingston at his elegant country house in Brooklyn Heights. These Massachusetts politicians felt that patriotism had "taken but shallow root in some places, particularly at New York."

An important man of business and commerce, Philip Livingston was drawn into much committee work in Congress for his province: on Indian Affairs, Marine, Commerce, the Treasury Board, and on the board of commissioners to inspect the army under General Washington. In his own state of New York, Livingston was a member of the Committee of One Hundred and of the Provincial Congress. Both he and his cousin, Robert R. Livingston, were chosen for the Second Continental Congress. But, as one had to be in New York while the other was in Philadelphia, it was Philip who signed the Declaration in early August although he could not secure an affirmative vote on the part of New York for Independence in July.

Livingston's duties in Congress were constantly being interrupted by the demands of his province. In 1777, he was chosen by the new state of New York as one of the senators to the new legislature. After attending these first meetings, he returned to Congress, which by that time was sitting in York, Pennsylvania, because the British were occupying Philadelphia.

This time his family did not want him to go because his health was poor. But he insisted on serving in public office until the end. He died in York, with only his son Henry at his bedside.

Philip Livingston had given much and lost much. His fine town house on Duke Street fell into the hands of the British invaders. His sumptuous country house, which had once been the scene of a conference between Washington and his generals, after being seized by the British and used as a naval hospital, was finally destroyed by fire. Not long before his death, he had had to sell some of his remaining property to preserve his credit. And he did not live to see the surrender of Lord Cornwallis, which made American victory certain and made heroes of the Signers.

Lewis Morris

April 8, 1726 — January 22, 1798

THE SIGNERS FROM NEW YORK COLONY were men of great wealth, either by inheritance or by their own industry. But both those who had inherited their wealth and those who had earned it had to work hard to keep it when war began. Patriotism does not buy bread, and serving the patriot cause often meant the sacrifice of much property.

Lewis Morris was the eldest son of Lewis and Tryntje Staats Morris, born in his mother's manor house, April 8, 1726. His father personally managed his early education, after which he took a Yale A.B. when he was twenty. That same year, his grandfather, another Lewis Morris, who had been the first royal Govenor of New Jersey, died. He had been the first lord of the manor of Morrisania, a vast estate he had acquired in beautiful Westchester County, New York. The Signer's father then became the second lord of the manor.

Returning from Yale to this attractive homestead to help his father manage the family estates, the younger Morris found that he enjoyed this so much that he preferred to go on collecting

quitrents and produce from the family's vast acres rather than devise new ways to increase the family fortune. Most people never
have enough, but Lewis Morris was not the go-getter that his forebears had been; and, of course, didn't have to be, thanks to them. He
felt it was better to use wisely what they had accumulated, while
himself taking time to enjoy it. And he did enjoy the life of an
aristocratic land-holder for sixteen years. But when trouble
threatened, he was ready to work for the continued existence of
the pleasant kind of civilized life he had always had.

On September 24, 1749, he married Mary Walton, daughter of
Jacob and Maria Beekman Walton, who brought him additional
wealth. The Beekmans were a prominent, wealthy, New York
family, and Beekman Place, along the East River, is still one of
the "best" addresses in New York City.

When his father died in 1762, the tall, handsome thirty-six-
year-old Lewis became the third and, as it turned out, the last lord
of Morrisania Manor. Coming into the inheritance of so vast an
estate placed upon him a great responsibility, which turned his
thoughts to politics, for on political questions depended his own
future welfare. After serving a term in the Provincial Assembly,
he began to realize where the British policy was leading.

Some of his Tory neighbors in Westchester objected to his resistance to British policy, saying that he was supporting the revolutionary movement only because he himself had not been given
better offices. In fact, Morris simply had more foresight than they.
But he was still representing only a minority in his county when
he persuaded some local politicians to issue a call for a meeting in
White Plains to choose Westchester's delegates to New York's
Provincial Convention. Bearers of such wealthy New York names
as DeLancey, Pell, Phillips, tried to defeat the aim of the meeting,
but Lewis Morris and his side carried the day, and eight deputies
were appointed to attend the Convention when it met in New York
on April 20, 1775.

Morris was named chairman of the delegation instructed to support a resolution to send representatives to the Second Continental Congress. He was hoping to be chosen a delegate himself
and he got his wish.

A little more than three weeks later, Lewis Morris took his seat
in the Congress in Philadelphia. Here his services had to do

mainly with administrative matters. He was put on the committee to select army posts in New York should trouble with England grow worse. Then he was assigned to the committee which was to supply ammunition and military stores. He was much occupied with the practical, business side of the Revolution, locating and purchasing tent cloth, gunpowder, or the sulphur and saltpetre used in making it. But, active though he was in practical affairs, Morris was not one of the debaters and speechmakers in Congress.

In September of 1775, Morris dealt with Indian affairs at Pittsburgh, and was later made a permanent member of the Indian Affairs Committee.

The following June he was home again as brigadier-general in command of the Westchester County militia, while his son was appointed brigade major. Believing that his military post would offer more opportunity for active service than proved to be the case, Morris secured a leave of absence from Congress and was therefore away from Philadelphia on the great day of decision in early July, 1776. Instead, he was attending the fourth New York Provincial Congress in White Plains which endorsed the Declaration of Independence. He went back to Philadelphia a short time afterward and signed the Declaration. He was then fifty.

In the autumn of 1776, Morris took part in the campaign in New York but after that his military service was interrupted by the responsibilities of his civil offices. He was county judge in Westchester for a brief time, and he served intermittently as member of the upper house of the new state legislature until 1790.

When the war ended, Morris retired with the rank of major-general and set about the heart-breaking task of rehabilitating his beautiful estates, which had been sadly plundered and burned by the British. Many of the fine houses and properties of American patriots were deliberately destroyed by the British, and Morris was one of their victims.

In his older years, Lewis Morris served as a member of the first Board of Regents of the University of the State of New York. His younger brother, Gouverneur Morris, played a prominent part in the drafting of the new Federal Constitution, and at the convention in Poughkeepsie in 1788, Judge Lewis Morris worked for its ratification.

Above everything, however, Signer Lewis Morris loved to preside over his beautiful Morrisania home and its fine grounds, and there he finally passed away at the age of seventy-two.

William Floyd

December 17, 1734 — August 4, 1821

WILLIAM FLOYD'S FAMILY had been in America since his great-grandfather Richard Floyd emigrated from Wales in 1654. The first Floyd settled at Setauket, Long Island, became a successful farmer, and interested himself in public affairs, serving as Judge of Suffolk County and as colonel of the militia. Richard Floyd was the founder of the family fortune and established the local reputation of the Floyds. By the time William, the Signer, was born in Brookhaven, Long Island, eighty years after his immigrant great-grandfather's arrival, the family was wealthy. Nicoll Floyd and his wife Tabitha Smith Floyd were the parents of the Signer.

Though William could have had the best of educations, he received only elementary schooling for when he was in his teens his father died, leaving him with the responsibilities of a landed proprietor. It is interesting to note that one of his daughters, Mary Floyd, became the first wife of Colonel Benjamin Tallmadge, chief of General Washington's secret service, who played an important part in catching Major André and uncovering the treason of Benedict Arnold.

William Floyd's family connections and the pleasure he took in extending generous hospitality naturally made him prominent in his community and, like his great-grandfather, he was active in both civic and military affairs. He served in Suffolk County's militia and eventually became a militia major general, though he was in Congress during most of the Revolution. Active resistance to British oppression had developed with especial strength among the settlers who had moved from the New England colonies to the eastern end of Long Island. Floyd was about forty when he aligned himself with the patriotic cause. Though this was against his interests as a large land-owner, such were his convictions and he stood by them.

In 1774, William Floyd was elected delegate to the First Continental Congress and took his seat on opening day. As a member of the Provincial Convention the next year, he was again elected and so was in Congress in 1776. He was one of those who, being neither aggressive nor brilliant enough to stand up and argue in the debates, "never quit their chairs" — as another delegate observed — but he served on many committees, and his independent judgment won the respect of his colleagues.

William Floyd and his family suffered severe hardships during the war. His property on Long Island was taken over by the British after the Declaration was signed, and his wife and family had to flee to Middletown, Connecticut. Difficult years followed, during which his duties separated him from his family. When he finally saw his home after seven years, it was in ruins.

At the end of the war, Floyd bought land in what is now Oneida County, New York, at the headwaters of the Mohawk River. He returned to Congress from 1789 to 1791 and was several times a presidential elector. In 1803 he finally moved to his new property and spent more and more time doing what he loved the most — cultivating his land. In 1808 he was elected state senator.

Floyd was a practical man of no special distinction, save for his stout and faithful patriotism. He was reserved, frank, independent, and well-liked, though he is known today only because his signature appears on the birth certificate of his country.

Francis Lewis

March 21, 1713 — December 31, 1802

NO LONGER YOUNG, Francis Lewis had retired from a successful career in business, which included much travel and some high adventure, by the time he went to Philadelphia to attend the Second Continental Congress at the age of sixty-three.

Lewis was not a native-born patriot. He was a Welshman, born in Llandaff, Glamorganshire, March 21, 1713, only son of the Reverend Francis Lewis and his wife, Amy Pettingal Lewis. His parents died while he was still a child, and he was brought up by his aunt in Caernarvon until he went to Westminster School in London. This was the end of his formal education. He became apprentice to a London merchant, working in the counting-house and thus preparing himself for a career in trade.

At the age of twenty-five, Francis Lewis came to New York, bringing a cargo of goods which, it is said, he had been able to buy with money he had inherited. Some of this cargo he took on to Philadelphia, where he remained for a year. He returned to New York, formed a partnership with a man named Richard Annely, and established permanent residence there. His continuously successful business necessitated considerable travel to England, and two visits to Russia. While on these business trips, Lewis was twice shipwrecked on the treacherous coast of Ireland.

When he was thirty-two, he married Elizabeth Annely, sister of his partner.

Serving as clothing contractor for the British troops during the French and Indian War, Lewis was at Fort Oswego during Montcalm's attack. Upon the surrender of the fort, when its garrison of sixteen hundred men became prisoners of war, Lewis was one of the thirty captives given to an Indian chief assisting Montcalm, but after some time, he was sent to France and there exchanged. The British government granted him five thousand acres for his military service.

Lewis accumulated a considerable fortune and became a man of influence and importance in New York. As British treatment of the American colonies became more intolerable, Lewis showed active interest in the patriot cause, serving as a member of the Stamp Act Congress in his colony.

A few years later, wishing to establish his elder son Francis in the business, he took the young man to England to make commercial connections there. Returning with a quantity of dry goods, they set up the firm of Francis Lewis and Son. But when the son was well launched, he carried on so successfully that the father retired. He never again engaged in business, but occupied himself wholly with public affairs which, by this time, were becoming very serious. He was wealthy enough to leave the city and live on his country estate at Whitestone, Long Island. Inevitably, all this obvious success made him enemies among jealous competitors who had not done so well.

Like Philip Livingston, another New York Signer, Lewis was a member of the important committees which organized the beginning of the rebellion: the Committee of Fifty-One, which later became the Committee of Sixty and, later yet, the Committee of One Hundred. The Fifty-One were really a committee of correspondence. Eventually Lewis and ten others resigned from the Fifty-One in protest against their "excessive caution" in opposing the British. Lewis favored a stronger stand and in April, 1775, the provincial convention agreed with him enough to pick him as one of New York's twelve delegates to the Second Continental Congress.

Though New York sent twelve members to the Second Congress, they were directed to arrange among themselves that only five would be attending Congress at the same time. Thus it was a matter of chance who the actual New York Signers were. These five were in favor of Richard Henry Lee's resolution declaring independence, but because their constituents had not instructed them to vote separation from Great Britain, they believed that they were not justified in voting on either side. They asked leave to withdraw from the question. This Congress granted, and that is why New York did not vote on July Fourth. Happily for the New Yorkers, the Declaration was not signed, except by John Hancock, on that day.

On July 9, when the New York provincial convention met at White Plains, letters from the New York delegates in Philadelphia and the Declaration itself were laid before them. That same evening they

> Resolved, unanimously, That the reasons assigned by the Continental Congress for declaring the United Colonies Free and Independent States are cogent and conclusive; and that while we lament the cruel necessity which has rendered that

measure unavoidable, we approve the same, and will, at the
risk of our lives and fortunes, join with the other colonies in
supporting it.

When, therefore, the Declaration had been engrossed and was
produced in Congress, the New York delegates were authorized to
sign it, and gladly did so.

In Congress, Francis Lewis was a member of the committee of
claims, of the committee to report a method of establishing a hospital, and of the committee to advise the best way of assigning
persons of character as intelligence agents and couriers. He was
also on the committee charged with inquiring "into the state of the
army and the best means of supplying their wants." He was indefatigable in this endless committee work. He was not one of the
congressional debaters, and Edward Rutledge considered him to
be one of the quiet ones. Nevertheless, Dr. Rush called him "a
very honest man, and very useful in executive business."

Lewis was again chosen a delegate to the Congress which had
to flee to York, Pennsylvania, when the British took Philadelphia.
Sometimes at that session, no more than nine members were present, and never more than eighteen. In January, 1777, Lewis wrote
that for several months he had been the only member attending
from New York, and this when Washington's army was in desperate need of food and clothing! But these congressmen at first all
had their own businesses to attend to.

Some of them lost their businesses, their fortunes, their homes
and their health as well, during the difficult years when they were
laboring for their country. Lewis was one of these devoted but
unfortunate men. After his staunch patriotism and hard work
in the cause of American liberty, Lewis was naturally a target for
British retaliation and suffered great losses. Less than a month
after he signed the Declaration, the British deliberately destroyed
his Long Island home, with all his books, papers, and furniture,
and carried Mrs. Lewis off to a New York prison. Lewis was dis-
tracted. About two months afterward, General Washington had
two Tory ladies placed under house arrest in their own Philadelphia houses until they could be exchanged for Mrs. Lewis. But
the experience and the worry about her husband's losses injured

her health and hastened her death, which occurred less than two years later.

During the disgraceful intrigues of the Conway Cabal against General Washington, when the plotters wanted to remove him and give General Gates the supreme command, Francis Lewis was Washington's strong supporter and played a part in defeating the plot.

In 1779, Lewis was elected for the fourth time to Congress but had to ask for leave of absence because of his wife's illness. He also endured the pain of having his only daughter married, clandestinely, to an officer of the British Navy. Thus lost to her father, she presumably went to live in England.

In December of this same year, Lewis became Commissioner of the Board of Admiralty; but after his wife died, he retired from public life.

In his ninetieth year he passed away, one of the few Signers to reach such an advanced age. His younger son, Morgan Lewis, who had been an officer in the Continental Army, was elected Governor of New York the next year.

VI

CONNECTICUT

Roger Sherman

Sam.ᵈ Huntington

Oliver Wolcott

Wᵐ Williams

Roger Sherman

Roger Sherman

April 30, 1721 — July 23, 1793

WITH NO EDUCATION save what he gained at home by his own efforts, Roger Sherman made himself, in the opinion of John Adams, "one of the most sensible men in the world. The clearest head and the steadiest heart." He was one of the five in Congress chosen for the committee to draft the Declaration of Independence. Thomas Jefferson, who composed it, recalled in after years: "I served with him [Sherman] in the old congress, in the years 1775 and 1776; he was a very able and logical debater in that body, steady in the principles of the revolution, always at the post of duty, much employed in the business of committees." Then he added: "I had a very great respect for him."

Roger Sherman was born in Newton, Massachusetts, just west of Boston. His parents were William and Mehetable Wellington Sherman, and his earliest American ancestor was John Sherman, who came from Dedham, in Essex, England, about 1636.

The boy was only two when his father moved to Stoughton, some twenty miles south of Boston and farther from the coastline. In those days, it was practically a frontier community, sparsely settled, with harmless Indian neighbors. Here Roger grew through boyhood and did not leave until he was a young man of twenty-two with responsibilities.

Schooling facilities were very poor in outlying communities like Stoughton. Young Roger was thirteen when the town built a schoolhouse and the boys were taught reading, writing, and arithmetic as far as fractions. The Stoughton school became a "grammar school." That meant Latin grammar, but Roger must have studied the correct use of English because, after he had become a prominent man, President Timothy Dwight of Yale, commented on his accurate use of his native language. Fortunately for a boy who enjoyed study and reading, his father possessed a small library of his own, and the Stoughton church had a Harvard-trained minister, the Reverend Samuel Dunbar, a great help to the studious Sherman. The boy thus achieved some knowledge of mathematics, physics, Latin, English poetry, history, economics, logic, philosophy, and theology. All this went on in the growing years while he plowed with a yoke of oxen, did the usual farm chores, and learned shoe-making from his father. A boy with such ambition and industry was bound to go far.

When he was twenty, his father died, and young Roger was left to care for his mother and the younger sisters and brothers. His older brother William had moved away to New Milford, Connecticut, and two years later Roger followed with the family, enticed by William's letters describing the attractions of western Connecticut. For those times, this was the "call of the West." It is reported that the family went by stage, but Roger walked the approximately fifty miles, carrying his sack of cobbler's tools upon his back.

Settlers in the frontier town found living conditions primitive. Everybody did some farming. The settler had to build his own house and outbuildings. Everybody in a family helped in the work, all year round. In the summers they grew their food. In the winters, the men cared for their animals, mended fences or stone walls, and made harnesses. The women spun, sewed, knitted. They had almost no money, but paid their debts and taxes in produce. Whatever they had — food, clothing, buildings, furniture — cost them endless labor. In addition to all this hard work, Roger Sherman continued to make shoes and, because he liked it, continued to study mathematics. He had had a surveyor grandfather, from whom, perhaps, he inherited his mathematical mind. This study led to his appointment, two years later, as surveyor of New Haven County, an office which he held for several years. Since surveying paid much better than cobbling, he put aside his shoe-making and, as the years passed, made money enough to buy land — and more land.

Commissioned by a neighbor to consult a lawyer in the county seat regarding a petition before the court, Sherman wrote down the items of the plea so as to have a clear and complete reference when the time came. During the interview in New Haven, the lawyer asked to see the paper Sherman was looking at. Handing it over reluctantly, he said it was only a memorandum he had made for himself and not likely to be helpful to the lawyer. But upon reading it, the attorney said, "My friend, you should fit yourself to be a lawyer."

When the surprised young man asked why, he was told that his notes, with a few alterations in form, were as good as any the lawyer himself could have prepared.

Undoubtedly the young man went on to Stoughton, his former home-town, while on this visit to the county seat. He made other visits to Stoughton during his first years in New Milford, for he had left a girl behind him there. In November, 1749, he married Elizabeth Hartwell, daughter of Deacon Joseph and Mary Hartwell of Stoughton, and took her back to the house he had bought the year before in New Milford.

The energetic Roger Sherman became active in town and church affairs, though he had not joined a church until he was twenty-one. (Perhaps it might be well to explain here that church membership in the strict Calvinistic congregations of that day was not easy to achieve, and since the early comers to New England were people who had broken away from the Church of England at home, partly because it was not strict enough, the descendants of seventeenth-century Americans were brought up to rigid rules.)

As a boy, Roger Sherman had been used to a Sabbath which began on Saturday at sunset. Sunday morning, at the sound of drum or conch-shell, the whole family walked to the cheerless meeting-house, children following the parents "in quiet procession." Between morning and afternoon service, there was an hour for lunch. No work and no play was permitted on Sundays, not even cooking or bed-making. This was the origin of the New England pot of baked beans, always made on Saturdays to last over. And, though children attended church, they could achieve membership only after examination and a careful observation by those who were already members. Becoming a deacon was a distinct achievement, an honor so important, indeed, that a deacon always used his title.

Sherman became town clerk of New Milford, served on the school committee, and before long was chosen "agent" to the assembly on the town's business. He and his brother opened New Milford's first store, of which he later became the sole owner. Sherman's friends and acquaintances persuaded him to write an almanac because of the astronomy and mathematics he had learned in his leisure hours. In those days when towns had no newspapers and not much else to read, almanacs were important publications. Roger Sherman wrote and published a series of almanacs for eleven years, beginning in 1750.

Early in 1754 he was admitted to the Litchfield bar and the next year represented New Milford (nineteen miles from Litchfield) in the General Assembly, which appointed him justice of the peace. One thing always leads to another, and four years later, he became a justice of the county court and, except for the two following years, he was constantly re-elected to the legislature until 1761, when he was forty years old. In 1755, during the French and Indian War, Sherman served on a committee to consider the financing of the expedition against the French stronghold at Crown Point. In 1759 he was appointed commissary for the Connecticut troops.

All these experiences helped to prepare him for a legislative career during the Revolution, especially in matters touching military supply and finance; and, by the time he was forty, Roger Sherman had made himself, with no help or fortune, a man of property with a considerable political reputation. He enlarged his business enterprise to open a store in New Haven and another in nearby Wallingford. Then, in 1760, his wife died and the next year Roger Sherman took his family to live in New Haven.

He now gave up the practice of law and devoted himself to merchandizing, which in New Haven included bookselling. His house adjoined his store on what is now Chapel Street, opposite Yale College. Since he loved books and reading, his store became a kind of rendezvous for the professors and preachers and educated men of the town — a little center for those interested in cultural pursuits.

Two years after moving to New Haven, Roger Sherman married again, and his second wife, Rebecca Prescott, gave him eight more children.

During the increasingly stormy years after the Stamp Act, Sherman was treasurer of Yale. A self-taught scholar who had lifted himself into a position of prominence altogether by his own efforts, study, and industry, he was given an honorary M.A. degree in 1768. Through the 1760's and 1770's he held many public offices, representing New Haven in the lower house of the legislature and then in the upper house, an office he held for nineteen years. From May, 1766, he was judge of the Superior Court of Connecticut and annually reappointed for twenty-three years thereafter.

The province of Connecticut had a homogeneous population, being then almost entirely Anglo-Saxon. There was a strong feeling against interference from without. As the years sped on into the agitated 1770's, Sherman stood in the conservative wing of the Revolutionary party, while denying the supremacy of the British Parliament over the American colonies. In 1774, John Adams wrote that Sherman thought that Parliament had authority to make laws for America "in no case whatever." The two had become acquainted when members of the First Continental Congress that same year.

Adams described Sherman as awkward and stiff when speaking in Congress, rigid as "a sophomore," standing with "his hands before him, the fingers of his left hand clenched into a fist, and the wrist of it grasped with his right." But, said Adams, "he has a clear head and sound judgment."

Sherman developed an interest in the Susquehanna Company, though he does not seem ever to have become a stockholder in it. This company was an extraordinary enterprise by an adventurous band of men who proposed to set up in Pennsylvania a new Connecticut county separated by more than a hundred miles from Connecticut itself. This happened because King Charles II, in granting a charter to Connecticut in 1662, had drawn its northern and southern boundaries carefully but had given its western boundary only as the Pacific Ocean! The king, of course, had no idea how far away that was. Nobody did until after the Lewis and Clark Expedition.

In 1753, a group of Connecticut men who were looking westward for land for themselves organized the company and bought from the Indians a tract around modern Wilkes Barre, Pennsylvania, nearly as big as the whole state of Connecticut. Here they set up a new Connecticut County. But when they tried to settle it Pennsylvania objected, and there was a series of little wars which the two states decided to call off as the Revolutionary War approached. Roger Sherman was on a Committee of the State Assembly to cooperate with Governor Trumbull in the matter. Before the Revolution was over, the dispute was peacefully settled, and the state of Pennsylvania kept her Susquehanna Valley lands. The state of Connecticut gave up its claim on land all the way to the coast, retaining only a "Western Reserve" in Ohio. This is now that part of Ohio which contains the city of Cleveland.

Every year Congress assigned Sherman to some committee dealing with finance. For raising money, he urged high taxes by Congress and by the states. He was against weakening the new government's credit through too many loans. This took courage as the people, unused to the taxes we have now learned to accept, voiced a strong resistance to parting with their cash. His business ability was repeatedly utilized by Congress. He was on committees for purchasing supplies and provisions, and for "supplying the army with shoes, hats, and shirts." Even earlier, the year before, when on a committee for investigating army contract frauds, Sherman surprised his colleagues by his familiarity with the making and selling of shoes.

Sherman went through a period of illness in 1776 and realized that he would have to slow down the next year. He wrote Governor Trumbull of Connecticut that his constitution would not permit "so close an application to business much longer." But he stayed on until 1781, and returned to Congress again in 1783 and 1784. With Benjamin Franklin on the committee to form the Articles of Confederation, under which the government operated before the Constitution was adopted, he proposed a plan of union which John Adams said was the best liked at the time although, he added, very little was taken from it when the Constitution was finally adopted.

The years 1783 to 1787 encompassed a very critical period in American history. Though the Pennsylvania-Connecticut controversy over the Susquehanna settlements had been officially settled, other states were in conflict. Some disputed their boundaries, others quarrelled over tariffs. Pennsylvania and Delaware had commercial differences, so did South Carolina and Georgia; Virginia and Maryland disputed over Chesapeake Bay. It soon became clear that the Articles of Confederation were weak and would have to be revised. Connecticut disregarded the call for a convention to revise the Articles until the May, 1787, session of the General Court. The legislators then appointed Roger Sherman as delegate to take the place of another delegate who had resigned. Now sixty-six, Sherman was the oldest of Connecticut's delegates, and his long years of business and legal experience, his broad general knowledge, and his forcible character made him the natural leader of the delegation.

In the Constitutional convention, Sherman was one of the most frequent speakers, credited with one hundred thirty-eight speeches. He made a strong impression. One thought him "as cunning as the Devil, and if you attack him, you ought to know him well; he is not easily managed, but if he suspects you are trying to take him in, you may as well catch an Eel by the tail." Another thought Sherman had "good sense to so high a degree that it might almost be called genius." His concise speech was noted: "With more well-digested thoughts to communicate than any other member of the Convention, he used fewer words to express his sentiments than any of his compeers." Another delegate described his appearance, not altogether favorably:

> Mr. Sherman exhibits the oddest shaped character I ever remember to have met with. He is awkward and unaccountably strange in his manner. But in his train of thinking there is something regular, deep, and comprehensive; yet the oddity of his address, the vulgarisms that accompany his public speaking, and that strange New England cant which runs through his public as well as his private speaking makes everything that is connected with him grotesque and laughable; and yet he deserves infinite praise, no Man has a better Heart or a clearer Head. If he cannot embellish he can furnish thoughts that are wise and useful. He is an able politician, and extremely artful in accomplishing any particular object; it is remarked that he seldom fails."

John Adams thought him "an old Puritan, as honest as an angel and as firm in the cause of American Independence as Mount Atlas." Thomas Jefferson said that Sherman "never said a foolish thing in his life." Mr. Macon of Georgia said Roger Sherman had "more common sense than any man" he knew.

There was a strong religious side to his character. Ever interested in theology, Sherman corresponded with several New England clergymen. During his years in Congress, it was his custom to buy a new Bible at the beginning of each new session, read in it every day and, upon his return home, give it to one of his children.

When he was seventy, he was elected to fill a vacancy in Connecticut's senatorial representation, and he was a United States senator at the time of his death, two years later.

In the summer of 1793, he was stricken with typhoid, and died on July twenty-third. After a large and impressive funeral he was buried in the cemetery behind the Center Church on the New Haven Green, but when the New Haven Green Cemetery was moved in 1821, his body was taken to the Grove Street Cemetery.

Roger Sherman has the special distinction of being the only one of all the Signers who signed all four of the greatest documents in the birth of his nation: the Articles of Association in 1774; the Declaration of Independence; the Articles of Confederation; and the Constitution itself.

Samuel Huntington

Sam.ᵈ Huntington

July 3, 1731 — January 5, 1796

MANY OF THE PATRIOTS who fearlessly resisted the threats and efforts of the British government to prevent the Declaration of Independence came from humble homes, yet by the vigor of their intellect and desire to learn, acquired for themselves a certain amount of education and commanded general respect. Like Roger Sherman, Samuel Huntington never had an opportunity to attend school and college.

His great-grandfather, Simon, came from England and was one of the thirty-five original proprietors of Norwich, Connecticut. After his death, his widow settled in Boston only thirteen years after the arrival of the Mayflower. Two generations later, Nathaniel Huntington was living in Windham, Connecticut, not far from Norwich, when his wife, Mehitable Thurston Huntington, gave birth to their first child, Samuel. Nine more children were to come.

Samuel grew up on his father's farm, helping with the chores as soon as he was old enough. He also helped in his father's clothing shop. Although three of his younger brothers attended Yale, Samuel had to stay on the farm until, when he was sixteen, he was apprenticed to a cooper and learned to make barrels.

However, he was studious by nature and had a desire to learn. He taught himself Latin and law, not easy subjects, and was admitted to the bar when he was twenty-seven. He had done it all himself, borrowing books to study in the hours he could snatch from farming and barrel-making. At twenty-eight, he gave up farming, entered a law office in Norwich, and soon began to win distinction in his profession. Four years later he was made King's Attorney (District Attorney) for Connecticut. But when relations became strained between the colonies and the mother country, Huntington, whose sympathies were with the patriots, resigned, feeling that he could no longer faithfully serve the king. He was conservative, however, and loyal to the mother country so long as there was hope of conciliation. When it became evident that there must be a separation, he supported the colonies.

At the age of thirty, Samuel Huntington married Martha Devotion, daughter of the Reverend Ebenezer Devotion, of Windham. Having no children of their own, they took two of Samuel's brother's children to raise, Joseph Huntington having married Martha's sister.

In the Stamp Act year, Samuel Huntington was chosen to represent Norwich in the General Assembly of Connecticut Colony, and this body appointed him a member of the committee for defense. In ten years, Samuel Huntington had made himself well enough known, liked, and respected to be elected assistant in the upper house of the legislature, to which he was re-elected every year until 1784.

Before the outbreak of the war, Huntington had been judge of the Superior Court. With General Jabez Huntington and the Honorable Benjamin Huntington, he had represented Norwich in the Connecticut Council of Safety. Three of the original nine members of this council came from Norwich and were named Huntington.

With his record it was not strange that this self-made gentleman was appointed a delegate to the Continental Congress. Samuel Huntington took his seat in 1776 with Roger Sherman, Oliver Wolcott, and William Williams, the other Connecticut congressmen. Huntington, who served on many committees, was regarded as "a sensible, candid, and worthy man."

In 1779 he was chosen President of Congress to succeed John Jay, who had been appointed minister plenipotentiary to negotiate a treaty between the United States and Spain. Two years later he had to resign because of poor health. He returned to Philadelphia and Congress in 1783.

The next year, Huntington was Chief Justice of the Connecticut Supreme Court. He then became lieutenant-governor of the state and Governor of Connecticut in 1786. Re-elected for eleven successive years, Huntington was still the governor at the time of his death in Norwich at the age of sixty-four. This self-taught man had been gratified by the honorary degree of LL.D. conferred upon him by both Yale and Dartmouth.

When George Washington and John Adams were elected to be the first President and Vice-President of our new nation in 1789, Huntington received two electoral votes for Vice-President.

With no formal education himself, he was careful to give his nephew and namesake, whom he had taken to raise, an opportunity to study at Dartmouth and Yale. This younger Samuel Huntington later moved to Ohio and became a governor of that state.

William Williams

April 8, 1731 — August 2, 1811

IN THE VILLAGE of Lebanon, somewhat east of central Connecticut, the Reverend Solomon Williams was pastor of the First Congregational Church when his wife, Mary Porter Williams, gave him the son who was to become a Signer. William was descended from Robert Williams, who came to Roxbury, Massachusetts, from Norfolk County, England, in 1637; so the family had been in America almost a hundred years.

William was given a preparatory education sound enough to enable him to graduate from Harvard at the age of twenty. Then he began to study theology with his father.

Four years later, however, having joined the staff of Colonel Ephraim Williams, his father's cousin, William served in the Lake George operations of the French and Indian War.

Returning to Lebanon after the Lake George campaign, William Williams resumed his activities in the town's affairs, became town clerk, and set himself up in business as a merchant. Judging by the number of offices he held, Williams must have been regarded as an exceedingly worthy citizen. He was town clerk for forty-four years, selectman for Lebanon for twenty-five years; he was a representative and later a councilor in the assembly for more than forty years, speaker for many years, and a colonel in the militia.

He was an ardent patriot, chosen to serve on several committees. Strong for independence, Williams not only gave money to the cause, he also wrote for it by setting down the colonists' claims in various journals, and helping to write many of the state papers of Connecticut's governor, John Trumbull, whose daughter Mary he married when he was forty years of age.

It was on Williams's promissory note that money was raised in 1775 for the cost of sending Connecticut troops to help in the capture of Ticonderoga. Appointed to represent his colony at the conferences of delegates from all the New England colonies, the next step finds him entering the national arena as delegate to the Continental Congress of 1776.

After voting for independence and signing his name to the Declaration, he helped to frame the Articles of Confederation, under which the country was governed before we had a Constitution. In 1777, he was elected to sit on the Board of War.

Throughout the struggle, Williams offered the hospitality of his house in Lebanon to any passing American soldiers, and he allowed French officers to live there when they were stationed in Lebanon through the winter of 1780–81.

After the war, Williams was a delegate to the Hartford Convention to consider Connecticut's adoption of the new Constitution of the United States. He voted in favor of it with one objection: He did not want the clause which forbade religious tests.

Another of those who served on the bench without having had legal training, William Williams was judge of the Windham County Court for many years, growing old while meting out justice.

A hardy New Englander, the old Signer lived to ripe old age, passing away on August 2, 1811, in the town where he had been born eighty years before.

Oliver Wolcott

November 20, 1726 — December 1, 1797

LIKE THE WILLIAMS FAMILY, the Wolcotts had been in the New World about a hundred years by the time Oliver Wolcott, the Signer, was born. The first Wolcott had been Henry, an Englishman of property, who had come to Connecticut in 1630 and had become one of the founders of the settlement at Windsor. He served in the first general assembly of the colony. Oliver's father was Roger, who went to work as a mechanic at the age of twelve. Industrious and thrifty, Roger acquired a considerable property and became governor in 1751. Thus, though Roger Wolcott had no formal education himself, members of his family had been serving in civil affairs and helping build up their colony since the first Henry crossed the Atlantic.

Roger married Sarah Drake, of Windsor. They had fourteen children, the youngest of whom was Oliver. He went to Yale, was at the head of his class for four years, and graduated in 1747. Before graduating he received a commission from the British Governor Clinton of New York to raise a company of volunteers. He did so and served as its captain during service on the northern frontier for some time.

After he returned home, Oliver Wolcott studied medicine with his older brother, Dr. Alexander Wolcott, intending to practice in Goshen. But in 1751, when Litchfield was organized as a county, he settled there on property his father owned. That was the year his father became governor.

Oliver was Litchfield's first sheriff and held this position for twenty years, during which time he devoted himself more and more to public life and legal affairs. Eventually he became judge of the County Court of Common Pleas and probate judge for the Litchfield district.

In 1755, he married Laura Collins, daughter of Captain Daniel Collins of Guilford, Connecticut. They had five children.

As discord between the mother country and her American colonies mounted toward open rebellion, Wolcott again engaged in military affairs. In 1771, he was made a major in the militia, in 1774 a colonel. In midsummer of the following year, after the Continental Congress had appointed him as one of the commissioners of Indian Affairs for the northern section, he traveled to Albany to a council with representatives of the Six Nations.

In October of that troubled year, 1775, he was elected to the Continental Congress and took his place among the new national figures in Philadelphia. He was now fifty.

Oliver Wolcott did not do much committee work in Congress. He joined in the early discussions about a declaration of independence and came to be recognized as a man who was not afraid to speak his mind. But by the end of June, 1776, illness forced him to leave.

Since he arrived home on the Fourth, the day of the all-important vote, Wolcott missed the chance to take part in the final great decision. Connecticut sent William Williams as a substitute and Williams cast the vote for independence that might have been Wolcott's. Later, however, both signed the Declaration.

In the next few weeks, Wolcott recovered his health. When General Washington requested more aid in the defense of New York from Connecticut's Governor Trumbull, Wolcott was able to take the field as brigadier general of the fourteen militia regiments ordered by the Connecticut governor and the Council of Safety to reinforce General Putnam on the Hudson River.

It should not be forgotten that the wives of these patriots who were eager to serve their country, did their full part in service, too. The ladies of Litchfield gathered in the rear of Wolcott's house and melted down the lead that had once formed part of King George's statue into bullets to be used against the king's redcoats. Wives are of the greatest help — or hindrance — to the public and patriotic service of their husbands. Mrs. Wolcott managed their small farm, preserved their property, and educated the children while her husband was away in the nation's service.

In October, Wolcott returned to Philadelphia and it was then, or possibly later, that he signed the Declaration. His name is at the bottom of the first column of signatures.

That winter, the members of Congress had to leave Philadelphia ahead of the invading British, and Wolcott went with them to Baltimore.

The next summer he was again active in military matters. After being in command of the sixth Militia Brigade in north-western Connecticut, he led a force of three hundred to four hundred volunteers from the brigade to join Gates against Burgoyne in September. It is said that among their supplies at this time were some of the bullets made from the melted statue of the king.

Early in 1778 Wolcott was again in Congress, now sitting in York, Pennsylvania. Elected again in 1780, he remained until 1784. For a time in 1779, however, he was once more on military service, as major general defending the Connecticut seacoast against raids by the Tory Governor Tryon, of New York. Before the war was over his eldest son, Oliver, was serving in minor campaigns.

After the peace, Wolcott resigned from Congress in order to pay more attention to the affairs of his own state. In 1784, he was commissioner at the Treaty of Fort Stanwix to make peace with the Indians of the Six Nations. Three years later he was chosen lieutenant-governor by the legislature. There were boundary disputes between New York and Vermont, and between Connecticut and Pennsylvania about the Wyoming Valley (in Pennsylvania) which he helped to settle. In 1789, he helped conclude a treaty with the Wyandottes in which they gave up their title to Connecticut lands in the Western Reserve, now part of Ohio.

Honors descended upon him. He received an honorary degree from Yale, he became President of the Connecticut Society of

Arts and Sciences and, upon the death of Samuel Huntington in January, 1796, he became governor and was elected to the office the following May. But his time as governor was brief and uneventful. He died while in office, at the age of seventy-one, on December 1, 1797. Before he died, he had the opportunity to vote, as presidential elector, for John Adams, second President of the United States.

A description of his person makes him appear the typical Connecticut Yankee: He was tall, dignified, of dark complexion, and with polished manners, considered to be a man of moderation, tolerant but very wary of new political theories. He was known for his integrity and his strong Puritan faith.

VII

RHODE ISLAND

Step Hopkins

William Ellery

Stephen Hopkins

Step. Hopkins

March 7, 1707 — July 13, 1785

By the time that great year of decision came upon our country, Benjamin Franklin and Stephen Hopkins were the oldest delegates in the Second Continental Congress. Both were practically self-taught; neither had had the opportunity of attending college. Both had represented their own colonies in the first assembly in this country, the Albany Congress of 1754. Consequently, both men had, by 1776, more experience in public affairs than any of the other fifty-four engaged in desperate consideration of the most serious problem that had yet faced the thirteen colonies — whether or not to insist upon independence.

Stephen Hopkins was born in Providence, Rhode Island, to William and Ruth Wilkinson Hopkins. His great-grandfather was Thomas H. Hopkins, who, about 1636, migrated from England to Providence, where he was assigned a lot in 1638. Stephen grew up as a farmer with little schooling. His mother taught him his first lessons, and his grandfather and uncle instructed him in elementary mathematics, for which he had a decided aptitude. Like several of his forebears, he became a surveyor and was much employed in establishing both private and public boundaries. This gave him a wide acquaintance throughout his colony.

Hopkins was only nineteen when he married Sarah Scott, descended from Rhode Island's first Quaker, Richard Scott. Three of their sons died at sea, a tragic but not unusual record for a seafaring New England family. After twenty-seven years of marriage, Mrs. Hopkins died and, two years later, Stephen married Mrs. Anne Smith. Although his mother was a Quaker, Hopkins now for the first time connected himself with the Society of Friends.

Until he was thirty-five, Hopkins worked at farming and land

surveying. Then he moved into Providence and took up a mercantile business with his brother. But he had begun public life
ten years earlier when, at twenty-five, he was chosen as a representative to the General Assembly. Devoted to the welfare of his
fellow citizens and working with tact, energy, and care for the
least detail, Hopkins had other offices thrust upon him. He was
town clerk, moderator of town meetings, and at the age of twenty-
nine was chosen to be one of the justices of the Court of Common
Pleas for Providence County.

Like other Signers from the northern colonies, Stephen Hopkins sat on the bench without having had legal training. In 1751,
he became Chief Justice of Rhode Island's Superior Court. Four
years later, the same year in which he married for the second
time, he was elected governor, an office in which he served
nine terms.

A rivalry had developed by this time between two classes in
Rhode Island: the rich and aristocratic citizens of Newport, and
the farmers and mechanics of the northern part of the state. Newport and Providence became rival towns. Both were leading
seaports, and Newport wished to remain the capital of the state.
Hopkins championed Providence as the capital, Samuel Ward,
wealthy landowner in Narragansett County, represented Newport.
For over a decade a feud existed between these men and their followers, especially in the contests for the governorship. But the
feud ended when both Ward and Hopkins withdrew in favor of
Josias Lyndon. Years later, both Ward and Hopkins were delegates to the First Continental Congress and worked there together, so that if any personal antipathy had existed, it was no
longer apparent. While Stephen Hopkins was engaged in commerce and had vessels that visited many foreign ports carrying
exports and imports, Providence became a great commercial port,
surpassing Newport.

Stephen Hopkins also owned tracts of land in Scituate and had
interests in an iron foundry where cannon were cast and iron
implements were made. But he never made a fortune because he
spent too much time in public activities instead of in work for
his own personal gain.

Hopkins first met Benjamin Franklin when both were attending
the Albany Congress of 1754. Franklin was then urging a plan

for colonial union, an idea which Hopkins also favored. After the Stamp Act of 1765, he became chairman of a committee to draft instructions to the Providence deputies in the General Assembly. He was Chief Justice when some Rhode Islanders, resisting British import duties, burned the British revenue schooner *Gaspée*. The Crown instructed its governor, Joseph Wanton, to arrest the men and have them sent to England for trial. The British plan was thwarted because Chief Justice Hopkins refused to apprehend any of the offenders "by his own order, nor suffer any Executive Officers in the Colony to do it."

In 1774, Stephen Hopkins was sent to Philadelphia as a delegate to the First Continental Congress. He was now sixty-seven, one of the oldest in that important assembly. Though a definite stand on independence for the colonies was avoided throughout that term, and many did not want to take such a bold and dangerous stand, the idea was in the air. People were talking about it. Hopkins of Rhode Island was a man with enough foresight to see, as he told members of that Congress, that "powder and ball will decide this question. The gun and bayonet alone will finish the contest in which we are engaged, and any of you who cannot bring your minds to this mode of adjusting this question had better retire in time."

After this straight talk, which Paul Revere must have heard as he was present in that first Congress, and after Hopkins's prophecy had been fulfilled in Lexington on the nineteenth of April in 1775, Hopkins was sent to the Second Continental Congress.

Here he was placed on the committee making plans for a navy, and on the committee for preparing the Articles of Confederation. As early as May 4, 1776, Rhode Island renounced its allegiance to King George III, and exactly two months from that day, Stephen Hopkins had the deep satisfaction of seeing a unanimous vote for national independence. All thirteen colonies were now arrayed against the king and war was on in earnest. In August, Hopkins signed the great document. But it was a difficult thing for him to do. We can see that his handwriting was shaky. He was now suffering from palsy and it was almost impossible for him to write.

The work that Hopkins did in connection with the Articles of Confederation was his last duty in Congress. Ill health compelled him to return home. During the first war years, he worked for independence in his own state as a member of the Rhode Island General Assembly.

He had never had the advantage of a systematic education, but Hopkins was an ardent reader and had cultivated literary and scientific tastes. Though books were rare, his grandfather had a small but choice library, which gave Hopkins the English classics to read. Since he had a real desire to learn and had made himself an educated man, he was naturally deeply interested in education and the establishment of schools. Active in founding Rhode Island College — now Brown University — Hopkins was its first chancellor, an office he held as long as he lived. He had helped found the *Providence Gazette and County Journal* in 1762 as a patriotic voice against the Tory *Newport Mercury*, or the *Weekly Advertiser*. He had contributed to its columns in the 1760's when unrest was growing, and his article on "The Rights of Colonies Examined" which appeared in 1764, was later issued as a pamphlet and reprinted throughout the colonies and in England. His desire to join the Philosophical Society of Newport as an out-of-town member, and his influence, in 1769, in having a telescope erected in Providence in order to observe the transit of Venus illustrates his wide interests. His public activities were equally varied. He was a "genial, entertaining Quaker, attractive alike to young and old."

This first citizen of Rhode Island passed away at the age of seventy-eight, not long after the final Treaty of Peace. He had lived to see his country free, independent, and at peace.

William Ellery

William Ellery

December 22, 1727 — February 15, 1820

IT IS BELIEVED that the great-grandfather of William Ellery came to America and settled in Gloucester, Massachusetts, sometime after the mid-1600's. His son Benjamin moved to Bristol, Rhode Island, and from there went on to Newport. These early Ellerys must have been successful and enlightened men, for Benjamin sent his son, another William, to Harvard, where he graduated in 1722. William returned from college to marry Elizabeth Almy and became the father of William, the Signer. The father held several public offices, himself directed the teaching of his son until he, too, was ready for Harvard. The younger William graduated there in 1742, only twenty years after his father!

William Ellery thus had all the formal education that the Quaker Signer of Rhode Island, Stephen Hopkins, had not been given. Yet he seems never to have achieved the wide popularity that Hopkins won, perhaps because he did not follow a single career and did not give so much of his time and effort to others. After leaving Harvard, he did not know quite what he wanted to do, since he was only fifteen. He first tried being a merchant, then served a period as a "naval officer" — that is, collector of customs — of his colony, and then, for two terms, was clerk of the General Assembly. But not until he was forty-three, when he took up the practice of law, did he find his real place and achieve success.

Three years after graduating, Ellery married Ann Remington of Cambridge. Thereafter until he was eighty, William Ellery made a yearly visit to Cambridge, so warm was his attachment to the scene of his college years and his first courtship. Ann died fourteen years after their marriage, and three years later the widower married his second cousin, Abigail Cary. It was not uncommon in those days for a woman to die young, worn out with child-bearing, and for the father to marry again to have help in raising his family. By these two wives, Ellery fathered seventeen children. Two of William Ellery's grandsons became authors: Richard Henry Dana, who wrote the American classic *Two Years Before the Mast* and William Ellery Channing, the nineteenth-century clergyman, writer, and philosopher, who counted Emerson, Hawthorne, and Thoreau among his friends.

Not until three years after his second marriage did William Ellery begin to practice law. By that time, he had served as clerk of the Court of Common Pleas. Perhaps it was this experience in the court room that turned his thoughts to a legal career.

As a lawyer he was so successful that his practice soon extended beyond the boundaries of the small colony in which he lived.

From the beginning of the colonists' dissatisfaction with Britain's mounting tyranny, Ellery was a patriot. He served on local committees organized to resist it, and upon the death of Rhode Island's congressman, Samuel Ward, was chosen to take his place in the Second Continental Congress. He took his seat in mid-May, 1776.

Soon after he arrived in that all-important assembly, Congress placed him on the Marine Committee, which dealt with naval and shipping problems. During the years he was in Congress he was on many other committees and took an active part in debates. In after years he used to like to tell about the signing of the Declaration of Independence: that he stood near the table and the secretary, Charles Thomas, because "I was determined to see how they all looked as they signed what might be their death warrant." He reported that all faces showed "undaunted resolution."

It is too bad that late in life Ellery requested his friends to preserve none of his correspondence; we might have had more intimate sidelights from him that could have brought some of those moments and men in Independence Hall into focus for us now, two hundred years after.

Only about four months after the signing, the British captured Newport and began a three-year occupation. In revenge for William Ellery's patriotism, they burned his house and destroyed his property. While all this was going on, Ellery, in Philadelphia, labored on committees: of the Treasury, for establishing expresses (mail routes), for providing relief for the war-wounded, and for army purchases. In 1779, he served on the committee for foreign relations; later, he worked on the committee for public accounts. In 1785, he was zealous in advocating the abolition of slavery in the new United States.

William Ellery was a round-faced, chunky and cheerful person, genial and kindly, well-blessed with friends, for he knew how to be a friend. As he moved into his nineties, an unusually old age for those times, he was also blessed in being free from, as he said, "sickness, pain and sorrow." Without glasses, he was reading Cicero — and in small print — sitting up in bed in his home in Newport when he passed away quietly as if going to sleep, the book still in his hand.

It was the fifteenth of February, 1820; the old Signer for Rhode Island was in his ninety-third year.

VIII

NEW HAMPSHIRE

Josiah Bartlett

Wm Whipple

Matthew Thornton

Josiah Bartlett

Josiah Bartlett

November 21, 1729 — May 19, 1795

IN PRE-REVOLUTIONARY TIMES, New Hampshire colony was sparsely settled. Having very little coastline, it had none of the first settlements like those that sprang up along the Atlantic seaboard where the ships came in. It is interesting, therefore, to see the difference in background and education of those Signers who represented the two colonies that did not touch salt water, or barely touched it (Vermont and New Hampshire), from those which naturally had a closer touch with the mother-land, where the first immigrants and much of their supplies came from. None of the three New Hampshire Signers was born in the colony.

The patriot Josiah Bartlett became a Chief Justice, Governor of New Hampshire, and a physician — all without either a law or medical degree. He was the son of Stephen and Mary Webster Bartlett, born in Amesbury, Essex County, Massachusetts. His early education was at an ordinary local school, the kind usually "kept" by a parson, but he had private tuition in Latin and Greek. At sixteen, when a modern American boy would still be in high school, he began to study medicine in the office of a relative, Dr. Ordway, who lived and practiced in the same town.

Under the doctor's guidance, young Josiah Bartlett read through such medical books as he could borrow in the libraries of his own and neighboring towns and observed what went on in Dr. Ordway's office. This was the only kind of clinical study and internship that was possible locally. In five years he was equipped, by the scientific standards of the period, to hang out his shingle. In 1750, when he was twenty-one, Dr. Bartlett began practice in Kingston, New Hampshire, where he was to live for the rest of his life.

In a short time he was "the Doctor" throughout the region and acquired a large practice. Interested in experiments, he discovered a successful treatment for an obscure but common disease by the use of Peruvian bark; and eventually he came to reject accepted treatments of some other diseases to introduce his own newer ones.

When he was twenty-five, Bartlett married his cousin, Mary Bartlett, of Newton, New Hampshire. They had twelve children. Three of his sons and seven of his grandsons became doctors.

Dr. Josiah Bartlett was also much interested in public affairs. Having earned a reputation for integrity and intelligence, his fellow townsmen chose him, the year after he was married, to represent Kingston in the Provincial Assembly of 1765, and continued to re-elect him until the beginning of the war. This was his introduction into public life.

For eight years, Bartlett had been colonel of a regiment of colonial militia. But by 1774 he was known to be a patriot, and the royal governor dismissed him. He was elected to the first Provincial Congress which, in turn, chose him as one of the New Hampshire delegates to the First Continental Congress in Philadelphia.

This last honor, Josiah Bartlett had to decline because his house had recently burned down, set on fire, as the doctor believed, by spiteful Tories. He was chosen again for the Second Continental Congress in 1775, accepted, and was the first man to vote in favor of the adoption of the resolution for independence.

Bartlett was a tall man, described as having a "fine" figure. His manner was affable though dignified. Very particular about his dress, he wore his auburn hair in the queue that was the custom of the day and wore short knee breeches with long silk hose and silver buckled shoes.

Bartlett was re-elected to Congress for 1777, but he was too exhausted by his labors in Congress the year before to serve. He had been on many committees, serving constantly without a break and taking great pains, so that he had become one of the most influential members in shaping legislation. The difficulty of travel between New Hampshire and Philadelphia was also exhausting. Again in Congress in 1778, he was the first to vote for the proposed Articles of Federation and Perpetual Union. He declined re-election the following year, whereupon his state appointed the doctor Chief Justice of its Court of Common Pleas.

He was promoted Associate Justice of the Superior Court in 1782, and Chief Justice six years later. His service on the bench ended in 1790.

It seems strange to us today to think of a layman elevated to the bench. But this occurred many times in some sections of our new country. Though no lawyer, Bartlett had been in close association with important lawyers while engaged in legislative work for fifteen years. Some of the ablest attorneys have expressed the opinion that justice had never been better administered in New Hampshire than when the judges knew very little law.

Josiah Bartlett was elected in 1790 to the highest office in his state when he became the chief executive. Ill health caused him to retire at the end of his term as New Hampshire's first governor, and it was not long until he died at his home in Kingston on May 19, 1795.

William Whipple

January 14, 1730 — November 10, 1785

WILLIAM WHIPPLE was a descendant of Matthew Whipple, who had immigrated to America from Essex County, England, at a date which is not quite certain but was earlier than 1638. The Signer was born at Kittery, Maine, the son of Captain William and Mary Cutt Whipple, in the house that had been the home of his great-grandfather on his mother's side. After some years of attending local schools, William Whipple, like many other New England boys of the eighteenth and nineteenth centuries, went away to sea while still in his early teens.

When he was about twenty-one, he became master of a sailing vessel, making many voyages in the European, West Indian, and African trade. Whipple was so successful that after about ten years he had saved up a respectable fortune and at twenty-nine gave up the rigors of life at sea and formed a partnership in a mercantile business with his brother Joseph in Portsmouth, New Hampshire. There he married his cousin, Catherine Moffatt, and went to live in her father's house, later designated as Number 70 Market Street. It is said to be the first three-storey house built in New Hampshire.

Sailors' lives make them independent, and in this sea-side town revolutionary ideas sprouted early. Captain Whipple took part in the resulting disputes, in favor of the colonists. As controversy became heated in the early 1770's, he decided to give up business and enter public life.

Captain Whipple was an immediate success as a public man. His fellow townsmen, placing the highest confidence in his integrity and patriotism, elected him to one office after another. Whipple was chosen to represent Portsmouth in the Provincial Congress in 1775; he was made a member of the council in 1776 when New Hampshire assumed its own form of government, with a House of Representatives and a Council of twelve; and he was also on the Committee of Safety and closely associated with the Portsmouth patriots. It was only another step onward when he was elected to the Second Continental Congress in Philadelphia.

William Whipple arrived in Philadelphia to attend Congress on February 29, 1776. In these first months, when many of the delegates were still hoping for better treatment after their pleas to George III, Whipple was already sure that only an American success in the field could achieve freedom. He did not think victory could come from diplomatic talk abroad. He wanted "spirited measures" against the Loyalists and speculators. He urged heavy taxation in order to spread the burden of war evenly on all the people. While serving on committees, Whipple observed with disgust a lack of national spirit in some places. The greed and selfishness of political life — which shows up in the inefficient public service which we see from time to time in any country — was not wholly absent then, and Whipple, coming in contact with it during his official work, expressed his feelings strongly in his letters. He was a firm and fearless congressman. Re-elected three times, Whipple remained in Congress until 1779, except for periods when he was on active military service.

Captain Whipple, erstwhile commander of a sailing ship, now became a soldier and, as General Whipple, was one of the few

Signers who saw active service in the Revolution. As brigadier general commanding the first of New Hampshire's two brigades of militia, he took part in the expedition against the British General Burgoyne, which resulted in a decisive defeat for the British and the great American victory which really made possible the French alliance. Burgoyne, who had at first viewed the men of New Hampshire and Green Mountains with contempt, was obliged to suffer a humiliating surrender after the battles of Stillwater and Saratoga, in which the New Hampshire troops won a large share of the honor due to the American army.

During the last years of the war, Whipple was active in the affairs of his state and he, like several other Signers, became an Associate Justice of the Superior Court, without any legal training.

When he was about fifty-two he began to be afflicted with a heart condition which was not understood by medical men in those days. He continued to ride horseback on his circuits for the court, though he often fainted and fell from his horse. He died while on circuit on November 10, 1785, at the age of fifty-five.

Matthew Thornton

Matthew Thornton

c. 1714 — June 24, 1803

THE THORNTONS were of English origin, though Matthew Thornton was one of the three Signers who were born in Ireland. Over the years, religious persecution had driven the Presbyterian Thorntons from one country to another. They emigrated first from England to Scotland; then, in order to escape the persecutions in Scotland under Charles I, they crossed to Ireland. Their descendants moved on to America, where they formed part of the group of immigrants known as the Scotch-Irish. This emigration began in 1717. On August 4, 1718, five small ships arrived in Boston with about one hundred twenty families, among whom was the family of James Thornton, including his small son, Matthew.

In the autumn, the Thorntons moved on again, presumably because they had nowhere to live, to Falmouth, Maine (now Portland). Here they spent an uncomfortable first winter still aboard the ship that had brought them. From the ship they moved at last to Worcester, Massachusetts, where Matthew went to school. Then, deciding to make medicine and surgery his profession, he studied under a locally eminent physician, Thomas Green of Leicester, a neighboring town.

Puritan religious intolerance drove the Presbyterian Thorntons out of Worcester, too. About a century later, the American humorist, Artemus Ward, described the Puritans as "that band of religious patriots who fled from the land of persecution to the land of freedom where they could not only enjoy their own religion but prevent every other man from enjoying his." And that was exactly the experience the Thornton family had.

Twelve years after arriving in this country, James Thornton had been able to buy a parcel of land in Worcester, but he felt so much discrimination that after ten years he sold it and moved on north with most of the Scotch-Irish families, to Pelham. His medical son, Dr. Matthew Thornton, however, decided to go still farther north and settle in the older and more thriving settlement of Londonderry, New Hampshire, where he soon established a large and profitable practice.

In 1745, during King George's War, a phase of the French and Indian War, Dr. Thornton accompanied the military expedition against the French Fort Louisburg, on Cape Breton Island. Resuming practice upon his return, he continued to be so successful that he was able to acquire a considerable estate. He bought his father's one hundred seventy acres at Pelham and three years later bought one hundred fifty acres more. Even after all this, he still continued to put money in land.

Dr. Thornton's first appearance in public affairs came in 1758, when he represented the town of Londonderry in the Provincial Legislature, serving for four years. Then he held many important offices. He was commissioned by the royal government as colonel of the Londonderry regiment of militia; became a selectman of the town, then moderator of its town meetings as the troubles with England grew worse through the early 1770's; and finally served as President of the Provincial Congress several times. In an address in 1760 before the royal governor, he expressed his desire for "fresh zeal for His Majesty's service." But within a few years he had to change his mind. In 1775, he denounced "the unconstitutional and tyrannical acts of the British Parliament." He had been revolted by the Stamp Act and joined the patriot agitators in the hue and cry which followed its enactment into law. After this, he found himself at the front of the local revolutionary party. As chairman of the local Committee of Safety and president of the Fourth Provincial Congress, Thornton inspired the people's confidence in him by his public addresses.

Many arduous duties were heaped upon him. He wrote his Committee of Safety in October, 1775, that he had not been able to take his clothes off for ten nights! After Christmas, he was appointed on the committee to draw up a plan for the government of the colony during its contest with Great Britain. The committee's report, made on January 5, 1776, was adopted the very same day. This swift action was taken without recurrence to the people's vote, so that it was "a stretch of power." But the people were satisfied, and the committee's report became a kind of constitution for New Hampshire until 1783. It was the first written constitution adopted by any of the American states.

Rather late in life, at the age of forty-eight, Thornton married Hannah Jack, of Chester, New Hampshire, who was only eighteen, and reported to be a great beauty. She, too, was of Scottish ancestry.

On the same day that New Hampshire's constitution was adopted, Dr. Thornton was elected Speaker of the House of Representatives. Within a week, he was also chosen Associate Justice of the Superior Court. After the New Hampshire House of Representatives reassembled on September 12, 1776, Dr. Thornton was chosen as delegate to the Second Continental Congress in Philadelphia. The day after he arrived, Thornton presented his credentials to Congress and signed the Declaration on November 4. He was the last to sign that year, and was one of the Signers who had not been in Congress to hear Lee's June resolution, nor the early July debates on the Declaration.

Thornton served only part of a year in Congress. Though he was appointed as delegate for 1777, he was unable to serve; for soon after he arrived in Philadelphia, he was inoculated for smallpox, which left him with such weak eyes that he was unable to work for a while. Later, he devoted his time to the affairs of his new state.

During his last years, he wrote political essays for the newspapers. His wife died in 1786, and his son the next year. These griefs and his own infirmities caused him to retire from public life.

While visiting his daughter in Newburyport, Massachusetts, in 1803, he passed away at the age of eighty-nine.

Judge Thornton was over six feet tall and of dark complexion. His manners were plain and unassuming. He was a sociable and communicative man, with a tenacious memory and a good sense of humor. John Adams wrote in a letter: "We have from New Hampshire a Colonel Thornton, a physician by profession, a man of humor. He has a large budget of droll stories with which he entertains company perpetually."

IX

MARYLAND

Charles Carroll of Carrollton

Thos. Stone

Wm Paca

Samuel Chase

Charles Carroll
of Carrollton

Charles Carroll of Carrollton

September 19, 1737 — November 14, 1832

THERE WERE SO MANY Carrolls, and even Charles Carrolls, among his relations in Maryland that the Charles Carroll who signed the Declaration of Independence habitually called himself Charles Carroll of Carrollton. His grandfather, descended from an old and noble Irish family, came to Maryland in the autumn of 1688 as attorney-general of the province. The Carroll family came to Maryland because they were Catholics who had suffered through England's religious struggles since Henry VIII's time.

Lord Baltimore, a Catholic, had founded a colony in Maryland about 1634, as a haven, not only for his fellow-Catholics but also for members of other persecuted sects — Puritans (who were being persecuted in Virginia), Presbyterians, Anabaptists, and others. Protestants then were attracted to this lovely province, and more and more came to live there. But by the time the attorney-general's son, Charles Carroll of Annapolis, was a man, Maryland's Protestants had brought their fear and hatred of the politics of the Roman Catholic Church with them and had begun a discrimination that infuriated the second Carroll, father of the Signer.

Incredible and ridiculous as it seems to us, people who had left the old country to seek religious freedom for themselves denied it to others. By the 1700's, Catholics in Maryland could neither vote nor hold public office. Catholic lawyers were not permitted to practice. Catholics could not be teachers of young children.

The Carrolls had, however, one commodity that was a great help to them, and that was money. The first American Carroll, who had been given large tracts of land, had become a successful planter. He had also had a prosperous legal practice (before discrimination became serious), had kept a store in Annapolis, and had eventually left a fortune to his son. This second Carroll was just as ambitious, but as a Catholic he was now not allowed to practice law. Instead, since he was very rich, he put his money to work for him by loaning it to reliable people on sound security and at good interest. By the time he married his beautiful cousin Elizabeth Brooke, they were the wealthiest people in Maryland, perhaps in all the colonies.

The third Charles Carroll, their only child, inherited all this wealth and used it wisely. The boy grew up in what must have been an ideal early-American environment, at the country estate of his father and grandfather, and at the town house in Annapolis. His mother taught him until he was about nine. Then he was sent to Bohemia Manor Academy, a Catholic school conducted — sub rosa — by the Society of Jesus. His cousin, "Jacky" Carroll, was there with him. But not for long. The two were soon sent to the Collège de St. Omer in French Flanders where young Charles's father had studied. The parents accepted the fact that, in order to give their son the best education, they would have to send him three thousand miles away, and that they would be separated for about fifteen years. His father asked him to write home "at least twice a year."

Charles was a good student, preferring Latin and "the maps" to "little figures" or arithmetic. He also studied dancing and, probably, fencing. After five and a half years, he studied at a Jesuit College in Rheims for a year, and then went to Paris to the Collège de Louis-le-Grand. By this time he and his cousin were no longer together, as Jacky had decided to become a priest. After about eight years' separation, Charles's father came to France and saw his son as a young adult. From Paris, Charles went to Bourges to study law, and after that he lived in London for about six years, studying law in the Temple. All this without any idea of ever practicing law. Born with a "silver spoon in his mouth," Charles Carroll never needed funds.

After sixteen years' education, he came home to Maryland in February, 1765, the Stamp Act year. His mother had said goodbye to a ten- or eleven-year-old boy. She saw him next as a man of twenty-seven or twenty-eight. His father presented his son with a ten-thousand-acre piece of land in Frederick County, at the mouth of the Monocacy river, which became the estate known as Carrollton Manor.

As a boy, Charles Carroll of Carrollton had been thin and delicate. Now a man, he was still thin, frail-looking, and small of stature, and he was always subject to chills and fevers. But he had a good figure, grace of movement, and polished, attractive manners. He made good company in the taverns, where the townsmen collected to exchange opinions on the political problems of the time. He made such good company, indeed, that he was soon invited to join the Hominy Club, to which his good friends, Samuel Chase and William Paca, and the young portrait painter Charles Wilson Peale already belonged.

Young Carroll, a new land-owner, was soon a staunch Marylander. Incensed by the Stamp Act, he described American feelings about it in a letter to a friend in London and, as early as 1767, was prophesying armed rebellion in other letters to friends across the sea.

It must have been a lovely day in Annapolis on June 5, 1768, when thirty-one-year-old Charles Carroll married his cousin Mary Darnall. She loved social affairs, and the young couple entertained constantly in their beautiful, hospitable home.

He took on the management of the family's business affairs, including the oversight and care of the vast plantations, the slaves, the sale of the tobacco they grew, the many accounts of loans and mortgages. For Carroll of Carrollton was as much of a money-maker as his father and grandfather before him.

Then came the troubled years of the 1770's. In the first November of the decade that saw the birth of a new nation, Maryland's royal governor raised the salaries for government officials. This meant more taxation of Americans without giving the taxpayers, from whom the money came, any voice in the matter.

A Tory lawyer named Daniel Dulany, a contentious man who had no sympathy at all for the patriots' feelings, began writing arguments supporting the royal governor's views on British taxation in the form of dialogues and printing them in the *Maryland Gazette*. In these dialogues, he called the first speaker, the man who posed the questions, "First Citizen." The man who answered, expressing Dulany's own views, was "Second Citizen." A month passed and still no one in the Patriot party had answered. Then articles began to appear over the signature "First Citizen," one of the names Dulany himself had used. In these, the new and different "First Citizen" took the patriots' view, attacking Dulany's statements. These articles continued in the form of letters between "First Citizen," on one side, and Dulany, who now signed himself "Antilon."

Readers of the *Gazette* were highly entertained by this battle in print, and the town buzzed with guesses as to the identity of "First Citizen." But in the clubs and taverns where he was so well known, his fellow members soon knew their man. The resulting publicity caused Charles Carroll of Carrollton to be placed on one important public committee after another.

He was now in public life: a member of the Annapolis Committee of Correspondence; of the first Maryland Convention; of the Provincial Committee of Correspondence; and the Committee of Safety. He was also teaching the province of Maryland that a Catholic could have some good ideas and might be of use to his country. He had become, in truth, the First Citizen of his region.

His father had never been able to hide the chip he carried upon his shoulder. He resented the prejudice against Catholics. He had a temper and it was galling to him that, as a Catholic, he could not vote, especially as he had always wanted to be in public life himself. His son, on the other hand, was able to appear to overlook all this. He was not looking for offense, neither was he ambitious for public office. He had an easy, delightful manner, charmed others by being a good listener, and delivered himself of positive ideas that were helpful.

By the middle of 1773, the Patriot party won a landslide victory in the local election. Carroll was publicly thanked by an open letter printed in the *Gazette*, for his "manly and spirited opposition to the arbitrary attempt of government to establish the fees of office by proclamation."

The first time Carroll was asked to be a delegate to the First Continental Congress, he refused. Though Marylanders did not admire Carroll's religion any more than they ever had, they now admired the man himself and felt that no one else could speak more ably and creditably for Maryland than he. But Carroll knew that, even if Marylanders trusted him to keep his religion in proper relation to other matters, delegates from other provinces would not feel that way. He would still have to convince them that a man's religion was his own affair. But he was too valuable a man to be left behind, and when Maryland's first congressmen set out for Philadelphia, Carroll of Carrollton went along as an unofficial member of the Maryland delegation.

The delegates told him everything that went on, and he gave them advice. He did not seem to mind this peculiar position; he was glad to serve his province even if others got the credit. But early in 1776, Congress was faced with a problem to which Maryland's "First Citizen" seemed to be the perfect answer. Hoping for an alliance with Canada, they sent a diplomatic mission consisting of Benjamin Franklin, Samuel Chase, and Charles Carroll of Carrollton. Carroll, they felt, was the ideal man to talk to the Catholic French Canadians for, of course, Carroll could speak French perfectly. He was asked to persuade his cousin, now a Jesuit priest, to accompany the mission.

This was the first American diplomatic mission to another country, and it failed. Canada preferred to remain with Mother England. But Carroll inspected forts along the way, thereby gaining military intelligence that was later valuable to Congress and to General Washington.

Returning to Philadelphia in June, Carroll was cheered to learn that Richard Henry Lee of Virginia had placed his resolution for independence before Congress. Later that month he was at the provincial convention, meeting in Annapolis, in which the important business was Maryland's decision whether to authorize her delegates in Philadelphia to vote for independence along with the other colonies. Carroll of Carrollton was the man principally instrumental in obtaining Maryland's vote for liberty.

On July Fourth, Maryland chose new delegates to Congress, and Carroll was again elected. This time he agreed to accept. Feeling that public service was a duty, and realizing that America must seek French aid, he knew he could be of special help. With the Maryland Convention still in session, it was July 18 before Carroll took his seat in Congress. He missed the early July excitement and discussions but, after all, he had wanted independence all along. He was on hand to sign the Declaration.

Charles Carroll was now a very busy man. His father was in his seventies and the care of the vast Carroll fortune and plantations fell upon the son. This in itself was a full-time job. But Carroll of Carrollton was also a leading figure in the Maryland Assembly; he was on the Board of War; he helped to draw up the Maryland Constitution; he was elected to Maryland's first Senate. But he opposed the confiscation of Tory property, deeming such action as tyrannical as the British measures Americans were fighting to be rid of.

Carroll was a stout supporter of General Washington when armchair critics raised their complaints. He was one of the committee that went to Valley Forge to investigate the sorry situation there.

Carroll was not sent on the mission to France, where he would have been of special value. Instead, the troublemaker, Arthur Lee, wanted to go, worked hard to secure the appointment, and became a member along with Dr. Franklin and Silas Deane. The French alliance was successfully consummated, without Carroll's help, in February, 1778. Carroll had already rendered very special service in Congress, even though it was not the service he had had in mind when he accepted. But when, that winter, he was asked to be President of Congress, he declined.

After the war, he represented his state in the first Federal Congress in 1789, and remained until he resigned in 1792. Sometimes he declined offers because of his health. He was always careful of his physical condition. Perhaps he had had this dinned into him when he was a puny child. He ended his political career in 1800 when he left the Maryland Senate to devote his time to the development of his estate, which had grown to gigantic proportions. He now owned between seventy thousand and eighty thousand acres of land in Maryland, Pennsylvania, and New York.

The years rolled on. One by one the Signers were dropping off. Carroll's father died; his wife died; and his son, Charles Carroll IV passed away. There was another war with England — the War of 1812 — to which Carroll was opposed, though there was nothing he could do about that. The whole country was growing and changing, and Carroll lived to see many of the changes. He was a member of the Potomac Company, which contemplated a water route to Ohio and the west; he was a member, too, of its successor, the Chesapeake and Ohio Canal Company, organized in 1823. He was on the first board of directors of the Baltimore and Ohio Railroad and laid its cornerstone amid respectful applause, on July 4, 1828, at the age of ninety-one. He saw three of the men he had known long ago in the Independence Congress become Presidents of the new nation — George Washington, John Adams, Thomas Jefferson. He went on living after they had all passed away. The time came when Carroll of Carrollton, who had always been the puny child, the small, frail man, became the sole surviving Signer!

As such, he became one of the sights to see. People made pilgrimages to Bunker Hill outside Boston, to Independence Hall in Philadelphia, and those who could went on to see the last Signer in Baltimore, just as they visited Fort McHenry. Here was a man in the flesh, who had become a national legend.

In his latter years, Carroll spent the winter months with his elder daughter Mary, who had married Richard Caton. Carroll had built a house in Baltimore for them when they were married.

Josiah Quincy, relative to John Adams, recorded visits he made in 1826: "I paid two visits to Charles Carroll (the signer of the Declaration of Independence), and dined with him . . . at Mr. Caton's, where the service, though the most elegant I had ever seen, in no wise eclipsed the conversation. . . . Old Mr. Carroll, courtly in manners and bright in mind, was the life of the party. He was then in his ninetieth year, but carried himself as if thirty years younger than his contemporary, John Adams. I have never seen an old man so absolutely unconscious of his age." When Mr. Quincy left the drawing-room, which was on the second floor, the old man jumped up and ran downstairs to open the front door. "Aghast at this unexpected proceeding," wrote Mr. Quincy, "I began to murmur my regrets and mortification in causing him the exertion."

" 'Exertion!' exclaimed Mr. Carroll, 'Why, what do you take me for? I have ridden sixteen miles on horseback this morning and am good for as much more this afternoon.' "

On into his nineties, Carroll of Carrollton took his daily constitutional on horseback. He thought it was good for him, and it probably was.

He could not be idle. He set regular hours for his time, mapping out courses of reading on which he took notes. He taught French to his great-grandchildren. He still kept the "plantation books," which included a record of all the slaves on his large estates. He took care of his own charities, and of course, because he was the wealthiest man in the country, his mail was flooded with begging letters. Even so, there is no record of his having given the vast sums to the Revolutionary War program that Robert Morris did. And here it might be mentioned that his father, Charles Carroll of Alexandria, had had the reputation of being very close with his money, never mixing business with charity. But then, in his day, when Catholics were so restricted in Maryland, he realized that the only way he could overcome religious prejudice in any degree was to possess himself of great wealth. And perhaps this was just what enabled his son, equipped by that wealth and with an excellent education, to have leisure for public affairs, and to accomplish what he did.

In the Spring of 1832, one of his callers was amazed to find the ninety-four-year-old Mr. Carroll still riding horseback. They rode around Baltimore together. But the old man had aged greatly in the last two years. By the time of his ninety-fifth birthday, in September, he was really ill — just too weak and old to go on living. He weighed under a hundred pounds. But even yet he did not want to stay in bed, reclining instead on an easy-chair or upon a couch.

Two months later, he passed away during the night.

After November 14, 1832, none of the Signers of the Declaration of Independence was left. Now they all belonged to history.

Thomas Stone

Thos. Stone

1743 — October 5, 1787

THOMAS STONE'S GREAT-GREAT-GRANDFATHER, William Stone, who came to America from Northamptonshire, England, landed in

Maryland in 1628, only a few years after the Mayflower adventurers reached Plymouth in 1620. He became Maryland's third "Proprietary Governor," that is, the governor representing Lord Baltimore, the proprietor who actually owned the colony, which had been given to him by the king.

His descendant, Thomas, the Signer, was born at Poynton Manor, Charles County, Maryland, in 1743, the eldest son of David and Elizabeth Jennifer Stone. He was taught by a Scottish school-master before he went to Annapolis to study law in the office of Thomas Johnson. Admitted to the bar in 1764, he began to practice in Frederick, Maryland.

Four years later he married Margaret Brown, who brought him a fine dowry of £1000, an enormous sum in those days and more than many newlyweds have today. The young pair bought land in Charles County near Port Tobacco and built a beautiful house, a stately dwelling that today is still considered one of the finest examples of colonial architecture in Maryland. They were settled and living in it about 1771.

When trouble with England came, Stone's sympathies were with the colonists, though he favored a mild course. Elected to Congress, he took his seat in mid-May of 1775. Thomas Stone seldom spoke in Congress, and as few of his letters remain, he is the least known nowadays of the Maryland Signers. His most important work in Congress was his service on the committee that later framed the Articles of Confederation. He voted for Independence and signed the Declaration when he was only thirty-three. He hated the thought of war, however, and was hoping, as late as September, 1776, that the Americans could still treat with Admiral Lord Howe for peace. But it was too late then to stop the war that had already begun a year and a half earlier at Lexington and Concord.

In 1783, Stone was again elected to Congress and, toward the end of this season, served as chairman, but he declined re-election thereafter and returned to his law practice. Later, when elected to the Constitutional Convention in Philadelphia, he declined because his wife was ill and he would not leave her. When she died in June, 1787, Stone was overwhelmed with grief.

He gave up his work and decided to take a trip to England, but he never got there. He was waiting in Alexandria for a ship when he died, at the age of forty-four, four months after he had lost his wife.

William Paca

Wm Paca

October 31, 1740 — October 13, 1799

LITTLE IS KNOWN of the forebears of Signer William Paca, though the name appears in America as early as the latter 1600's and may perhaps be Italian. The family were already prosperous planters when William was born to John and Elizabeth Smith Paca on their plantation near Abingdon, Harford County, Maryland. He was given sound early schooling, probably by tutors, including a good grounding in the classical languages, before he was sent to the College of Philadelphia at the age of fifteen. By the time he was nineteen, he had received an M.A. degree and went to Annapolis to study law in the office of Stephen Bordley.

Annapolis was Maryland's chief city in those days, fashionable and entertaining. Here Paca met two other future Signers, then also apprentices in the law. Samuel Chase, a year younger than he, was reading law in the office of Hammond and Hall; and Thomas Stone, three years younger, came to Annapolis to read law in the office of Thomas Johnson. All three of these young lawyers were to be chosen as Maryland's delegates to the Congress at Philadelphia and would sign the Declaration of Independence.

Before seeking admission to the bar, William Paca went to London to complete his legal training at the Inner Temple. Then, after some foreign travel, he came home and married Mary Chew, daughter of wealthy Samuel Chew of Annapolis.

In the next few years, he earned a reputation as a lawyer and, five years after he was married, entered public life as a member of the Provincial Legislature.

With Samuel Chase, Paca held the view that the royal governor's proclamation regulating the fees of civil officers should be recalled. In this, they thought, the king's representative was going too far. Proclamations such as this were becoming more frequent and were antagonizing the freedom-loving colonists. When a poll tax was arbitrarily to be collected from all Marylanders for the support of the clergy of the Church of England only, William Paca led the opposition. After all, the very first people to come to America left England to get away from that kind of interference in their personal affairs. And it was obviously wrong to tax all voters for the benefit of one religious denomination only.

It was during this controversy that Paca, Chase, and Thomas Johnson wrote an article in reply to one signed by the Tories Daniel Dulany and James Holliday defending the tax. This was reprinted in London, and of course brought the names of Paca and the other two protesting Whigs into prominence. Paca became the local leader of the patriot cause, as the Revolution came to a boil in the 1770's.

While serving on the Maryland Committee of Correspondence, he was elected to the First Continental Congress in June, 1774. After his sojourn in Philadelphia, he was back in Annapolis in the autumn, serving as one of the city's representatives in the Provincial Congress. Also elected to the Second Continental Congress, he remained a delegate until 1779.

In Congress, William Paca was numbered among the quiet ones. Dr. Benjamin Rush called him "a good tempered worthy man, with a sound understanding which he was too indolent to exercise, and hence his reputation in public life was less than his talents." But Rush added, "He was beloved and respected by all who knew him, and considered at all times as a sincere patriot and honest man."

After the war started, William Paca, as a member of the Maryland Council of Safety, spent several thousand dollars of his own money outfitting troops. He was also a member of the convention that framed a constitution for his new state and was elected one of the first of Maryland's state senators when the new state government was established.

In 1777 he married again, his first wife having died in 1774. But his second wife, Anne Harrison of Philadelphia, was to live only three years longer. She saw her husband appointed Chief Justice of the Court of Appeals in Admiralty and Prize Cases; but she did not live to see him elected Maryland's third governor. Unanimously re-elected twice, he finished his last term in 1785. As governor, he paid much attention to the welfare of soldiers returning from the war.

In 1789, George Washington appointed Paca Federal District Judge, but this judicial service was short, for the next year, at the age of fifty, he died at "Wye Hall," his country estate in Talbot County.

Samuel Chase

Samuel Chase

April 17, 1741 — June 19, 1811

THE REVEREND THOMAS CHASE, father of Samuel, the Signer, came to America from England. His wife did not live long after the birth of their son in Somerset County, Maryland, and he moved to Baltimore to become the rector of St. Paul's Church. A classical scholar himself, he took charge of his son's education until the boy, at eighteen, went to Annapolis to study law. Two years later, Samuel Chase was admitted to practice.

He was twenty-one when he married Anne Baldwin of Annapolis, and twenty-three when, elected to the Maryland Assembly, he began his public career of twenty years' service to Maryland.

From the beginning, Samuel Chase was opposed to the irritating measures of the royal governor and, as the turbulent 1760's wore on, this young patriot was always an active leader in insurrection. After he had taken part in a demonstration against the Stamp Act, the mayor and aldermen of Annapolis denounced him as a "busy, restless incendiary, a ringleader of mobs" and "an inflaming son of discord." Chase replied that his critics were "despicable tools of power," and pointed out that what they called "mobs" were actually "men of reputation and merit."

By the time he was thirty-three, each colony had organized its Committee of Correspondence. Samuel Chase was on the Maryland committee and was sent as a delegate to the First Continental Congress. Throughout the next year or so, the busy lawyer was also serving on the Council of Safety, was a member of the Maryland Convention, and attended the Second Continental Congress in Philadelphia, where he urged a total embargo on trade with Great Britain.

In the cold February of 1776, he was appointed, with Benjamin Franklin and Charles Carroll, to go to Canada to ask for Canadian support for the colonies. When the Canadians declined, Chase returned to carry on in Maryland a vigorous agitation that was badly needed, because Maryland, like other middle colonies, was undecided. As a result of Chase's campaign, Maryland rescinded previous instructions to the delegates and at last advised them to vote for independence. Vastly relieved, though still anxious, Samuel Chase rode one hundred fifty miles in two days to get to Philadelphia in time for the final vote.

On the morning of July 1, thanks to Chase's efforts, the unanimous vote of Maryland's Convention was read before Congress. Busy as a hive of bees, Congress prepared for the final vote to make the United States of America one nation of its own.

A few days later, in a letter to John Adams, Samuel Chase wrote, "Oppression, Inhumanity and Perfidy have compelled Us to it," and asked: "How shall I transmit to posterity that I gave my consent?"

His chance came on August 2 when the Declaration had been engrossed and was ready for signatures. Seeing how strongly he felt, he must have been a happy man when he wrote down his name for posterity. He was then thirty-five and he had been working for this moment for over ten years.

Like Washington, Chase was a very tall man, over six feet tall and large in proportion. His appearance was striking, and his broad face was ruddy — so much so that some of his colleagues in the Maryland bar called him "Bacon face." We can just imagine how red he became when he was condemning British oppression.

This ardent patriot was reappointed to the Congress for two more years. He served on numerous committees, perhaps the most important of these being the one consisting of himself, Richard Henry Lee, and Gouverneur Morris, to prepare a paper discrediting British peace proposals in 1778. This document is supposed to have been largely Chase's work.

When intrigues against General Washington flared up in Congress, Samuel Chase strongly and steadfastly opposed them, and Washington always remembered this.

Maryland sent Chase to England in 1783 to recover, from two fugitive Loyalists, bank stock that had belonged to the state when it was a Crown colony. Chase started suit in the British Court of Chancery, which has always had a reputation for prolonged delays. The case dragged on and on for years, but it was ultimately settled in Maryland's favor — not by Chase himself but by William Pinckney, whom Chase had encouraged to study law and taken into his own office as a student. While he was in London, Chase met the English statesmen William Pitt, Charles Fox, and Edmund Burke, Whigs who had done their best for America before the Revolution.

Toward the end of the war, his friends urged him to move to Baltimore, where he eventually became Chief Judge of the Criminal Court and later Chief Judge of the General Court. In 1795, President George Washington received a letter from his friend Joseph McHenry, suggesting Chase for Federal office. Washington intended to appoint him attorney general, but in January, 1796, nominated him instead to the United States Supreme Court. Chase's judicial opinions while on the Supreme Court bench showed his intellectual caliber, and many of them are cited to this day. His performance on the bench was notable.

It is the more astonishing, then, to learn that his political opponents, led by John Randolph of Virginia, managed to secure Chase's impeachment. But Chase was acquitted, resumed his seat, and remained until his death. It is remarkable that Thomas Jefferson in part instigated the charge against his fellow Signer.

Samuel Chase's forceful manner of speaking earned him the title of the "Demosthenes of Maryland." Of the four Maryland Signers, it was he who was most instrumental in bringing about the unanimity of Maryland's vote on independence in those first July days of 1776. Dr. Rush noted that Samuel Chase "rendered great services to his country by awakening and directing the public spirit of his native state in the first years of the Revolution."

As Samuel Chase grew older and as his thick hair became white, one man thought he was the living image of Dr. Samuel Johnson, "in person, in manners, in unwieldy strength, in severity of reproof, in real tenderness of heart, and above all in intellect."

The years passed on, and the old judge began to suffer from gout. Ill health prevented him from serving on the bench during the 1806 term, and no court was held at all the year of his death, 1811, when he was seventy.

X

DELAWARE

Cæsar Rodney

Tho M:Kean

Geo Read

Caesar Rodney

Caesar Rodney [signature]

October 7, 1728 — June 26, 1784

WILLIAM RODNEY, GRANDFATHER OF THE SIGNER, came to America about 1681 and settled in Kent County on the beautiful Delaware River. Here, during his lifetime, he built up a considerable estate, which was inherited by his son Caesar.

Caesar Rodney married a daughter of the Reverend Thomas Crawford, who had been the first missionary sent to Dover, Delaware, by the Society for the Propagation of the Gospel in Foreign Parts. This pair had eight children. The eldest was the second Caesar Rodney, who was to play a dramatic part in his colony's vote for independence.

Signer Rodney was born on his father's farm near Dover, Delaware. Since theirs was a cultivated home, his parents no doubt taught him his first lessons and perhaps sent him to the local parson's school, but there is no record of his having done any formal advanced study. Since his father died when the boy was only seventeen, Caesar had to be placed under the guardianship of Nicholas Ridgely, the clerk of the peace of Kent County. As the eldest child, he is supposed to have remained at home, helping his mother manage the plantation.

The young man's guardian seems to have led him into public life, which began with his being commissioned high sheriff of Kent County in 1755 when he was only twenty-two. During the next few years, he served his county as register of wills, recorder of deeds, clerk of the orphan's court, clerk of the peace, and justice of the peace. He was thirty when he was elected for the first time as delegate from Kent County to the colonial legislature at New Castle, and he served continuously — with the exception of the assembly of 1771 — for fifteen years. During four of those years he was speaker, and he held that post until the end of colonial government under the Crown in 1776.

Rodney was chosen representative of Kent County to the Stamp Act Congress, together with Thomas McKean, another of Delaware's Signers. George Read, Delaware's third Signer, was designated, along with Rodney and McKean, to form a Committee of Correspondence and they were instructed to prepare an address to the king.

In the summer of 1774, Caesar Rodney organized a meeting to protest British aggression and, at this time, the three men were chosen as Delaware's delegates to the First Continental Congress in Philadelphia.

On September 5, the First Congress in America assembled in Philadelphia. After Caesar Rodney and John Adams of Massachusetts were introduced to each other, Adams described Rodney in his diary as the "oddest looking man in the world; he is tall, thin and slender as a reed, pale; his face is not bigger than a large apple, yet there is sense and fire, spirit, wit, and humor in his countenance."

One can imagine with what eagerness these men, all of whom were regarded as the most influential personalities in their own colonies, anticipated meeting each other: to see what manner of men they were; to hear how they talked; to listen to their views on the most critical issues touching their country and their very lives.

During those 1770's, when the colonies' political pot was coming to a boil, there was a steady crescendo of excitement and activity. It was in 1774 that Caesar Rodney became colonel of the "Upper" regiment of the Kent County militia, and in September of 1775 he was made brigadier-general of that militia and of the western battalion of Sussex County. He was returned to the Second Congress, along with McKean and Read. These were the three Delaware representatives whose signatures are preserved for all time on the famous document of 1776.

In June of 1776, however, Rodney was presiding over the colonial assembly in New Castle, which gave new instructions to the three Delaware congressmen, authorizing them to cooperate with the other colonies. Often, as in this case, active patriots found they really ought to be in two places at the same time. Rodney was one of these, only this time his predicament was more serious than usual. On the twenty-second, he hurried to Sussex County on receiving news of a threatened Loyalist uprising. The Tories there were holding up Delaware's consent for independence. Upon his return home, he received an "express" (a message sent "expressly" by a messenger on horseback) from McKean, urging him to hasten to Philadelphia at once, as his vote was required on Richard Henry Lee's resolution for independence. McKean was voting for it. Read, still influenced by Tory sentiment and hoping for reconciliation, was *not* voting for it. Therefore the third Delaware vote was necessary to overcome the tie, and make it possible for Delaware to vote independence.

July 2 dawned cloudy and dark after a night of rain. It is thought that Rodney received McKean's message sometime in the night and started off at once. Heavy rain developed before ten in the morning, but Rodney pushed on traveling the eighty miles on horseback, and arrived in the afternoon, drenched and weary, but in time to cast his vote for independence. Rodney was present in Congress, then, while the Declaration was being discussed on the third and fourth of July, and he voted for its adoption in the afternoon of the Fourth.

Later in July, after all the excitement in Congress, Rodney was back in New Castle, presiding over the last session of the colonial assembly, which he himself had called for the purpose of fixing a date for Delaware's constitutional convention and arranging for the election of delegates. Thus engaged, he was unable to give time to his own political endeavors and was defeated as a delegate to the new convention, and also to the first state legislature.

Outwardly undisturbed by this show of ingratitude, Caesar Rodney's patriotic ardor turned again to military affairs. In November of 1776, he was made chairman of the Kent County branch of the Council of Safety. The next month, when Washington was retreating across New Jersey before turning suddenly to capture the Hessians at Trenton, and when Congress had fled to Baltimore, Rodney was busily recruiting Kent County militia and sending soldiers on to aid Washington. He was placed in command of the post at Trenton after Washington's main army had gone into winter quarters at Morristown. The Signer was in command of the Delaware militia with the rank of brigadier general when the

British invaded the state in September, 1777. All this time he kept in close touch with General Washington. Only a few days later, Thomas McKean, acting governor of the state, commissioned Rodney as major general of the Delaware militia.

By this time, Caesar Rodney was known to be the best man to depend on when danger threatened. His political star rose once more, and in December, 1777, he was again elected to Congress. In the Spring, he was elected "President" of his state for a three-year term.

As wartime excecutive, Rodney furnished the state's quota of troops, making sure they were clothed and armed. He also raised money and supplied provisions to meet a series of distressing appeals from General Washington for aid to his hungry and poorly clad soldiers. Even in 1780, Washington was still writing Rodney: "The army is again reduced to an extremity of distress, for want of provision — we have *this* day but *one* day's supply (of flour) in camp."

While he was laboring at all his tasks, Rodney was far from well himself. He suffered recurrent attacks of asthma, and he had a cancerous growth on his face that had been sapping his strength since the 1760's. He had consulted physicians in Philadelphia and submitted to an operation in 1768. Had he gone to England for treatment as he had then been advised, he might have been helped. But having received temporary relief, and being caught up in the war, he had put it off, and by the time the Americans began to win, it was too late to make the journey.

When, in 1782, he was again chosen as a delegate to Congress, he declined. His health was deteriorating, and he was now having to hide his disfigured face behind a green silk veil. He sought medical and surgical aid in Philadelphia, but nothing could be done.

Caesar Rodney was still serving, however, as speaker in the upper house of his state's legislature when, at the age of sixty-five, he died in June, 1784. His grave remained unmarked for about a hundred years, when a small stone was placed over it. In 1888, the body was moved to Christ Episcopal Churchyard in Dover, and on July 4, 1923, an equestrian statue was unveiled in Rodney Square, Wilmington, by the citizens of his state.

Thomas McKean

March 19, 1734 — June 24, 1817

THOUGH HE REPRESENTED the province of Delaware in both Continental Congresses, Thomas McKean was later to become both chief justice and governor of his native state, Pennsylvania, and to command Pennsylvania troops.

He was descended from William McKean, of Argyllshire, Scotland, who moved a little to the westward when he went to Londonderry, Ireland, about 1674. The Signer's father, another William, was brought as a child farther west across the ocean and became a tavern keeper in Chester County, Pennsylvania. He married Letitia Finney of a prominent and wealthy Scotch-Irish family who had also settled in Pennsylvania. The second son of this pair was Thomas.

After his first lessons, learned as a child at home, Thomas and his older brother, Robert, were sent to the Reverend Francis Allison's Academy at New London, Pennsylvania, where Thomas remained for seven years. He must have known another future Signer, George Read, very well indeed, since they were both schoolboys at the academy at the same time. When he was through at the Allison school, Thomas McKean went to New Castle, Delaware, to study law under his cousin, David Finney.

His legal studies seem to have given McKean the idea that he would like to hold office. Apparently he had very little trouble getting started and, once he had his foot on the ladder, he rose rapidly. First he became a junior clerk in the office of the Prothonotary of New Castle County, Delaware. (In Delaware, Pennsylvania, and some other states, the register or chief clerk of a court is called the prothonotary, a late Latin word, first used by the Church to mean a chief notary, or clerk.) He was only eighteen when he was appointed deputy prothonotary and recorder for probate of wills in the county. Two years later he was admitted to the bar in the Lower Counties of Delaware, then became deputy attorney general and clerk of the Delaware Assembly. At twenty-four he was admitted to practice before the Supreme Court of Pennsylvania. In 1758, he went to London to round out his legal studies. After that, for ten years, he practiced law in the three provinces of Delaware, Pennsylvania, and New Jersey, and for a time was enrolled in "Richard William's company" of infantry, in Newcastle County.

His growing prominence, his success in the law, and his various public offices naturally roused jealousies. But McKean had no time for these petty feelings. He only studied harder.

In October of 1762, McKean was elected a member of the assembly from Newcastle County. The people liked him so well, they elected him every year for the next seventeen years, though during the last six years of that time he lived in Philadelphia. He kept his house in Newcastle probably because his business frequently called him back. He declined further re-election on October 1, 1779.

At the age of twenty-nine, he married Mary Borden, eldest child of Colonel Joseph Borden, of Bordentown, New Jersey. Thomas McKean's connection with this prominent and wealthy family at once broadened his political horizon and influence. After ten years of marriage, Mary McKean died, not long after the birth of her sixth child. A year and a half later, McKean married Sarah Armitage, of New Castle, and moved to Philadelphia.

Thomas McKean's second marriage was solemnized in September, 1774, and by that time the political troubles of the colonies had become so serious that there was much correspondence between local committees and also between influential local leaders. In Delaware, McKean led the movement for a colonial congress. When this met, it selected him as one of its delegates to attend the First Continental Congress in Philadelphia on the first Monday of September, 1774. Caesar Rodney and George Read were the other Delaware delegates, and these three again took their seats when the Second Continental Congress met in May, 1775. McKean served on over thirty committees, including the five standing committees. He was regarded as particularly useful on the Secret Committee.

Strongly in favor of Richard Henry Lee's resolution for independence, McKean was horrified to find, at the last moment, that his vote for it would mean nothing without Caesar Rodney, who was in New Castle investigating Tory activity there. George Read, the third Delaware delegate, opposed independence and meant to vote against the Declaration, thereby canceling McKean's vote. When the date was set for the final vote, McKean sent an express at his own expense, asking Rodney to return.

Though he was a resident of Delaware, McKean had also put his name down among the persons dwelling in the middle ward of Philadelphia who were "able and willing to bear arms." The moment the Independence vote was won, Colonel Thomas McKean rushed off to command a group of Pennsylvania "Associators," at Perth Amboy, New Jersey. For this reason he was not able to sign the Declaration when it was engrossed and ready for signatures in early August.

Long after the war, McKean wrote in a letter to John Adams: "After the 4th July I was not in Congress for several months, having marched with a regiment of associators as colonel, to support General Washington. . . . When the associators were discharged, I returned to Philadelphia, took my seat in Congress and signed my name to the Declaration on parchment," probably in January, 1777.

In the autumn of 1776, he helped to frame Delaware's first constitution. Well-known as a rebel, McKean failed re-election to Congress at this time because of Tory opposition, and worked in his state's assembly, instead. But his interests had been steadily turning to Philadelphia, where his home now was, and in 1777 he became Chief Justice of Pennsylvania, while remaining active in Delaware politics. He held offices in both states for six years. This was bound to create jealousies.

On Christmas, 1780, McKean wrote a letter to the Delaware legislature, saying that both his health and his fortune were impaired by his constant attention to public business and asking to be excused from attending Congress. But this modest request was refused. Against his will, he was kept on until the preliminary agreement of peace was signed in 1783.

McKean's political enemies had been jealously protesting his two positions, wanting him to relinquish either the Pennsylvania chief justiceship or the Delaware seat in Congress. But his friends in both states claimed him. He wrote to John Adams that he was "hunted like a fox by the enemy — compelled to remove my family five times in a few months, and at last fixed them in a little log-house on the banks of the Susquehanna . . . and they were soon obliged to move again on account of the incursions of the Indians."

After the war, McKean, as a Federalist, worked for the ratification of the Federal Constitution in the Pennsylvania convention of 1787. He thought this frame of government "the best the world has yet seen." As the years passed, he became much less "liberal" in his views, and his much more conservative decisions as Chief Justice, a position he held for twenty-two years, brought about some conflicts either with the assembly, or the council, or with the military authorities. Nevertheless, his decisions went to the heart of the matter and revealed his honesty and his high sense of justice. Even his enemies had to admit his honesty, ability, fairness and frankness.

In manner, Judge McKean was somewhat harsh and domineering, according to some observers, but he had many admiring friends. Among these was the Massachusetts Signer John Adams, who once described McKean as one of the three men in Congress who "appeared to me to see more clearly to the end of the business than any others of the whole body."

After 1792, McKean became a Jeffersonian. He could not accept Federalist foreign policy, for he was a friend to France and never got over his aversion for England. In 1800, he warmly embraced Thomas Jefferson's election to the presidency.

Throughout his life McKean held many high offices and he was also a recipient of many honorary degrees, diplomas, and other honors. As a member of the American Philosophical Society, he must have known Benjamin Franklin well before they met in Congress.

When he died in June of 1817 at a ripe old age, only a very few Signers were left. Though some of the Signers lost everything they had during the revolutionary struggle, some were imprisoned, and some left with broken health, Thomas McKean was fortunately still possessed of large tracts of Pennsylvania land.

George Read

Geo Read

September 18, 1733 — September 21, 1798

THE FATHER OF GEORGE READ was John, born in Dublin, Ireland, sixth in descent from Sir Thomas Read, of Berkshire. John Read came to America after the sudden death of the girl he loved; and amid new scenes and people, in the province of Maryland near the head of Chesapeake Bay, he found another girl, Mary Howell, daughter of a planter of Welsh descent. They were married and to them were born six sons, the first being George, the Signer.

Soon after George's birth on the family farm near North East, in Cecil County, Maryland, his parents moved to New Castle County, Delaware, and George grew up on a farm that overlooked the wide and pleasant meadows and slopes beside the beautiful Delaware River.

He was sent to school first in Chester, Pennsylvania, then to an academy run by the Reverend Francis Allison in New London. Here he came to know fellow students who would later be associates in political life. In fact, the Reverend Mr. Allison taught more than one boy who was to become a Signer. George left the academy in his fifteenth year to study law in the office of John Moland, a Philadelphia attorney.

When he was twenty, George Read was admitted to the Philadelphia bar, where he began his practice. Dissatisfied when his first year's earnings proved inadequate, he moved to New Castle, drawn back to the scenes of his childhood and his father's large plantation. Here he was soon being called the "honest lawyer," and regarded as possessing "profound legal learning, clear reasoning and calm deliberation."

Though George Read at first used to say that men of ambition should never marry, he did finally take a bride when he was about thirty. She was a widow, Mrs. Gertrude Ross Till, the sister of George Ross, the Pennsylvania Signer.

That same year, George Read was appointed attorney general

of Delaware's three Lower Counties. This was his first political appointment. He held it for almost twelve years, until he resigned on being elected to the First Continental Congress. He felt he could not serve in this body of American patriots while holding office under the king, and he preferred to serve the patriots.

When New Castle heard of Boston's hardships under the Boston Port Bill, the people appointed a committee, which naturally included George Read, to raise subscriptions for relief. Boston received nine hundred dollars from this one Delaware county. Samuel Adams himself wrote a letter of thanks to Read.

The next year, 1765, Read was protesting the Stamp Act, declaring that "if this or any similar law imposing an internal tax for revenue were enforced" the colonists would fear they were about to become "slaves of Great Britain." To avoid that, they would resist. He said they would try to be "as independent of Great Britain as possible." It is not surprising that, with this attitude, he was returned to the Second Continental Congress.

Even so, Read was only a moderate Whig, cautious at first about taking the bold step of separation from the mother country. Probably because of the preponderance of Tory sentiment throughout the middle colonies, especially in Sussex County, he thought Lee's resolution for independence premature and refused to vote for it. It was this negative stand by Read that led Thomas McKean to dispatch an express to Caesar Rodney, the absent Delaware member, urging him to come quickly because his vote was needed.

After the resolution had been adopted, however, George Read at once fell in step and "zealously upheld it," later supporting the new republic at the risk of his life. In that first year of American independence, he was president of the Delaware Constitutional Convention, and a member of the committee that drafted his state's first constitution. He was thought to have more influence in his state's politics than any other member of the new government.

When the British took Wilmington in September, 1777, and captured Delaware's Governor John McKinly, Read had to assume the governor's duties. Hurrying back from Philadelphia by a roundabout route, he drove with his family along the Jersey shore of the Delaware river to Salem, as secretly as possible. But as they rowed across the river, a British man-of-war, sighting them, sent an armed barge in pursuit. At this critical moment, Read's boat grounded offshore and they were caught. Read, however, explained politely that he was a country gentleman returning home — which was true! — and the British sailors helped carry his wife, mother, and children to dry ground, unaware that the country gentleman was also an important "rebel."

As the head of his colony, Read now labored to raise troops, clothing, and provisions for the Army, and to remove a widespread disaffection to the patriot cause among the people. Gradually, he succeeded in sparking a new spirit.

Early in 1778, Read observed to George Washington in a letter, "My situation is rather an unlucky one, in a government very deficient in its laws, and those greatly relaxed in their execution." He did his best, but the next year, ill health required his resignation from the assembly and he had to decline re-election to Congress.

Three years later he was well enough to accept when Congress elected him Judge in the Court of Appeals in admiralty cases. But he was discouraged when Congress, in 1786, ordered the salaries of judges to be stopped, while keeping the court for any cases that might arise.

Read was one of his state's first United States Senators. A loyal Federalist, he supported such measures as the national bank and the excise law. Twice senator, he resigned in 1793 to become Chief Justice of Delaware, a post he held until his death in 1798.

George Read was a tall man, slight, and with fine features. Punctilious in dress — as most lawyers are — he was agreeable and dignified in manner, and a strict moralist. During the many years of his public life, he maintained his family mansion with its extensive gardens and stables overlooking the broad views of the beautiful Delaware River valley at New Castle. He was not one of the wealthy Signers, nor, on the other hand, one of those who lost vast properties and possessions during the war.

XI

NORTH CAROLINA

John Penn

Joseph Hewes,

Wm Hooper

William Hooper

Wm Hooper

June 17, 1742 — October 14, 1790

WILLIAM HOOPER was born in Boston, Massachusetts, the eldest son of Reverend William Hooper and his wife, Mary Dennie Hooper. He attended the Boston Latin School and then entered Harvard as a sophomore, graduating at eighteen. The next year he began to study law under James Otis, one of the first and most ardent of the revolutionaries. In such close contact with his legal instructor's patriot ideas, William Hooper's thoughts were now being shaped. He soon became a stout patriot, though his family remained loyal to the king throughout the Revolution. After he was admitted to the bar, Hooper left home, perhaps to rid his parents of the embarrassment of having a patriot son, and went south to Wilmington, North Carolina. Here, in 1764, he set up his law practice.

Hooper was a handsome young man whose cultivation, brilliance, and agreeable manner soon won him acceptance in the Lower Cape Fear region, a congenial community of strongly patriotic views. Three years later he married Anne Clark, a daughter of Thomas Clark, one of the early settlers of Wilmington.

Hooper's troubles began when he was appointed deputy attorney general.

William Tryon, the royal Governor of North Carolina, was a brutal and domineering man whose administrative officials oppressed landholders with false and exorbitant fees. This led to the organization of a group called "Regulators," who rose in protest, violent and otherwise. Mobs of Regulators grew bold enough to enter courtrooms and manhandle attorneys, and William Hooper suffered some rough treatment at their hands, simply because of the official position he held. When Governor Tryon led a military expedition against the Regulators in 1771, Hooper was a mem-

ber of the expedition. He was, after all, one of Tryon's officials.
The Regulators were crushed, but their discontent and bitterness
remained. The heavy hand of the royal governor was felt out in
the backwoods, and the great frontiersman, Daniel Boone, in his
home on the Yadkin River, shared this discontent though he had
no part with the Regulators. He preferred to go farther away —
far beyond to the free and beautiful land of Kentucky where he
would meet nothing but wild animals and Indians.

Two years later Hooper was elected to the assembly, where he
remained until the royal government was overthrown, but by this
time he was taking the side of the North Carolina colonists. Josiah
Quincy, of Boston, who had come south to help set up patriot
Committees of Correspondence, was at a dinner party for twenty
people at Hooper's home in March of 1773. Afterward he noted in
his diary that Hooper was now "apparently in the Whig interest"
and had "taken their side in the House" — in spite of his Tory
ancestry.

The dark clouds were gathering fast. Hooper soon achieved a
place of leadership among the patriots and was placed on the
Committee of Correspondence. He presided over the meeting that
appointed the committee to call the first Provincial Congress and
was, of course, himself elected. By this congress, he was chosen
to attend the First Continental Congress in Philadelphia. Foreseeing
the trouble with England, he had already written in a letter of
April, 1774, that the colonies were "striding fast to independence,
and ere long will build an empire upon the ruins of Great
Britain."

In Congress, Hooper served on many committees and took part
in many debates. In fact, John Adams considered him an orator
comparable to Richard Henry Lee and Patrick Henry. Though
Hooper remained a member of Congress until 1777, he was absent
in July, when the vote on independence was taken, but he was
back again in time to sign the Declaration.

Resigning from Congress in the Spring of 1777, Hooper returned
to "Finian," his home on Masonboro Sound near Wilmington. He
had lost his private income through his public service and wished
to return to his remunerative law practice.

About five years later, when it looked as if Wilmington might be captured by the enemy, Hooper was forced to flee. He left his family at home, fearing the consequences to them if he were caught and they were with him. There followed a period of intense anxiety and distress, during which he became dangerously ill of malaria. In the end, his family was restored to him, but much of his property was destroyed, and his health was permanently damaged.

In 1782, William Hooper moved to Hillsboro and two years later was again a borough member in the House. He strongly advocated gentle treatment of the Loyalists, no doubt thinking of his Tory family in the North, or perhaps remembering that he, too, had once been an official of the king's government. Thomas Jefferson once remarked: "We had not a greater tory in Congress than Hooper." But this was not quite fair. Hooper was a patriotic American who made many sacrifices for his country. But he did fear the too rapid rise of the power of the masses in a democratic state.

Hooper was never a popular leader. He was too plainly the aristocrat, unable to approach the people easily, holding himself aloof from all except intimate friends who understood him. He was not a strong character and, under the blows of personal misfortune, became discouraged. No doubt recurring attacks of malaria caused his latter years of painful physical decline.

William Hooper died when he was only forty-eight years old, but he had lived to see the Constitution ratified.

Joseph Hewes

Joseph Hewes,

January 23, 1730 — November 10, 1779

THE NORTH CAROLINA SIGNER Joseph Hewes was born in Kingston, New Jersey, of Quaker parents, Aaron and Providence Worth Hewes. After his school years, he was apprenticed to a Philadelphia merchant, in whose office he spent several years learning business methods. At the age of thirty, he was able to establish a mercantile and shipping business of his own in Edenton, North Carolina.

With him, he took a nephew, Nathaniel Allen, Jr., son of his older sister, Sarah Hewes Allen. Nathaniel later became a partner and eventually inherited much of his uncle's fortune. For, though successful in business, Joseph Hewes had suffered a tragedy in his private life. He had become engaged to Miss Isabella Johnston, a sister to Samuel Johnston, president of the North Carolina Provincial Assembly and later governor, but a short time before they were to have been married, she died. Hewes never married.

A few years after he became a North Carolinian, he started his public career by winning election to the colonial assembly in 1766. He served until the royal government ended in 1775. A member of the Committee of Correspondence, he was appointed delegate to the newly organized Provincial Congress. The next step was his election to the First Continental Congress in 1774.

It is not hard to see why Hewes won political office so quickly and so easily. He had a pleasant disposition and an agreeable manner which made his fellow-townsmen in Edenton think him "one of the best and most agreeable men in the world." And, though he hesitated over voting for independence, he was an out-and-out patriot from the beginning. "I consider myself now head and ears in what the ministry call rebellion," he said in 1775. And he added that he felt no compunction "for the number of our enemies lately slain in the battle at Bunker Hill." He hoped to be there himself "next campaign." Not bad for a Quaker pacifist! No wonder Hewes was one of a small group specially denounced by the king's governor.

His service in the Continental Congress consisted mostly of committee work. He did not make speeches or take part in discussions, but his committee work was endless. One of his letters explained that he could not return to North Carolina to attend the Provincial Congress because he was attending sessions of the Continental Congress every day and working on committees every night. He often worked twelve hours a day without stopping, the result being that he began to feel the effects on his health.

Though he was well aware that a policy of non-importation of

British goods would be disastrous to his own business, Hewes, as a patriot, supported the policy. He also helped prepare the statement of colonial rights in the first session of Congress. He remained a year in Philadelphia and later returned for the Second Continental Congress. Hewes was one of many sincere patriots who did not, at first, want a break with England. He simply wanted more freedom in making the colonies' laws. This was the reason why he held back his support of Lee's resolution for independence, even against the views of his own Provincial Congress. What finally persuaded him was the great speech of John Adams in early July. Then, seeing that the popular opinion, as shown by documents received from all the thirteen colonies, was for independence, Hewes cried out:

"It is done! and I will abide by it."

John Adams was to say, years later, "The unanimity of the States finally depended upon the vote of Joseph Hewes, and was finally determined by him." This is his special distinction.

His experience in private life as a ship-owner naturally caused him to be placed at the head of the committee to fit armed vessels; to be chairman of the committee of marine; and to be the first executive head of the United States Navy. In North Carolina he had known John Paul Jones, and it was he who brought Jones into the Navy and found a ship for him.

Joseph Hewes and John Penn voted for North Carolina in favor of independence. In early August together with William Hooper, they signed the Declaration. When it was proclaimed in Halifax, North Carolina, on August 1, the crowd that had assembled to hear it broke out in a surge of rejoicing and prayer.

Hewes kept at the committee work as long as he could. He paid for gunpowder and other war supplies to be sent to the troops. For this he was afterwards reimbursed by Congress. Absent for a time, he returned when he was again elected and took his seat in 1779. But not for long. His health had been ruined by overwork and irregular bachelor hours. In November of that year, he suddenly collapsed and died soon afterward. He was only forty-nine.

Hewes was buried in the Christ Church cemetery in Philadelphia.

John Penn

John Penn

May 6, 1740 — September 14, 1788

JOHN PENN WAS BORN in Caroline County, Virginia, the only child of Moses and Catherine Taylor Penn. At the time of his father's death, he was eighteen and had had only a few years at a country school. But after inheriting his father's comfortable fortune, he was able to concentrate on study. He applied himself diligently in the excellent library of his relative, Edmund Pendleton, mastered the books on law he found there, and was licensed to practice at the age of twenty-one.

Two years later, he married Susannah Lyme and for about twelve years practiced law successfully in Virginia. Then, in 1774, he moved to Granville County, North Carolina, where many of his relatives had preceded him.

John Penn is said to have possessed an attractive personality and to have been a good speaker (though Benjamin Rush said later that Penn seldom addressed Congress). As he began to take part in North Carolina's public affairs, he soon made it clear that his personality attracted and influenced the local voters and that, as a political orator, he was able to win their agreement to his way of thinking. Penn quickly became a leader in his new community and, only a year after his arrival in the colony, was chosen to attend the Provincial Congress. Here he served on many committees and was noted for tireless attention to his work. In less than a month, the Provincial Congress elected him to the First Continental Congress in Philadelphia.

In those early days, when overland travel was by horse only, and nobody traveled very much, it was a wonderful new experience for those leaders in their own communities to come together, see each other, and exchange ideas. Listening to the discussions and reports of the representatives from the other colonies, John Penn soon abandoned any thought of their ever being able to work with the royal government. He had written a letter from Philadelphia as late as February, 1776, in which he said: "My first wish is that America may be free; and second that she may be restored to Great Britain in peace and harmony and upon Just terms." But now he knew that tyranny had gone too far and realized that a return to the Empire was beyond hope.

Like the rest of those men in the Revolutionary Congress, Penn served at great personal sacrifice. They all had to give up their own private businesses, had to let their properties and estates deteriorate while, away from home, they gave their time and their effort to establishing their country's liberty, and risked complete destruction of their homes by British troops.

In April of that significant year, both Penn and Hooper were in Halifax, North Carolina, attending the Provincial Congress and urging a vote for independence. Joseph Hewes, the other North Carolina congressman, was in Philadelphia, but he was still opposing the stand for independence. By July, Penn and Hooper had returned to Congress; and Hewes, at last persuaded by John Adams's great speech, joined the others in voting for independence. In early August, all three North Carolinians signed their names on America's birth certificate.

John Penn remained in Congress until 1777. Elected again the following year, he served until 1780.

While he was in Philadelphia, Henry Laurens, the President of Congress at that time, challenged Penn to a duel. It so happened that both men were boarding at the same boarding-house and thus took breakfast together on the morning of the day set for the duel. They decided to walk together to the meeting place and, starting off, found they had to cross a difficult spot in the street. It may have been snow drifts or rain puddles, or the dirt street may have been pock-marked with holes. At any rate, the younger man, Penn, assisted his opponent across the street.

After negotiating the crossing, Penn suggested they drop the idea of fighting a duel. It did seem rather foolish, since he had just been helping his antagonist. The older man agreed and, in better spirits, they turned back. The duel never took place.

No one knows what this quarrel was about. But Laurens, though he disapproved of duelling on principle, had a savage tongue, which several times led to challenges. He accepted the challenges but seems usually to have fired his pistol in the air. At least once he stood to be shot at, but himself refused to fire at all.

In 1780, Penn became a member of the Board of War. Within the next year or so, he declined a judgeship because his health was failing. What time he had for work, he devoted to his law practice. But in September, 1788, he died at the early age of forty-eight. Not one of the North Carolina Signers ever lived to see his fiftieth birthday.

XII

SOUTH CAROLINA

Edward Rutledge J.

Thos Heyward Junr.

Thomas Lynch Junr.

Arthur Middleton

Thomas Heyward, Junior

[signature: Thos Heyward Junr.]

July 28, 1746 — March 6, 1809

THOMAS HEYWARD was designated "Junior" because there were other Thomases in the family, though his father was Colonel Daniel Heyward. The colonel was one of the wealthiest of the South Carolina planters. He and his wife lived at Old House plantation, in what is now St. Luke's Parish, South Carolina, where their eldest son, Thomas, was born.

The boy was given the usual preparatory education that became the son of a gentleman of means and, again like many other boys whose fathers could afford it, was shipped off to London to study law. He was admitted to the Middle Temple, and after five years was called to the bar. The next year, 1771, upon his return home, he was also admitted to the bar in the province of South Carolina.

Given his education and social position, it was natural that the young lawyer should enter public life. In September of the next year, he was elected one of three members from St. Helena's Parish to the Commons House of Assembly. At that time, in South Carolina as in other colonies, there was a bitter controversy between the Commons and the royal governor over taxation by the British Parliament. A revolutionary party, once formed, grew so swiftly that within two years it was in political control of the colony.

When the news that the British had closed the port of Boston reached South Carolina, a convention of the people of the province was called. A general committee of this convention ordered an election to be held for delegates to a Provincial Congress to meet in Charleston, January, 1775; and Heyward was voted a delegate. The new Provincial Congress took over government of the colony, replacing the old royal British government.

South Carolina and Virginia were the two southern colonies most disturbed by British treatment of Massachusetts, and in the former, Thomas Heyward was an important and busy worker. As the year 1775 drew to a close, it became clear to all patriots that the colonies would have to set up new constitutions on which to base new governments of their own. Heyward was on the committee to prepare the new constitution for South Carolina, and in February, 1776, he was elected delegate to the Second Continental Congress in Philadelphia. After the General Assembly adjourned in April, Heyward went at once to Philadelphia and was there during the deliberations on independence and the final vote on July Fourth. He was just turned thirty when he signed the Declaration of Independence.

Re-elected more than once, Heyward served in Congress until the end of 1778. After that he returned home and became a circuit judge.

As we are indebted to John Adams and Dr. Benjamin Rush for writing down their impressions of some of the Signers and so giving us a glimpse of them, it is well to note what was recorded of Thomas Heyward. Dr. Rush found him a "firm Republican of good education and most amiable manners," who "possessed an elegant poetical genius, which he sometimes exercised . . . upon the various events of the war."

When the operations of war moved into the South, Heyward, in common with all other citizens between the ages of eighteen and forty-five, became a member of his state's militia. He was captain of a battalion of artillery in Charleston. This battalion fought in Moultrie's defeat of the British on Port Royal Island, where Heyward was wounded. He was able to take part in the defense of Charleston the next year, but when the city fell on May 12, 1780, Heyward found himself a prisoner of war. Although he was paroled at first, Sir Henry Clinton soon recalled the paroles of many militia officers and state officials and sent them to prison. Heyward was held at St. Augustine, Florida, until exchanged in July, 1781. He filled in his time by composing patriotic verses to British tunes. The British, meanwhile, plundered his beautiful plantation, "White Hall," and took away his slaves.

After he returned home, Thomas Heyward represented Charleston in the legislature for two more years before resuming his work as circuit judge until 1789. Then he retired in order to devote his whole time to agriculture and to rebuilding White Hall.

In 1773, Heyward had married Elizabeth Mathewes. She died some years later, and in 1786 he married Elizabeth Savage.

In his sixty-third year, Thomas Heyward, Jr., died and was buried in the family burial ground on his father's plantation, Old House, where he had spent his childhood. In this quiet spot, there stands a lonely monument to the "patriot, statesman, soldier, jurist."

Arthur Middleton

Arthur Middleton

June 26, 1742 — January 1, 1787

THE MIDDLETONS had been a family of inherited wealth for generations before Arthur Middleton signed the Declaration of Independence. The first American Middleton was an Edward who, having inherited much property in England, traveled with his brother Arthur to Barbados, and from there to Carolina in 1678. Edward obtained a large grant of land in Berkeley County, North Carolina, where he at once entered local politics.

Edward's grandson, Henry, inherited both the family fortune and the desire to build up the new country. He was the father of Arthur, the Signer. Henry and his wife, Mary Williams Middleton, were living at Middleton Place on the Ashley river, near Charleston, South Carolina, when Arthur was born.

When he was twelve, Arthur was sent away to study in England. After a total of nine years abroad, during which he studied at Westminster School (associated with Westminster Cathedral in London), at St. John's College, Cambridge, and at the Inner Temple, London, the young American rounded off his education with a two-year tour of Europe before returning to his native land. He arrived at Charleston on the ship *Nancy*, the day before Christmas, 1763. Twelve years old when he sailed away, he was twenty-one when he returned, ready to think about finding a wife and entering local politics.

In mid-August, 1764, after his return, Arthur Middleton married Mary Izard of Cedar Grove, St. George's Parish, Dorchester. He had come home when Americans were everywhere becoming embroiled in political conflict. Even his conservative father was exerting his influence in persuading the colony to embrace the patriot cause. Holding the same opinion, Arthur found himself chosen, the next year, a member of the committee which was to correspond with the colony's London agent. This led to his decision to travel to England again and, with a party of relatives and friends, Mr. and Mrs. Middleton sailed in May, 1768, on the *Nancy,* the same ship that had brought him home four years before.

The Middletons traveled in England and southern Europe for three years. In Rome, the young husband indulged in a study of music and painting, for he was fond of the fine arts and literature. After their return in September, 1770, they went to live at Middleton Place, the large estate which Arthur inherited through his mother.

While Arthur was studying abroad, his father was as active in the political life of the king's government in South Carolina as he later became in resisting the royal government, though he was never a believer in independence. Under the king, Henry Middleton was a member of the Commons House of Assembly, its speaker in 1747, 1754, and 1755, and a member of His Majesty's Council for South Carolina. But conservative though he was, he resigned from the Council in 1770 to lead the opposition to the British.

Arthur Middleton returned from abroad the same year that saw his father take a stand with the patriots. He followed his father's example of activity in the American cause, and wrote political essays on the questions of the hour. He signed them "Andrew Marvel." A year after his return, he was elected to the House of Assembly and, a few months later, to the first Provincial Congress representing Charleston. When, in June, 1775, the assembly decided to place the province in a position to resist oppression, three regiments were recruited and a Council of Safety organized. Middleton was active in this work and, as one of three chosen for the Council of Safety, he advised some very bold moves including one which apparently frightened the new royal governor, Sir William Campell, into seeking protection from angry rebels by boarding a British ship.

Early in 1776, Middleton was appointed one of a committee of eleven to prepare a constitution for South Carolina. His father had been chosen as the state's representative in the First Continental Congress in 1774. But as he felt American sentiment sweeping on toward independence, he resigned and let his son, who was much more radical, succeed him as a South Carolina delegate in the Second Continental Congress. Being duly elected, Arthur Middleton departed for his new duties after the adjournment of the General Assembly.

The Pennsylvanian Dr. Benjamin Rush has left us a bit of description of Middleton. From this, one gathers that he was rather a snob, an attitude all too easy to fall into when one has always been surrounded by the elegance of inherited wealth. Rush considered him a "man of cynical temper, but of upright intentions towards his country." He points out that Middleton was a critical Latin and Greek scholar, and liked to read Horace and other "classicks" during recesses from Congress. Middleton spoke often in Congress, Rush says, and "always with asperity or personalities." Middleton refused to serve on the Committee of Accounts because he said he hated accounts, never kept his own, and knew nothing about them. He of course was always able to pay someone else to attend to this uninteresting side of his business. Middleton sat in Congress during the deliberation preceding the Fourth, voted on that day for Independence, and later signed the Declaration. He served until the end of 1777.

When Charleston was besieged by the British in the Spring of 1780, Middleton fought in the state militia, to which he, in common with all men of military age, belonged. When the city fell, on May 12, he was paroled as a prisoner of war. But the parole, with those of many others of the civil and militia officers, was soon revoked by Sir Henry Clinton, and Middleton was sent to prison in St. Augustine, Florida. In the general exchange of July, 1781, he was released and resumed his duties in Congress. The war was coming to an end.

After the surrender at Yorktown, Middleton proposed to Congress that Lord Cornwallis should not be exchanged but rather be regarded as a "barbarian who had violated all the rules of modern warfare and had been guilty of innumerable cases of wanton cruelty and oppression." Congress did not pass this resolution.

Having seen the ugly devastation the British left behind them in South Carolina, Middleton could not help but feel bitter. His own beautiful family estate, Middleton Place, was on the enemy line of march, and of course they occupied it. The buildings did not suffer, but the Signer's rare collection of paintings was damaged.

In 1782, Middleton was again elected to Congress.

When the Constitution was adopted, he was appointed to a committee to prepare a seal for the state of South Carolina. He personally drew the reverse side of the design that was adopted and is still official — mute evidence, perhaps, of his art study in Italy as a young man.

At the age of forty-five, Arthur Middleton died at his home on Goose Creek when his younger son was only two years old.

Edward Rutledge

November 23, 1749 — January 23, 1800

EDWARD RUTLEDGE was only twenty-seven when he went to Philadelphia as congressman from South Carolina.

His father, Dr. John Rutledge, had come from Ireland in 1735 and married Sarah Hext when she was a mere slip of a girl. Their oldest son, John, was born when Sarah was only fifteen, and she was twenty-seven when her husband died, leaving her with seven children. Edward, the youngest, was then just a year old.

The boy was taught his school lessons by the Anglican minister of Christ Church and learned the Greek and Latin classics from a tutor in Charleston. Later he was sent, like his brother John, to England to finish his education by studying law at the Middle Temple in London. He was admitted to Middle Temple at eighteen and five years later was called to the bar. He returned the following year.

He had been home a year and had been admitted to the bar of South Carolina when his public and his married life began. In 1774, he married Henrietta Middleton, sister of the Signer; and when she died, eighteen years later, he married Mary Shubrick Eveleigh, a widow. Edward Rutledge's public life began when he was elected on July 7, 1774, to the First Continental Congress. He had made himself popular by instituting legal proceedings to protect the publisher of *The South-Carolina Gazette,* Thomas Powell, who had been imprisoned for printing his *Gazette* on unstamped paper, thereby violating the much resented Stamp Act.

Edward Rutledge's older brother John was also a delegate to the First Continental Congress. Both took part in heated discussions there, young Edward upholding his brother's arguments; in fact, the two Rutledges talked and argued so much in the debates that John Adams became impatient. He thought "young Ned Rutledge" was "a peacock" who wasted time debating upon "points of little consequence." Adams considered Edward Rutledge an "uncouth and ungraceful speaker; he shrugs his shoulders, distorts his body, nods and wiggles with his head, and looks about with his eyes from side to side, and speaks through his nose." Dr. Rush, however, thought Edward was a "sensible young lawyer," very useful in Congress, but he, too, remarks upon the young man's "great volubility in speaking." Still, allowances must be made. Edward Rutledge was then only twenty-seven, raw and green compared to many of the other delegates. Young Rutledge was no doubt very pleased with himself, to be included in that group of very important men from all over the thirteen colonies.

In February, 1776, he was again elected by the Provincial Congress to the Second Continental Congress, so that he was present, and a staunch supporter of the Declaration, in July. His brother was also re-elected, but he left Philadelphia and returned home to be on hand there for the discussions being considered in the Provincial Congress. Through the hot debates that went on during June about the question of independence, Edward Rutledge held off action, restrained by the indecisiveness of his constituents at home, while John was there talking for independence. Finally, on July 2, after the votes from the home parishes had come in "yea," the South Carolina delegates could at last take a stand in favor of the Declaration of Independence. Edward signed the document when it was prepared.

In November, 1776, Rutledge went home to take part in the defense of his new state. He belonged to the Charleston Battalion of Artillery, in which he was soon made a captain. He participated in General Moultrie's defeat of Major Gardiner on Port Royal Island in February, 1779.

In the autumn of that year, he was returned to Congress to fill a vacancy. But early in 1780, when the British commenced a third invasion of South Carolina, Captain Rutledge was back at this post, taking part in the defense of Charleston, until it fell to the enemy in May. He was captured and sent to St. Augustine, Florida, as prisoner of war and, like Middleton and Heyward, exchanged in July, 1781.

At the beginning of 1782, Edward Rutledge was back in his state's legislature, where he drew up the bill proposing the confiscation of the properties of all Loyalists, feeling this measure was necessary to repair the enemy destruction in the state.

Honors in public life and success in his law practice came in the post-war years. From 1782 to 1796, he represented Charleston again in the House. He was an efficient worker and at one point was chairman of nineteen committees!

Rutledge was a stiff conservative, and as an influential Federalist, he was a presidential elector in 1788, 1792, and again in 1796 when, Federalist or not, he voted for Thomas Jefferson for President.

He was elected to the state Senate twice, and in 1798 he became Governor of South Carolina. By this time, however, his health was poor, and he was performing his duties under physical distress. Within a year of the end of his term, Governor Rutledge, next youngest of the Signers, died in Charleston on January 23, 1800, at the age of fifty-one.

Thomas Lynch, Junior

Thomas Lynch Jun

August 5, 1749 — c. 1779

SOUTH CAROLINA'S DELEGATES to the 1776 Congress were all from wealthy families; their fathers were planters or country-gentlemen;

they all went to England to round off their educations; and they all studied law.

Thomas Lynch, the only son of Thomas and Elizabeth Allston Lynch, born in Prince George's Parish, Winyaw, South Carolina, was the youngest man to sign the Declaration. He was not quite twenty-eight at the time. His grandfather had come from Ireland to South Carolina soon after the first settlement was started there. His son Thomas, the Signer's father, discovered a method of growing rice on the lowlands, which were periodically covered by tidal water. By taking grants for large tracts of tidal areas on the North and South Santee rivers, Thomas, Senior, laid the foundation of a fortune.

His son, Thomas, Junior, received the education, probably by tutors, that country gentlemen usually gave their sons, and when he was fifteen, he was sent to Eton College in England. After two years there, he entered Gonville and Caius College, Cambridge, and topped off his studies with the law at Middle Temple in London. He came home again in 1772. The boy of fifteen returned a man of twenty-three.

Now that he was home, however, young Thomas Lynch did not want to carry on in the legal profession. His father good-naturedly allowed him to drop it, gave him Peach Tree plantation, and urged him to enter public life. On May 14, 1772, Thomas, Junior, married Elizabeth Shubrick, and the young pair settled at Peach Tree in St. James Parish on the North Santee River.

Since his wealthy and patriotic father was active in politics, Thomas, Junior, had little difficulty winning the offices for which he was a candidate. He was a member of the First and Second Provincial Congresses and a member of the First General Assembly of his state. In June of 1775, the Provincial Congress appointed him a captain in the First South Carolina Regiment. In July, he went to North Carolina to recruit a company and there contracted "swamp fever," or malaria, which affected him for the rest of his short life.

Under the constitution which the younger Lynch had helped to draft in the General Assembly, he was elected to the Second Continental Congress.

The Thomas Lynches, father and son, were the only such pair in the Second Continental Congress, though the elder Lynch did not live to become a Signer. Thomas Lynch, Senior, had been elected to both the First and Second Congresses, but a stroke of paralysis rendered him nearly helpless early in 1776. His son was elected as a sixth South Carolina delegate, in part at least so that he might care for his father.

Unhappily, the younger Lynch's health was also deteriorating, and he was too feeble to expend effort in public concerns though he was on hand at the July meeting to vote for Independence and, later, to sign the Declaration.

One may notice a space left open for another signature among the South Carolina names on the Declaration of Independence. This is a mute and pathetic reminder that it was hoped the older Lynch would live to sign.

But it was soon evident that the two Lynches could not remain in Philadelphia. The father had had a slight recovery, and doctors hoped that he might live to reach the home where he longed to be. The son tried to arrange a journey southward by easy stages for his father, and the two sick men set off together. But at Annapolis, Maryland, the father had a second stroke which killed him. The unhappy son, after burying his father there, continued his journey, reaching home with not much hope for a long life of his own.

After two years of illness, he and his wife took passage for a voyage to the West Indies, in the hope that he might regain his health in that benign climate. From the West Indies they shipped, as they intended, for the south of France, but their ship was never heard of again. All on board were probably lost at sea.

This was in 1779. Thomas Lynch, Junior, rich, well-educated, the young Signer who had everything but health, was thirty years old when he vanished.

XIII

GEORGIA

Button Gwinnett

Lyman Hall

Geo Walton.

Lyman Hall

Lyman Hall

April 12, 1724 — October 19, 1790

THIS SIGNER FOR GEORGIA, acknowledged as the most powerful factor in persuading his colony to independence, was born and spent half of his life in Connecticut. In the charming town of Wallingford, which still has over a hundred pre-Revolution houses, Lyman Hall was born on April 12, 1724.

He was the son of John and Mary Street Hall. His first New England ancestor was another John Hall, who came from Coventry, England, to Boston in 1633, moved on to New Haven, Connecticut, and finally settled in nearby Wallingford. The Signer's mother, Mary Street, was a Wallingford girl whose grandfather, the Reverend Samuel Street, was the first pastor in Wallingford.

Lyman Hall prepared for college with his uncle, the Reverend Samuel Hall, a Yale graduate of 1715. He himself went to Yale and graduated in 1747. After that, he studied theology under this same uncle and was ordained by the Fairfield West Consociation, the local church organization. Trouble developed in the congregation, however, and Hall was dismissed, though he continued preaching by filling vacant pulpits. But the ministry was not for him. When he left it to study medicine, Dr. Hall was on the road to success and prosperity.

In 1752, he married Abigail Burr, of Fairfield, but she lived only a year after her marriage. Two or three years later, Hall married again. His second wife was Mary Osborn, another Fairfield girl, daughter of Samuel and Hannah Osborn.

In the stories of the South Carolina Signers, we have mentioned the migration of New England settlers to the South. Lyman Hall may have thought that he could build up a practice more quickly in a newly settled part of the country; he may have liked the prospect of having milder winters; or he may have wanted to venture into a different region. At any rate, he moved south to

Dorchester, South Carolina, when he was thirty-two. About the time the Halls joined the colony, earlier settlers were moving on farther south. Lyman Hall was among the group who followed on to Georgia and founded the town of Sunbury in the Midway Settlement. This was in the parish of St. John, where patriot feeling became so strong that it was known as the Southern Cradle of Liberty.

The country thereabouts was densely wooded and abounded in game. The settlers made clearings and planted corn, potatoes, and peas in the uplands; but there were many swamps that had to be ditched and drained for the cultivation of rice, and where there are swamps, there are mosquitoes that carry malaria. The doctor was in demand. He soon had a big practice and wealth enough to buy a plantation.

Of all the thirteen colonies, Georgia had been granted the mildest treatment by the mother country. England had sent the settlers there large sums for silk culture and similar purposes. Consequently, as rebellion spread throughout colonies to the north in the 1760's, there existed a great difference of opinion in Georgia. The people of St. John's Parish naturally were deeply interested in the events that were taking place in the northern colonies of their birth. When seeds of revolt began to sprout in Georgia, the royal governor reported that the head of rebellion could be located in St. John's Parish, where the descendants of New England Puritans were asserting their strong feelings. The "Puritan element" were the first Georgia patriots, and Dr. Lyman Hall was the leader.

In July, 1774, the patriotic groups called a meeting — in opposition to the royal governor of the province — at the Liberty Pole at Tondee's tavern in Savannah. Dr. Hall, who of course represented St. John's Parish, and many of the others, had hoped that a majority of the parishes would unite with them in sending deputies to Congress. But this proposal met no response.

Dr. Lyman Hall, "being blessed with the art of oratory to an unusual degree," spoke far and wide and, in March, 1775, succeeded in persuading his neighbors to elect him a delegate to the Continental Congress. When he left for Philadelphia, he took with him, as a gift from his people to the suffering Massachusetts patriots, one hundred sixty barrels of rice and £50 sterling. He presented his credentials on May 13, 1775, and was unanimously admitted as a delegate from the Parish of St. John in the Colony of Georgia, but the colony of Georgia as a whole was not represented in the First Continental Congress. Dr. Hall therefore could not vote, since all questions were decided by vote of the colonies. He took part in debates, however, declaring "that the example which had been shown by the parish which he represented would be speedily followed and that the representation of Georgia would soon be complete." His prediction came true two months later when, in July, 1775, Georgia's Provincial Congress voted to join the confederated colonies in the cause of liberty. In this decision, the influence of Dr. Lyman Hall was of great weight.

The following February, Hall was elected again and sent to attend the Second Continental Congress. By this time, his neighbor, Button Gwinnett, a warm personal friend, arrived in Philadelphia as a second Georgia delegate.

These two, with the third Georgia delegate, George Walton, were on hand to vote for the Declaration of Independence and to sign it.

It was natural that Dr. Hall, in Philadelphia, should associate with the representatives of his native state. He and Roger Sherman became friends. Later — for Dr. Hall was elected to Congress for three successive terms — their opponents complained that "Georgia always votes with Connecticut." Hall declined a fourth nomination to Congress.

When, in December, 1778, Savannah fell and the entire coastal region of Georgia came under British hands, Dr. Hall's residence and rice plantation were destroyed. He moved his family north for the duration, visiting relatives in Wallingford. On his return in 1782, he settled in Savannah, resumed his medical practice, and was elected Governor of Georgia. He made an impressive and dignified chief executive, for he was six feet tall, with polite manners and easy deportment.

During his one term as governor, the northern boundary of Georgia was adjusted, the public debt arranged, land offices established, and treaties made with the Cherokee Indians. Hall's recommendation that a parcel of land be set aside for the endowment of an institution of higher learning led to one of the first

state-supported colleges in America, Franklin College, the heart
of what is now the University of Georgia.

Dr. Hall bought a plantation in Burke County when he retired
in 1790, but he was not given much time to build up his new
estate. In October of that year, he died, in the sixty-seventh year
of his age.

Button Gwinnett

Button Gwinnett

c. April, 1735 — May 16, 1777

BECAUSE HE WAS BAPTIZED in St. Catherine's Church, Gloucester,
England, on the tenth of April, 1735, it is supposed that Button
Gwinnett was born in that month. He was named Button for his
godmother, Miss Barbara Button, descended from Sir Thomas
Button, admiral and arctic explorer.

The name Gwinnett, pronounced with the accent on the last
syllable, Gwin-*nett*, was originally the Welsh, *Gwynedd*, the name
of the northern part of Wales.

The home of the Buttons, however, was in Glamorganshire, in
South Wales. Miss Barbara Button never married, and having
inherited wealth, was able to do much for her cousin, Anne Emes
Gwinnett, who, no doubt as a mark of appreciation, named her
second son for her cousin.

Samuel Gwinnett, the father of the Signer, entered the church,
and in 1727 was given a living at Down Hatherly. He married Anne
Emes of Twyning and brought his bride to the vicarage, where
they lived for more than forty years. Here was born their second
son, Button, who was to become a Signer of the Declaration of
Independence in far-off America.

Nothing is recorded of the boy's education. His older brother
Samuel became a clergyman and married Emilia Button. When
the future American, Button Gwinnett, was twenty, his godmother
died, leaving him £100. He is thought to have started his business
career in Bristol under the guidance of his uncle, William Gwinnett, a Bristol merchant.

At the age of twenty-two, he married Ann Bourne, of Wolver-hampton, and for some time worked in partnership with his father-in-law, Aaron Bourne. He became interested in exporting goods to America and, for a time, was the sole owner of the brig *Nancy*. Though he carried on extensive mercantile operations, they were not successful, and his debts to a Bristol firm lost him the *Nancy*, which was seized under an attachment and sold by the sheriff to liquidate his indebtedness. Debts were to plague Button Gwinnett all his short life.

It is not known just when Button Gwinnett arrived in Savannah, Georgia — certainly after his three daughters were born, since their births are recorded in the registry of the Collegiate Church in Wolverhampton. The last date recorded is 1762. But by October, 1765, Gwinnett had secured a store property in Savannah and had begun to advertise, in the *Georgia Gazette*, his recently exported merchandize.

Not long after his own advertisement appeared, he saw one that took his fancy: St. Catherine's Island was for sale.

All along the coastline of Georgia runs a line of islands, sepa-rated from the mainland by winding waterways, salt marshes, and bays, into which Georgia's rivers empty into the sea. Between the mouth of the Medway and Sapelo Sound River lies St. Catherine's Island, about ten and one-half miles long and three and one-half miles wide at its widest part. Looking across to the mainland, less than ten miles away, one could see in Gwinnett's time the busy town and harbor of Sunbury, rival port of Savannah, some forty miles to the north. Sunbury was the home of Lyman Hall, who became a warm friend to Gwinnett and also a Signer. Sun-bury was Gwinnett's landing place on the mainland, his base of supplies, and his refuge when British war vessels and patrols came too near his island home.

It was in the Stamp Act year of 1765 that Button Gwinnett bought the island with high hopes of becoming a planter. Having become the owner of vastly more than the required fifty acres of land needed to qualify as an elector of the province, Gwinnett was commissioned His Majesty's Justice of the Peace for the par-ishes of St. John and St. Andrew. Within the next few years he was becoming better known, with the result that he was appointed to more and more committees dealing with public affairs. After his work in the Common House of Assembly, Gwinnett seems to have dropped out of public life for a time. His own personal affairs were probably too demanding.

Neither he nor the colony of Georgia took an early interest in colonial independence. Georgia was the youngest, the most remote and sparsely settled of the thirteen colonies. Moreover, her governor, Sir James Wright, was an able, sympathetic, and wise administrator. Under his guidance the province had prospered, and the British Parliament had given her many thousands of pounds, so that Georgia was more contented than her sister colonies to the north, which were being exasperated, then harassed, and finally outraged by tyrannical acts of Parliament. For this reason Georgia was the last to join her sister colonies in the common cause of the 1770's. Gwinnett himself had been rooted in England for almost thirty years before being transplanted to American soil.

New Englanders had been migrating to Georgia, bringing news of the troubles in the North, but not until July, 1774, did Georgia make her first remonstrance against the treatment of the colonies by Great Britain. This was at an open meeting held on the twenty-fourth at the Liberty Pole at Tondee's tavern in Savannah. Dr. Lyman Hall of Sunbury was there, but not many attended, and most of those present were from the two parishes of Christ Church and St. John. They tried for a more representative meeting the next month, at which resolutions were passed reciting a long list of colonial grievances, but few of them applied to Georgia. Georgia was the only one of the thirteen colonies not represented at the First Continental Congress in Philadelphia, though Dr. Lyman Hall was there as an observer.

Probably through his friendly association with Hall, Gwinnett became a Whig. In January, 1776, he attended one of the weekly meetings of the Georgia Council of Safety in Savannah. Though he may not have been a member at the time, he attended to report that British warships were lying off the coast. At Georgia's Second Provincial Congress, he was elected as a delegate to the Second Continental Congress.

Just before this, Gwinnett had been a candidate for the command of Georgia's battalion of eight companies. He very much wanted to see active service. But a popular Savannah merchant,

Samuel Ebert, also an aspirant for the colonelcy, had had some military training. As there was some opposition to Gwinnett, it was agreed that, for the sake of keeping harmony, both should withdraw, whereupon Lachlan McIntosh was chosen as a compromise. Ebert was made lieutenant colonel, and Gwinnett was sent to Congress.

The appearance of five British ships off the coast, followed by an attack on Savannah in March and the consequent swift movement of events, delayed the departure of the delegates, and not until May 20, 1776, could Gwinnett and Hall take their seats in Congress.

When writing his autobiography, John Adams remembered that Hall and Gwinnett were both intelligent and spirited men, "who made a powerful addition to our Phalanx." In a letter to Roger Sherman, Dr. Hall wrote, "Gwinnett is, if possible, a Whig to excess." Gwinnett must have been thrilled with the mounting excitement in Congress that preceded the great Fourth.

Button Gwinnett was appointed to serve on several of the important committees. He seldom spoke in public and wrote very little. His name in his handwriting on the Declaration of Independence is the only thing that draws our attention to him now — two hundred years later. Were it not for that, his amusing name would be lost in the mists of time.

After having served ten weeks in Congress, Gwinnett left Philadelphia and was back home in Georgia by late August, headed for trouble. He never returned to Congress.

A patriot who had wanted to be a soldier, Gwinnett hoped to be a general of Georgia troops, but he never achieved his desire. Instead, he was elected speaker of the Georgia Assembly and, though he was re-elected as delegate for the Fall term to the Continental Congress, there is no record of his attendance.

In the Georgia Assembly, Gwinnett helped draft Georgia's first constitution and also helped to defeat schemes for South Carolina to absorb Georgia. In the Spring of the following year, 1777, upon the death of Governor Archibald Bulloch, Gwinnett was made governor of the new state of Georgia and, of course, commander in chief of its army. He held these positions for only two months.

The Georgia patriots were disturbed by British forces so near in

East Florida. On the same day, March 4, 1777, that Button Gwinnett was chosen to be governor, he was directed by the Council of Safety to draft militia and volunteers for a campaign against the British in which they were to cut off all supplies for the garrison at St. Augustine. Little more than a week later, Gwinnett received the letter that was to raise the curtain on the final tragic act.

The letter was from none other than John Hancock, President of the Continental Congress then sitting in Baltimore, dated January 8, 1777. It said:

> "I have the honour to inclose you a copy of an intercepted letter from the Governour of East-Florida to Lord George Germaine, containing, among other things, the most convincing proof of the treasonable conduct of Mr. George M'Intosh of your State. This Gentleman it seems, is a Member of the Congress in Georgia, and under that character is secretly supporting, by every act in his power, the designs of the British King and Parliament against us.
>
> The United States of America have hitherto suffered extremely from the misrepresentations of their enemies, but much more from the baseness and perfidy of their pretended friends. I have it therefore in command from Congress to request, that you will cause the said George M'Intosh to be immediately apprehended, and take every other step in this matter which shall appear to you to be necessary for the safety of the United States of America. . . ."

The intercepted letter referred to here was from Governor Patrick Tonyn of East Florida, reporting to Lord George Germaine on receiving supplies of rice from the rebel colony of Georgia. Tonyn said that he expected one thousand more barrels to arrive and that Mr. Panton (a Georgia Tory) executed the business and was greatly assisted by Mr. George McIntosh "one of the Rebel Congress of Georgia."

George McIntosh was a brother of General Lachlan McIntosh who had allied himself with the conservative section of the Whig party, and had received the command of the First Battalion — a post Gwinnett had wanted — after which he was made brigadier general in command of the Georgia brigade. Button Gwinnett had achieved his high mark in politics. His office as governor and commander in chief of Georgia's army placed him above General McIntosh, a bitter pill for the general to swallow. Thus rivalry between the conservative Whig whose brother was in disgrace and the extreme Whig who was now ordered to arrest him had already begun. It is very likely that Gwinnett may have had his suspicions. Both the McIntosh brothers had been members of Georgia's First Provincial Congress, and George had even been a member of the Council of Safety, sitting in that body with Gwinnett many times. They were neighbors whose two parishes adjoined. Gwinnett's appointments had not only been great honors but showed that he had won the public's confidence in his integrity and ability. The McIntoshes probably hated Gwinnett, envious of his success.

As Governor of Georgia, Gwinnett did as he was ordered to do by Congress. George McIntosh was charged with treason against the United States and placed in irons. But the McIntoshes had their friends, too, and, as people did not know everything about the case, opinions were aired in a badly divided community.

Then came the East Florida expedition in the Spring of 1777, and it was bungled. General McIntosh ordered Colonel Ebert to lead the ill-fated expedition. But even though he had not himself led it, a large part of the people of Georgia lost confidence in General McIntosh's loyalty and integrity. When an inquiry followed in the assembly and the question was raised whether it was civil authority that had hampered military authority, or vice versa, McIntosh's hot temper flared. For this raised the question of whether Gwinnett as governor and commander in chief was to blame or whether it was the fault of General McIntosh.

The inquiry upheld Gwinnett.

General McIntosh, enraged, cried out before the assembly that Gwinnett was a "scoundrel and a lying rascal."

The insult was not to be borne. Gwinnett promptly challenged McIntosh to a duel. He was certainly no coward to take on a general with pistols.

The duel took place the following morning, just outside the town of Savannah. Both men hit their marks and both were wounded. The general recovered, but Gwinnett died three days later.

The burial place of Signer Button Gwinnett is unknown, and

there is no reliable picture of him. Though he had daughters, there are no descendants living to this day, so far as is known.

Only one thing remains of this Georgia Signer — his hand-written signature on the Declaration of Independence, and thirty-six other signatures, most of them owned by research libraries, universities, and historical societies. Gwinnett's are the rarest of Signer signatures and correspondingly expensive. One Gwinnett document alone brought $28,000 at an auction in 1926. Another sold in 1927 for $51,000, though that was also signed by John Hancock, Robert Morris, and others.

George Walton

Geo Walton.

c. 1741 — February 2, 1804

THE FIRST AMERICAN WALTON of George Walton's family was his grandfather, who emigrated from England in 1682; and the emi-grant's son, Robert, was living near Farmville, Prince Edward County, Virginia, when his own son, George, was born in 1741. Both parents died while their boy was very young, and the child was taken to live with an uncle. When he was old enough, the uncle apprenticed him to a carpenter.

The carpenter seems to have seen qualities that had escaped the uncle. Impressed by George's intelligence and character, he released him from apprenticeship so that he could go to school, while giving him a portion of his wages. But even so, the boy had so little formal schooling that he is said to have been practically self-taught.

Nothing more of his early life is known until, at the age of twenty-eight, he moved to Savannah, Georgia, and began to study law. He was admitted to the bar in 1774 when he was thirty-three years old and the next year married Dorothy Camber, herself a patriot, though daughter of a loyal British subject.

In Savannah, Walton fell in with the local Whigs and must soon have become acquainted with Lyman Hall and Button

Gwinnett. He took part in the first meetings called by the patriot party that same summer, served on committees, and vehemently condemned British colonial policy. He was one of the group that called the meeting at the Liberty Pole at Tondee's tavern, which was the beginning of the Georgia Provincial Congress.

Chosen unanimously to be the secretary of this body, George Walton was then elected president of the newly formed Council of Safety. When the Provincial Congress met in February, 1776, to elect delegates to the Second Continental Congress, Walton was one of the men elected. The exact date of his arrival in Philadelphia is not known, but it was probably about June 29, though the journals of Congress do not mention him until July 17.

George Walton showed himself a strong advocate of independence, noted for his ability and zeal. Perhaps he had, at times, too much zeal — which can cause trouble. In Congress, Walton took an interest in Indian affairs and went to Easton, Pennsylvania, in January, 1777, when a treaty was negotiated with the Six Nations of the Iroquois.

Back in Georgia by spring, he was one of the "Conservative Whigs" who made life hard for Button Gwinnett. He was, in fact, the leader of the opposition to Gwinnett, and a friend of the firebrand, General McIntosh, who was later responsible for Gwinnett's untimely death. During the next two years, the patriot party in Georgia was itself divided by dissension.

In January, 1778, George Walton was commissioned colonel of the Georgia militia's First Regiment. During the siege of Savannah his leg was broken by a cannon-ball, he fell from his horse, and was captured by the British. The next year, he was exchanged and sent home in time to be elected governor, a position which he held for only two months.

This little man, small of stature, but good-looking, impressed others as being haughty, dignified and stern. This impression was not altogether fair, for though Walton did have a violent temper, he could be counted on to do what he said he would do, which is not always true of politicians. Bitter with his enemies, he was warm with his friends. Unfortunately, he chose to hate his colleague, Button Gwinnett, and to be friendly with Gwinnett's enemy, General McIntosh. Going to the extent of sending a doubtful letter to Congress in trying to defend McIntosh after the general had killed Gwinnett in the duel, Walton was censured by the legislature in 1783. This forced the attorney general to bring charges against him. But Walton had his backers and, of the three Georgia Signers, he served longest in the Second Continental Congress. Except for the years 1778 and 1779, when he was first fighting the British, then held as a British prisoner, he appeared regularly in Congress until 1781.

He was commissioned in 1783 to negotiate a treaty with the Cherokees in Tennessee, after which he served six years as Chief Justice of Georgia. In 1789, he was a presidential elector and was for the second time elected governor.

During this term a new constitution for Georgia was established, the capital was definitely located at Augusta, and after many frontier difficulties, the Creek Indians were pacified.

The next year, in 1790, Walton retired to his estate, "Meadow Garden," but was soon called back to public life as judge of Georgia's Supreme Court.

In 1795, he built a new home which he called "College Hill," but he was not given time to enjoy it long. Within a few months, he died there at the age of fifty-four. He was buried in Rosney Cemetery nearby. For the 1848 celebration of the Day of Independence, however, citizens erected a new monument in Augusta to the three Georgia Signers, and the bodies of Lyman Hall and George Walton were reinterred there.

BIBLIOGRAPHY

Adams, Charles Thornton. *Matthew Thornton of New Hampshire*. Philadelphia: Dando Printing and Publishing Company, 1903.

Allan, Herbert S. *John Hancock, Patriot in Purple*. New York: The MacMillan Company, 1948.

Biddle, Honorable Edward W. *James Wilson, James Smith, and George Ross, Three Signers of the Declaration of Independence who were members of the Cumberland County Bar*. Historical address delivered in the Court House, Carlisle, Pennsylvania, April 4, 1902.

Boardman, R. S. *Roger Sherman, Signer and Statesman*. Philadelphia: University of Pennsylvania Press, 1938.

Buchanan, Roberdean. *McKean Family of Pennsylvania*. Lancaster: Inquire Printing Company, 1890.

Burlingham, Charles C. *Francis Lewis*. Philadelphia: Historical Sketch read at the Sesqui-Centennial International Exposition, September 20, 1926.

Butterfield, L. H., ed. *Letters of Benjamin Rush*. 2 volumes. Princeton: Princeton University Press, 1951.

The Adams Papers. Diary and Autobiography of John Adams. 4 volumes. New York: Atheneum, 1964.

Carroll, Charles. *Journal During His Visit to Canada in 1776*. Baltimore: John Murphy for the Maryland Historical Society, 1876.

Corner, George W., ed. *The Autobiography of Benjamin Rush*. Princeton: Princeton University Press, 1948.

Drake, Francis. *Dictionary of American Biography*. 2 volumes. Gale, 1879.

Fay, Bernard. *Franklin, the Apostle of Modern Times*. Boston: Little Brown & Company, 1929.

Franklin, Benjamin. *Autobiography*. Art-Type edition. New York: Books, Incorporated.

Gurn, Joseph. *Charles Carroll of Carrollton*. New York: P. J. Kennedy and Sons, 1932.

Hart, Ann Clark. *Abraham Clark*. San Francisco: The Pioneer Press, 1923.

Historical Society of Delaware. *A Biographical Sketch in Letters to and from Caesar Rodney*. Philadelphia: University of Pennsylvania Press, 1933.

Huntington, Susan D. "Samuel Huntington." *The Connecticut Magazine.* Volume 6, Number 4, May–June, 1900.

Jenkins, Charles Francis. *Button Gwinnett.* Garden City: Doubleday, Page and Company, 1926.

Lee, Richard H. *Memoir of the Life of Richard Henry Lee.* 2 volumes. Philadelphia: H. C. Carey and I. Lea, 1825.

McGee, Dorothy Horton. *Famous Signers of the Declaration.* New York: Dodd, Mead, and Company, 1955.

Shewmake, Oscar L. Esquire. *The Honorable George Wythe.* Delivered before the Wythe Law Club of the College of William and Mary, Williamsburg, Virginia, 1921.

Smith, Ellen Hart. *Charles Carroll of Carrollton.* Cambridge: Harvard University Press, 1942.

Thoms, Herbert, Dr. *Lyman Hall, Physician, Patriot, Signer.* President's Address, New Haven County Medical Association, New Haven, Connecticut, April 28, 1927.

Van Doren, Carl. *Benjamin Franklin.* New York: Viking Press, 1938.

Whipple, William. *Collections and Proceedings of the Maine Historical Society.* Series 2, Volume VI. Portland, 1895.

Woods, David Walker Jr. *John Witherspoon.* London: Fleming H. Revell Company, 1906.

Young, Eleanor. *Forgotten Patriot.* New York: The MacMillan Company, 1950.